COMPUTER-AIDED DRUG DEVELOPMENT

THEORY AND APPLICATIONS

M. DURGA BHAVANI, DR. K. SARITHA, DR K. RAVI SHANKAR, DR. G. RAGHAVENDRA

Contents

Computer-aided Drug Development

Theory and Applications

AUTHORS

Ms. M. Durga Bhavani

Assistant Professor,
Department of Pharmaceutical Chemistry,
Narasaraopeta Institute of Pharmaceutical Sciences (Autonomous),
Narasaraopet, Andhra Pradesh, India

Dr. Saritha Karnati

Professor,
Department of Pharmaceutical Chemistry,
K.V. Subba Reddy Institute of Pharmacy (Autonomous),
Kurnool, Andhra Pradesh, India

Dr. K. Ravi Shankar

Associate Professor,
KVSR Siddhartha College of Pharmaceutical Sciences,
Vijayawada, Andhra Pradesh, India

Dr. Raghavendra Kumar Gunda

Associate Professor, Faculty-In-Charge,
Department of Pharmaceutics,
Narasaraopeta Institute of Pharmaceutical Sciences (Autonomous),
Narasaraopet, Andhra Pradesh, India

Editor

Dr. A. Muralidhar Rao, M.Pharm., Ph.D.

Principal,
St. Mary's College of Pharmacy,
Secunderabad, Telangana, India

Published by Notion Press

Notion Press, Inc.

800, West El Camino Real #180,
California, USA 94040

Notion Press Media Pvt Ltd

#7, Red Cross Road,
Egmore, Chennai, Tamil Nadu 600008

Email ID:publish@notionpress.com

Phone Number: +91 44 46315631

Preface

The pharmaceutical sciences have witnessed a tremendous transformation with the advent of computer technologies. What once took years of trial-and-error research is now accelerated through computer-aided tools, modeling, and simulations. Recognizing the growing need for future pharmacy professionals to understand this intersection of computers and pharmaceutical development, we have envisioned this book, **"Computer-Aided Drug Development: Theory and Applications."**

This book has been thoughtfully structured to provide students, researchers, and professionals with a comprehensive yet accessible exploration of how computational techniques are integrated at every stage of modern drug development. Beginning from historical evolution and fundamental concepts, the book walks the reader through critical areas such as computational modeling of drug disposition, computer-aided formulation design, biopharmaceutical characterization, pharmacokinetic and pharmacodynamic simulations, clinical development applications, and the role of emerging technologies like Artificial Intelligence, Robotics, and Computational Fluid Dynamics (CFD) in pharmaceutical research.

Our goal has been to present not just the theoretical foundations, but also practical insights and real-world applications. We have ensured that the chapters build intuitively, anticipating the common questions a learner might have, while linking complex concepts to clinical relevance and industrial practices. The emphasis has been on clear explanations, structured flow, examples, and the incorporation of up-to-date knowledge without overwhelming the reader with unnecessary technicality.

Each chapter has been carefully developed with the aim to bridge the gap between classroom learning and the needs of the pharmaceutical industry. Special attention has been given to include review questions, multiple-choice questions (MCQs), and practical examples to reinforce understanding and promote active learning.

This book is the collective effort of a team of committed educators and researchers:

Ms. M. Durga Bhavani, Assistant Professor, Department of Pharmaceutical Chemistry, Narasaraopeta Institute of Pharmaceutical Sciences (Autonomous), Narasaraopet, Andhra Pradesh, India.

Dr. Saritha Karnati, Professor, Department of Pharmaceutical Chemistry, K.V. Subba Reddy Institute of Pharmacy (Autonomous), Kurnool, Andhra Pradesh, India.

Dr. K. Ravi Shankar, Associate Professor, KVSR Siddhartha College of Pharmaceutical Sciences, Vijayawada, Andhra Pradesh, India.

Dr. Raghavendra Kumar Gunda, Associate Professor and Faculty-In-Charge, Department of Pharmaceutics, Narasaraopeta Institute of Pharmaceutical Sciences (Autonomous), Narasaraopet, Andhra Pradesh, India.

Each of us brings diverse academic and research experience to this project, united by a common vision — to contribute a practical, academically sound, and industry-aligned resource to pharmacy education.

We sincerely hope that **"Computer-Aided Drug Development: Theory and Applications"** will serve as a reliable guide for students, educators, and practitioners alike, and inspire further exploration into this exciting and ever-evolving field.

We welcome constructive feedback from readers and educators that will help us refine future editions and continue contributing meaningfully to pharmaceutical sciences.

Authors

CHAPTER ONE

Introduction to Computers in Pharmaceutical Research and Development

1.1 Historical Evolution

1.1.1 Emergence of computers in pharmaceutical sciences

The initial emergence of computers in pharmaceutical sciences was influenced by the broader industrial and technological developments of the mid-20th century. In the 1950s and 1960s, the pharmaceutical industry started experiencing significant growth in experimental data generated from pharmacological, toxicological, and clinical research. Managing, calculating, and interpreting such data manually was not only slow but also error-prone. During this time, mainframe computers were introduced in select research facilities for basic statistical processing and mathematical modeling. Early usage was focused primarily on tasks like statistical quality control in manufacturing, pharmacokinetic data analysis, and simple inventory management. However, these machines were bulky, expensive, and required specialized knowledge in programming languages such as FORTRAN and COBOL, which limited their accessibility to most researchers.

By the 1970s, the introduction of mini-computers and the development of time-sharing systems made computational resources more widely available. Pharmaceutical scientists started using computers for plotting dose-response curves, fitting pharmacokinetic models, and performing linear and non-linear regression analysis. The scope of computational applications began to expand into areas like drug solubility modeling and chemical structure representation using simple line notations. The early evolution of chemoinformatics started to take shape, allowing researchers to digitize chemical structures and store molecular information in basic databases. These foundational developments laid the groundwork for more complex applications in the future.

1.1.2 Milestones in pharmaceutical computing

Several technological milestones have shaped the evolution of computers in the pharmaceutical field over the decades. In the late 1980s and early 1990s, the development of dedicated pharmaceutical software marked a major shift. Programs like WinNonlin were introduced for pharmacokinetic and pharmacodynamic modeling, while software like SYBYL, ChemDraw, and ISIS/Draw allowed researchers to visualize chemical structures and simulate molecular behavior. The Human Genome Project, initiated in 1990, accelerated the integration of computational biology and bioinformatics into drug discovery. This milestone contributed to the creation of vast biological databases and sequence alignment tools that allowed pharmaceutical scientists to explore genetic and protein targets for new drugs.

The late 1990s saw the implementation of electronic data capture (EDC) systems in clinical research. These platforms replaced paper-based case report forms and brought automation to clinical trial data collection and management. Around the same time, high-throughput screening (HTS) technologies were introduced in drug discovery, enabling rapid testing of thousands of compounds. The massive datasets generated by HTS created an urgent need for robust data processing tools, database management systems, and integration with laboratory information management systems (LIMS). Regulatory milestones also influenced pharmaceutical computing during this period, such as the release of FDA's 21 CFR Part 11 in 1997, which defined requirements for electronic records and signatures in clinical trials and manufacturing.

Moving into the 2000s, advancements in internet technology and data connectivity enabled global collaboration and cloud-based research environments. Software for in silico modeling, such as AutoDock and MOE, became popular for structure-based drug design. Computational tools were now used for virtual screening, lead optimization, protein-ligand docking, and prediction of ADME properties. The rise of -omics technologies — genomics, proteomics, and metabolomics — further enhanced the role of computers, as specialized algorithms were developed for multi-dimensional data analysis. Open-source software platforms also began to emerge, making high-end computational tools more accessible to academic researchers and smaller pharmaceutical firms.

1.1.3 From manual records to AI-driven R&D

The transformation from manual records to AI-driven research and development in pharmaceuticals has been both revolutionary and inevitable. Traditionally, drug discovery workflows relied heavily on handwritten laboratory notebooks, paper-based data entry, and physical charts. These methods made record-keeping tedious, data analysis slow, and regulatory compliance challenging. Even formulation trials and stability studies were conducted using printed protocols, and documentation often lacked integration and traceability. This system was not scalable for the demands of modern pharmaceutical research, which increasingly required handling of large volumes of data with high accuracy and consistency.

With the adoption of digital systems such as electronic laboratory notebooks (ELNs), enterprise resource planning (ERP) systems, and global document management systems, pharmaceutical companies gradually eliminated paper records and centralized their data infrastructure. Integration of these systems with advanced instruments, automated data logging, and barcode-based inventory tracking marked the beginning of digitally managed laboratories. Clinical trials also underwent a parallel transformation with the use of cloud-based clinical trial management systems (CTMS), automated patient enrollment systems, and AI-based risk-based monitoring.

In the last decade, artificial intelligence and machine learning have taken center stage in pharmaceutical R&D. AI algorithms are now used for predicting drug-target interactions, optimizing chemical structures, identifying biomarkers, and analyzing real-world data for pharmacovigilance. Natural language processing (NLP) tools are used to scan scientific literature and generate hypotheses for novel therapeutic targets. Deep learning models like convolutional neural networks (CNNs) and recurrent neural networks (RNNs) are applied to image-based drug screening and time-series clinical data, respectively AI has also enabled digital twins for virtual simulation of organs and patient behavior, drastically improving the design and success rate of clinical trials. These advancements have shifted pharmaceutical R&D from a reactive and manual approach to a proactive, data-driven, and predictive ecosystem powered by computing intelligence.

1.2 Role and Scope of Computers in Drug Development

1.2.1 Drug discovery and design

The process of drug discovery and design has been profoundly enhanced by the use of computers. Traditionally, discovering a new drug involved extensive experimental screening of thousands of chemical compounds, which consumed both time and resources. The introduction of computer-aided drug design (CADD) has changed this paradigm by allowing scientists to predict how potential drug molecules will behave even before they are synthesized. Computers are now extensively used in both **structure-based** and **ligand-based** drug design approaches. Structure-based drug design relies on the knowledge of the 3D structure of a biological target, usually a protein, and uses techniques such as molecular docking, molecular dynamics simulations, and energy minimization to predict the best binding interactions between the drug and its target. These simulations help researchers identify lead molecules that have a high probability of showing biological activity.

In ligand-based drug design, when the structure of the target is unknown, computers are used to analyze the properties of known active molecules to develop quantitative structure-activity relationship (QSAR) models. These models help predict the activity of new compounds by comparing their chemical features to known active compounds. Pharmacophore modeling, another important computational tool, allows researchers to identify the essential chemical features required for biological activity. Large virtual libraries of drug-like molecules can be screened using in silico methods, dramatically reducing the number of candidates for physical testing. Computational chemistry tools also assist in optimizing the physicochemical properties of lead molecules such as solubility, lipophilicity, and metabolic stability. This integration of computational tools into the early stages of drug discovery has significantly increased the success rate and efficiency of identifying new drug candidates.

1.2.2 Preclinical and clinical research

Computers play a central role in both preclinical and clinical phases of drug development by enabling data analysis, modeling, simulation, and regulatory compliance. In preclinical research, computers are used to simulate pharmacokinetic (PK) and pharmacodynamic (PD) profiles of drugs through predictive models. These models are developed using data from in vitro studies and animal experiments and help in estimating human responses even before clinical trials begin. Physiologically based pharmacokinetic (PBPK) modeling is widely used for extrapolating drug behavior from animals to humans. This approach considers organ-specific drug distribution, enzyme activity, and transporter involvement, and provides insights into optimal dose selection and expected variability.

During clinical research, computers are used in the design, execution, and monitoring of trials. Clinical trial protocols are developed with the help of simulation software that allows researchers to predict recruitment rates, dropout trends, and endpoint sensitivity. Electronic data capture (EDC) systems are used to collect patient data in real time, eliminating the need for manual entry and reducing errors. Clinical trial management systems (CTMS) and interactive web response systems (IWRS) help in randomization, drug supply management, and patient follow-up. Adverse event tracking, safety monitoring, and statistical analysis of trial data are handled through validated software that complies with international regulatory standards. Computers also aid in performing interim analyses, generating clinical study reports, and managing clinical trial master files (TMFs). The integration of artificial intelligence in clinical trials has made it possible to predict patient eligibility, analyze electronic health records, and support adaptive trial designs, thereby accelerating the development timeline.

1.2.3 Regulatory submission and market access

Regulatory submission is a highly structured process that requires accurate, traceable, and well-organized documentation of all activities conducted during drug development. Computers are indispensable in compiling, formatting, validating, and submitting regulatory documents to agencies such as the USFDA, EMA, and CDSCO. Most regulatory authorities now mandate electronic submissions through platforms like the electronic Common Technical Document (eCTD). Specialized software tools are used to create, hyperlink, and publish submission dossiers according to regulatory specifications. These tools ensure proper formatting of Module 1 to Module 5, and validate them using region-specific tools before submission.

In addition to submissions, computer systems are used to track regulatory queries, manage correspondence, and maintain compliance throughout the product lifecycle. Regulatory information management systems (RIMS) help companies handle multiple submissions across different markets and maintain global alignment. These systems store data related to variations, renewals, product licenses, and approval status. For market access, computers support pricing analytics, health technology assessment (HTA) modeling, and real-world data analysis. Predictive models are used to assess the economic impact of a new drug in different healthcare systems, helping companies position their products strategically. Post-marketing surveillance, pharmacovigilance, and risk management plans are also supported by computer software that integrates data from adverse event reports, electronic health records, and patient registries. Thus, computers have become an integral part of regulatory strategy and market.

1.3 Statistical Modeling in Pharmaceutical R&D

1.3.1 Introduction to modeling approaches

Statistical modeling plays a vital role in pharmaceutical research and development by enabling researchers to understand complex biological systems, optimize formulations, interpret experimental data, and make data-driven decisions. Modeling refers to the creation of mathematical or computational representations of real-world biological or pharmaceutical processes. In the context of drug development, models are used to describe the relationship between input factors and responses, predict outcomes under various scenarios, and support regulatory submissions with scientifically valid justifications. The models can be simple linear regressions or advanced nonlinear dynamic systems depending on the research objective and the nature of the data involved.

In pharmaceutical R&D, models are developed from experimental data obtained during drug discovery, preclinical studies, clinical trials, and manufacturing processes. These models help in identifying significant factors affecting drug performance, understanding variability, and designing robust experiments. For example, modeling can be used to predict how a change in pH or excipient concentration will affect the dissolution rate of a formulation. Modeling approaches can be broadly divided into two types: empirical or descriptive models and mechanistic models. Both have distinct roles and are used according to the complexity and purpose of the study. Statistical software like SAS, R, JMP, MATLAB, and Minitab are commonly used to develop and evaluate these models, ensuring reproducibility and compliance with regulatory requirements.

1.3.2 Descriptive vs. Mechanistic Modeling

Statistical modeling approaches in pharmaceutical science can be broadly categorized into **descriptive** and **mechanistic** models. Each serves a different purpose in the drug development process. Descriptive models, also known as empirical models, are built directly from observed data without incorporating any knowledge of the underlying mechanisms. These models focus on describing patterns, relationships, or trends in the data. On the other hand, mechanistic models are based on prior knowledge of the physical, chemical, or biological processes involved in the system being studied. They are typically built using differential equations or logical relationships and aim to explain the cause-and-effect mechanisms.

Descriptive models are usually easier to construct and require fewer assumptions, making them useful in the early stages of development when detailed knowledge of the system is limited. They are commonly used in regression analysis, design of experiments (DoE), and process optimization. Mechanistic models are more complex but provide deeper insights and can be used to simulate system behavior under different conditions. These models are essential in pharmacokinetics, pharmacodynamics, drug absorption, and disease progression modeling. The choice between descriptive and mechanistic modeling depends on the research question, available data, and desired level of understanding.

1.3.2.1 Characteristics and applications

Descriptive models are characterized by their focus on empirical relationships and statistical significance. They often involve fitting mathematical functions such as linear, polynomial, or exponential equations to observed data. These models are ideal for applications like dose-response analysis, stability studies, and screening of formulation variables. In a typical factorial design experiment, for example, a second-order polynomial model may be used to identify which combination of excipients yields the best dissolution profile. The strength of descriptive models lies in their simplicity, speed, and flexibility when dealing with real-world noisy data.

Mechanistic models, in contrast, are characterized by their ability to represent the underlying processes that govern the system. They often involve solving sets of differential equations that describe mass transfer, reaction kinetics, transport mechanisms, or physiological pathways. Applications of mechanistic models include predicting plasma drug concentration using compartmental models in pharmacokinetics, modeling enzymatic degradation in biopharmaceuticals, or simulating gastrointestinal absorption using physiologically based pharmacokinetic (PBPK) models. Mechanistic models are also used in quality-by-design (QbD) frameworks to simulate how variations in raw materials or process parameters affect product quality. Although they require detailed input data and strong domain knowledge, these models provide predictive power and are favored for risk assessment and regulatory submissions.

In summary, descriptive models are valuable for identifying trends and optimizing experimental conditions, while mechanistic models provide a deeper understanding of how and why processes behave in a certain way. Both types of modeling are complementary and are often used together in modern pharmaceutical development to ensure both efficiency and scientific rigor.

1.3.3 Common Statistical Parameters

In pharmaceutical research and development, understanding statistical parameters is essential for designing experiments, analyzing data, and making valid scientific conclusions. These parameters are used to summarize data, assess variability, and evaluate the significance of observed effects. They form the foundation of all statistical models and provide the tools necessary for making informed decisions in both preclinical and clinical studies. Researchers and regulators alike rely on these parameters to interpret results, determine the reliability of findings, and assess whether a drug or formulation meets the desired standards. A clear understanding of these core concepts enables the proper application of statistical techniques throughout the drug development process.

1.3.3.1 Mean, median, variance, SD, p-value

The **mean**, also known as the average, is the most common measure of central tendency and is calculated by summing all observed values and dividing by the number of observations. In pharmaceutical contexts, it is frequently used to report the average concentration of a drug in plasma, the average tablet weight, or the average dissolution rate. The **median** is the middle value when the data are arranged in order and is less affected by extreme values, making it useful in skewed data distributions such as patient response times or adverse event durations.

The **variance** is a measure of how much the data values differ from the mean. It provides insight into the spread or dispersion in a dataset, which is important in understanding batch-to-batch consistency or variability in biological response. The **standard deviation (SD)** is the square root of the variance and is expressed in the same unit as the data. It is often reported alongside the mean to describe the degree of variability in clinical trial results, assay performance, or formulation stability. For example, a drug formulation with a mean dissolution time of 30 minutes and an SD of 2 minutes indicates tight control, whereas a higher SD would suggest inconsistency.

The **p-value** is a statistical measure that indicates the probability of observing a result as extreme as, or more extreme than, the actual observed result, under the assumption that the null hypothesis is true. In pharmaceutical studies, a p-value is used to test hypotheses and determine whether observed differences are likely due to chance. A p-value less than 0.05 is typically considered statistically significant, suggesting that the result is unlikely to have occurred by random variation alone. For example, when comparing the effect of two different formulations on bioavailability, a p-value below 0.05 indicates that the difference is statistically meaningful and not due to chance.

1.3.4 Estimation and Confidence Regions

Estimation is a fundamental concept in statistical modeling where values obtained from a sample are used to make inferences about a population. In pharmaceutical R&D, estimation is used in a wide range of applications such as determining average drug concentrations, estimating pharmacokinetic parameters like half-life or clearance, and predicting future outcomes in clinical trials. There are two main types of estimation: point estimation and interval estimation. Point estimation provides a single best guess of a parameter, such as the mean plasma concentration. However, point estimates do not convey the uncertainty associated with the estimate, which is why interval estimation is often preferred in regulatory and scientific reporting.

1.3.4.1 Interval estimation and interpretation

Interval estimation involves constructing a range, known as a **confidence interval (CI)**, within which the true population parameter is expected to lie with a certain level of confidence, usually 95%. For example, a 95% confidence interval for the mean blood pressure reduction by a new drug might range from 8.2 mmHg to 12.6 mmHg. This means that there is a 95% probability that the actual mean reduction lies within this interval, assuming the data follow the assumptions of the statistical model. The width of the confidence interval depends on factors such as the sample size, variability in the data, and the desired confidence level. Narrow intervals indicate high precision, while wide intervals reflect greater uncertainty.

In pharmaceutical research, confidence intervals are crucial for interpreting the results of bioequivalence studies, clinical efficacy trials, and stability assessments. Regulatory authorities such as the USFDA require that the 90% confidence interval for the ratio of pharmacokinetic parameters like AUC (Area Under the Curve) and Cmax (maximum concentration) fall within the acceptance range of 80% to 125% for generic drug approval. In formulation development, confidence intervals help determine the robustness of a product's performance across different manufacturing conditions. By providing a range instead of a single estimate, interval estimation gives a more realistic view of uncertainty, helping scientists make decisions that are both statistically sound and scientifically meaningful.

1.3.5 Nonlinearity at the Optimum

Nonlinearity is a common feature in pharmaceutical systems due to the complex interactions between formulation components, biological systems, and processing variables. When developing statistical or mathematical models to optimize a formulation or process, it is often observed that the relationship between the independent variables (such as concentration of excipients, pH, or temperature) and the response variable (such as drug release or bioavailability) is not linear. Nonlinearity at the optimum refers to the phenomenon where the response surface becomes curved or distorted around the region of maximum or minimum response. This behavior is critical to understand because it affects the accuracy and reliability of optimization results, especially in quality-by-design (QbD) studies and design of experiments (DoE) applications.

In a linear system, the response changes proportionally with changes in the input variables. However, in nonlinear systems, small changes in input can lead to unpredictable or exaggerated changes in output. This behavior is especially relevant when working near the optimum point of a formulation or process. For instance, adjusting the ratio of two surfactants in a microemulsion system might lead to a drastic change in droplet size or stability near the critical composition, which would not be predicted by a simple linear model. Recognizing nonlinearity helps scientists avoid misleading conclusions and encourages the use of higher-order models or response surface methodologies to better capture the real behavior of the system.

1.3.5.1 Model fitting challenges

Fitting a model to data that exhibits nonlinearity poses several challenges. One major issue is that traditional linear regression techniques are inadequate for capturing the curved nature of the response. In such cases, polynomial models or nonlinear regression techniques must be employed, which require more advanced statistical tools and careful selection of model terms. Another challenge is the presence of multiple local optima on the response surface, which can lead to incorrect identification of the global optimum. This problem becomes more serious in multidimensional models where interaction effects between variables further complicate the surface geometry.

Moreover, the assumptions of normality, homoscedasticity (equal variance), and independence of residuals may be violated in nonlinear systems, affecting the validity of statistical tests and confidence intervals. Nonlinear models also tend to be more sensitive to outliers and require larger datasets for stable parameter estimation. Optimization algorithms such as gradient descent, Newton-Raphson, or evolutionary algorithms are often needed to accurately locate the optimum in such cases. Despite these challenges, addressing nonlinearity is essential in pharmaceutical modeling because it leads to more accurate predictions, better understanding of process behavior, and more robust product development.

1.3.6 Sensitivity Analysis

Sensitivity analysis is a powerful tool used in pharmaceutical modeling to evaluate how changes in input variables influence the output or response of a model. It helps researchers identify which parameters are most critical to the performance of a formulation, process, or biological system. In the context of drug development, sensitivity analysis is used at various stages, including formulation optimization, pharmacokinetic modeling, and risk assessment. For example, when modeling the dissolution profile of a tablet, sensitivity analysis can reveal whether the amount of binder or the compression force has a greater impact on the final release rate. This knowledge allows scientists to focus on controlling the most influential parameters to ensure consistent product performance.

Sensitivity analysis also aids in the identification of robust operating conditions, where small variations in input variables do not significantly affect the output. It plays an important role in quality-by-design approaches, where it helps establish a design space by determining the range of acceptable values for critical process parameters. Moreover, sensitivity analysis supports regulatory submissions by providing justification for parameter ranges and risk control strategies. It also enhances model validation by revealing potential weaknesses or assumptions in the model structure.

1.3.6.1 Local and global sensitivity

Sensitivity analysis can be categorized into **local** and **global** approaches based on the range and method of evaluation. **Local sensitivity analysis** involves changing one parameter at a time, usually by a small amount, while keeping all other parameters constant. This method is simple and computationally efficient but is limited to the specific region around a nominal value. It is most suitable when the model is linear or when the interaction between variables is minimal. For example, in a pharmacokinetic model, local sensitivity analysis can assess how a small change in clearance affects the plasma concentration profile.

Global sensitivity analysis, on the other hand, evaluates the influence of parameters over their entire range and often considers the combined effects of multiple variables. It provides a more comprehensive understanding of model behavior, especially in nonlinear and complex systems. Methods like Monte Carlo simulations, Sobol indices, and variance-based techniques are commonly used in global sensitivity analysis. These methods generate random or structured input samples across the full parameter space and analyze the resulting output variability. In pharmaceutical applications, global sensitivity analysis is particularly useful in identifying high-risk variables, prioritizing experiments, and designing robust formulations. By capturing both individual and interactive effects of parameters, global sensitivity analysis helps in making better-informed decisions in drug development.

1.3.7 Optimal Design of Experiments

Optimal design of experiments is a crucial aspect of pharmaceutical research where the goal is to extract maximum information from a limited number of experimental runs. Traditional experimental designs such as full or fractional factorial designs work well in many cases, but when the number of variables is large or the cost of experimentation is high, optimal design methods are preferred. These designs are mathematically planned in such a way that they provide the most precise estimates of model parameters with the least number of trials. In pharmaceutical R&D, optimal designs are widely used in formulation optimization, analytical method development, and process validation. They not only improve efficiency but also help meet regulatory expectations under quality-by-design (QbD) frameworks by identifying the design space and understanding parameter relationships.

Optimal designs are based on criteria that seek to minimize variance or maximize information content. These criteria are derived from the statistical properties of the design matrix and the variance-covariance matrix of parameter estimates. Unlike conventional designs, optimal designs can be customized for complex models, irregular constraints, or specific experimental regions. They can be generated using specialized software such as JMP, Design-Expert, and MODDE. By using optimal design, pharmaceutical scientists can model nonlinear systems, identify critical process parameters, and develop robust formulations even with limited resources.

1.3.7.1 D-optimal, A-optimal, Latin square

D-optimal design is one of the most widely used optimal design methods in pharmaceutical research. It focuses on minimizing the determinant of the variance-covariance matrix of the estimated regression coefficients. In simpler terms, it aims to obtain parameter estimates with the smallest possible confidence region. D-optimal designs are particularly useful when the experimental region is constrained or when the model is nonlinear. They are flexible and can handle missing data, mixture designs, and irregular factor spaces. For instance, in developing a nasal spray formulation, a D-optimal design can help identify the best combination of pH, viscosity enhancer, and preservative level using fewer trials than a full factorial design.

A-optimal design, on the other hand, minimizes the average variance of the parameter estimates. It focuses on improving the overall precision of the estimates rather than the size of the confidence region. A-optimal designs are helpful when all parameters are equally important, and the goal is to reduce uncertainty uniformly across the model. Though less common than D-optimal designs in pharmaceutical applications, they are still valuable in method validation and analytical optimization studies.

Latin square design is a special type of experimental design used to control for two sources of variability simultaneously. It is structured in a way that each treatment appears only once in each row and column. This design is especially useful when conducting tablet compression studies, bioavailability tests, or sensory evaluations where the variability due to position, order, or subject can affect results. Latin square designs are simpler to construct and analyze compared to optimal designs and are often used in early-stage studies where control over external factors is essential.

Each of these designs serves a specific purpose in pharmaceutical research, and their selection depends on the complexity of the system, the number of variables, and the availability of resources. By applying these designs appropriately, researchers can save time, reduce costs, and generate scientifically sound conclusions.

1.3.8 Population Modeling

Population modeling is an advanced approach used in pharmaceutical sciences to study how a drug behaves across a population rather than in a single individual. This method considers the variability among individuals in terms of their physiological, genetic, demographic, and disease-related characteristics. Unlike traditional pharmacokinetic (PK) and pharmacodynamic (PD) models that are based on average profiles, population models aim to describe the distribution of parameters within a population and identify factors that contribute to variability. This technique is especially valuable in clinical drug development, where understanding differences between patients can lead to better dosing strategies, improved efficacy, and reduced adverse effects.

Population modeling integrates data from many individuals, often collected from clinical trials, and fits a single model to describe both typical responses and the extent of variability. These models are built using nonlinear mixed-effects modeling (NLME), which combines fixed effects (common to all individuals) and random effects (specific to each individual). Specialized software such as NONMEM, Monolix, and Phoenix NLME are used to develop and evaluate these models. Regulatory agencies encourage the use of population models to support dose selection, labeling recommendations, and risk-benefit assessments.

1.3.8.1 Inter-individual variability modeling

Inter-individual variability modeling is a core component of population pharmacokinetics and pharmacodynamics. It involves quantifying how much individual responses differ from the population average and identifying the sources of that variability. Factors such as age, weight, sex, organ function, genetic polymorphisms, and co-medications can all influence drug absorption, distribution, metabolism, and excretion. By incorporating these covariates into the model, researchers can explain a significant portion of the observed variability and tailor treatments more effectively.

For example, a population PK model for an anticancer drug may show that elderly patients with reduced renal function have slower drug clearance, requiring dose adjustment. Similarly, a PD model might reveal that certain genotypes respond differently to a beta-blocker, leading to personalized therapy. Inter-individual variability modeling is also useful in bridging studies, pediatric extrapolations, and special population assessments. It enhances the understanding of drug behavior in real-world settings and supports the move toward precision medicine in pharmaceutical practice.

Review Questions

1. What was the initial use of computers in pharmaceutical sciences?

In the 1950s and 1960s, computers were used mainly for basic statistical processing, inventory control, and pharmacokinetic data analysis using mainframes and early programming languages like FORTRAN.

2. What were the main limitations of early computers in pharma R&D?

Early computers were bulky, expensive, and required programming expertise, which restricted their use to specialized research centers.

3. What role did mini-computers play in pharmaceutical development during the 1970s?

Mini-computers made computational tools more accessible, enabling dose-response analysis, regression modeling, and early chemoinformatics applications.

4. Name two early software tools used for chemical structure drawing.

ChemDraw and ISIS/Draw were among the first tools for digital molecular structure representation.

5. How did the Human Genome Project influence pharmaceutical computing?

It accelerated the integration of bioinformatics, allowing researchers to analyze genes and proteins for drug discovery and target identification.

6. What is the function of electronic data capture (EDC) systems in clinical trials?

EDC systems replace paper-based forms, allowing real-time, accurate digital data collection in clinical research.

7. What is 21 CFR Part 11 and why is it important?

It is an FDA regulation that defines standards for electronic records and signatures in pharmaceutical environments to ensure data integrity.

8. Mention any two open-source tools used in modern pharmaceutical R&D.

AutoDock (for molecular docking) and R (for statistical analysis) are commonly used open-source tools.

9. How has AI transformed pharmaceutical R&D in recent years?

AI is used for drug-target prediction, structure optimization, adverse event analysis, and virtual clinical simulations.

10. What are digital twins in the context of pharma R&D?

Digital twins are virtual simulations of organs or patient behavior used to test drug effects and improve clinical trial outcomes.

11. Define computer-aided drug design (CADD).

CADD refers to using computational methods to design drug molecules with improved activity, safety, and pharmacokinetic properties.

12. What are the two main approaches in CADD?

Structure-based drug design and ligand-based drug design.

13. What is QSAR modeling?

Quantitative Structure-Activity Relationship (QSAR) models predict biological activity based on chemical structure features.

14. What is a pharmacophore model?

It represents the essential features of a molecule required for biological activity and is used in virtual screening.

15. What is PBPK modeling used for?

Physiologically Based Pharmacokinetic (PBPK) modeling predicts drug absorption, distribution, metabolism, and excretion using physiological parameters.

16. How do computers aid in clinical trial design?

Computers simulate patient enrollment, dropout rates, and endpoint sensitivity to optimize trial protocols.

17. What is the role of IWRS in clinical research?

Interactive Web Response Systems manage randomization, drug supply, and patient tracking in real time.

18. Mention one use of AI in clinical trials.

AI can predict patient eligibility using electronic health records and support adaptive trial designs.

19. What is the eCTD format in regulatory submission?

The electronic Common Technical Document (eCTD) is a standardized format for submitting drug approval documents digitally.

20. What is the function of Regulatory Information Management Systems (RIMS)?

RIMS track regulatory submissions, manage approvals, and ensure compliance across global markets.

21. Name a statistical software used in pharmaceutical modeling.

JMP, Minitab, and SAS are popular statistical tools for pharmaceutical data analysis.

22. What is the difference between descriptive and mechanistic models?

Descriptive models use observed data patterns, while mechanistic models are based on known physical or biological processes.

23. What is the purpose of a confidence interval?

It estimates the range within which a population parameter is likely to lie with a specific confidence level (e.g., 95%).

24. Define p-value in hypothesis testing.

The p-value indicates the probability that observed differences occurred by chance under the null hypothesis.

25. Why is standard deviation important in pharmaceutical data?

It reflects the variability in results, helping assess batch consistency or clinical outcome variation.

26. What does nonlinearity at the optimum mean?

It refers to a curved response surface near the optimum, requiring advanced modeling techniques for accurate optimization.

27. What is local sensitivity analysis?

It studies the effect of small changes in one parameter while keeping others constant, to evaluate model responsiveness.

28. Define global sensitivity analysis.

It assesses the impact of all parameters across their entire range, capturing interaction effects and high-risk variables.

29. What is D-optimal design used for?

It minimizes the confidence region of regression parameters, ideal for constrained or nonlinear models.

30. What is population modeling?

It describes drug behavior across varied individuals, accounting for inter-individual variability to support personalized dosing.

MCQS

1. In which decade did mainframe computers first appear in pharmaceutical research?

A) 1940s

B) 1950s

C) 1970s

D) 1980s

2. Which programming language was commonly used with early pharmaceutical computers?

A) Java

B) Python

C) FORTRAN

D) HTML

3. Early computers in pharma were mainly used for:

A) Data encryption

B) Statistical analysis

C) Genetic editing

D) Virtual reality

4. What development in the 1970s increased access to computational resources?

A) Personal computers

B) Mini-computers and time-sharing systems

C) Cloud computing

D) Blockchain

5. Which field started emerging due to digitization of chemical structures?

A) Genomics

B) Chemoinformatics

C) Robotics

D) Pharmacogenomics

6. WinNonlin software was mainly used for:

A) Molecular modeling

B) Clinical trial randomization

C) PK/PD modeling

D) Hospital billing

7. ChemDraw software helps in:

A) Clinical trial monitoring

B) Drawing chemical structures

C) Blood pressure monitoring

D) Data encryption

8. The Human Genome Project began in:

A) 1980

B) 1990

C) 2000

D) 2010

9. High-throughput screening (HTS) helped mainly in:

A) Automating marketing strategies

B) Rapid compound testing

C) Designing hospital software

D) Monitoring patient health

10. LIMS stands for:

A) Laboratory Information Management System

B) Learning Integrated Medical System

C) Limited Information for Medical Software

D) Logistic Inventory Management Service

11. What regulation mandates standards for electronic records in pharma?

A) HIPAA

B) 21 CFR Part 11

C) GDPR

D) PCI DSS

12. Virtual screening is used in:

A) Drug packaging

B) Protein-ligand docking

C) Clinical trial site selection

D) Vaccine distribution

13. Which software is commonly used for in silico drug modeling?

A) Adobe Illustrator

B) AutoDock

C) Microsoft Excel

D) Oracle CRM

14. Electronic Data Capture (EDC) systems mainly replace:

A) Hard drives

B) Paper case report forms

C) Handwritten prescriptions

D) Clinical devices

15. Structure-based drug design requires knowledge of:

A) Drug price

B) Chemical reactivity

C) Protein 3D structure

D) Solubility curves

16. QSAR models are used when:

A) Clinical trials are over

B) Target structure is unknown

C) Drug labeling is needed

D) Patient recruitment begins

17. Pharmacophore modeling identifies:

A) Drug manufacturing defects

B) Essential features for biological activity

C) Supply chain bottlenecks

D) Tablet hardness parameters

18. PBPK models are useful for predicting:

A) Drug clearance in humans

B) Labeling design

C) Brand positioning

D) Pharmaceutical marketing

19. Electronic laboratory notebooks (ELNs) help in:

A) Drug packaging

B) Managing experimental records

C) Managing hospital beds

D) Auditing pharmacy stores

20. AI models now assist in:

A) Optimizing lab space

B) Predicting drug-target interactions

C) Writing medical novels

D) Managing cafeteria logistics

21. Natural Language Processing (NLP) in pharma helps:

A) Translate package inserts

B) Extract insights from literature

C) Manufacturc drugs

D) Manage cold chains

22. Digital twins simulate:

A) Manufacturing costs

B) Chemical stability

C) Organs and patient behavior

D) Equipment maintenance

23. Deep learning is used in pharma for:

A) Project management

B) Clinical imaging analysis

C) Staff training

D) Customer surveys

24. Early computer use in pharma was limited because of:

A) High power supply

B) Expensive costs and expertise needed

C) Poor software availability

D) Lack of researchers

25. Cloud-based CTMS supports:

A) Hospital inventory

B) Clinical trial management

C) Drug pricing models

D) Adverse event reporting to patients

26. What transformed paper-based clinical trial data collection?

A) SMS alerts

B) Electronic Data Capture (EDC) systems

C) Print journals

D) Barcode labeling

27. Which of the following improved global collaboration in pharma R&D?

A) Local servers

B) Internet technology

C) Fax machines

D) Typewriters

28. The first use of computers in pharma mainly helped with:

A) Drug advertisement

B) Pharmacokinetic data analysis

C) Manufacturing vaccines

D) Managing hospital pharmacies

29. Computational tools now allow:

A) Faster product advertising

B) Virtual screening of drug candidates

C) Tablet coating quality control only

D) Monitoring office attendance

30. AI and machine learning are enabling pharma to shift towards:
A) Reactive paper-based documentation
B) Proactive predictive data-driven R&D
C) Manual case studies only
D) Delayed trial reporting

Answer Key

1. **B** – 1950s
2. **C** – FORTRAN
3. **B** – Statistical analysis
4. **B** – Mini-computers and time-sharing systems
5. **B** – Chemoinformatics
6. **C** – PK/PD modeling
7. **B** – Drawing chemical structures
8. **B** – 1990
9. **B** – Rapid compound testing
10. **A** – Laboratory Information Management System
11. **B** – 21 CFR Part 11
12. **B** – Protein-ligand docking
13. **B** – AutoDock
14. **B** – Paper case report forms
15. **C** – Protein 3D structure
16. **B** – Target structure is unknown
17. **B** – Essential features for biological activity
18. **A** – Drug clearance in humans
19. **B** – Managing experimental records
20. **B** – Predicting drug-target interactions
21. **B** – Extract insights from literature
22. **C** – Organs and patient behavior
23. **B** – Clinical imaging analysis
24. **B** – Expensive costs and expertise needed
25. **B** – Clinical trial management
26. **B** – Electronic Data Capture (EDC) systems
27. **B** – Internet technology
28. **B** – Pharmacokinetic data analysis
29. **B** – Virtual screening of drug candidates

30. **B** – Proactive predictive data-driven R&D

CHAPTER TWO

Quality-by-Design (QbD) in Pharmaceutical Development

2.1 Introduction to QbD

2.1.1 Concept and rationale

Quality-by-Design (QbD) is a scientific and systematic approach to pharmaceutical development that begins with predefined objectives and emphasizes product and process understanding and process control, based on sound science and quality risk management. The concept was formally introduced by the U.S. Food and Drug Administration (FDA) as part of its "Pharmaceutical cGMPs for the 21ˢᵗ Century" initiative. The core idea of QbD is that **quality should be built into the product from the beginning**, rather than tested into it at the end. This is achieved by understanding how various formulation and process variables affect product quality and by designing manufacturing processes that can consistently deliver products that meet predefined quality criteria.

In traditional pharmaceutical development, quality was often ensured through final product testing, with minimal understanding of how the process variables influenced the outcome. This approach could lead to batch failures, regulatory issues, and expensive post-approval changes. QbD replaces this reactive approach with a proactive methodology where critical quality attributes (CQAs), critical material attributes (CMAs), and critical process parameters (CPPs) are identified and controlled through robust experimental designs and statistical modeling. It emphasizes the importance of linking the physical, chemical, and biological properties of the drug and excipients with process design, using tools like risk assessment, design of experiments (DoE), and control strategies. The rationale behind QbD is that increased process understanding leads to greater flexibility in manufacturing, higher product reliability, better compliance, and faster regulatory approvals. Moreover, QbD lays the foundation for continuous improvement and lifecycle management of the pharmaceutical product.

2.1.2 Need for scientific risk-based development

The need for a scientific and risk-based development approach in pharmaceuticals arises from the increasing complexity of drug molecules, formulation technologies, and regulatory expectations. Regulatory authorities across the globe, including the FDA, EMA, and ICH, have recognized that a traditional "one-size-fits-all" quality control approach is insufficient to guarantee product quality, especially in the case of biologics, highly potent drugs, and personalized medicines. In this context, QbD provides a structured framework to identify, evaluate, and control risks that could potentially impact product quality, safety, or efficacy.

Scientific risk-based development involves the systematic identification of potential failure modes using tools like Failure Mode and Effects Analysis (FMEA), Ishikawa diagrams, and fault tree analysis. It allows developers to focus their efforts and resources on areas that are most critical to product performance. For example, in the development of an oral solid dosage form, the particle size of the active pharmaceutical ingredient (API), the type of binder, and the granulation method may be identified as high-risk variables that need stringent control. By using scientific data and statistical tools, developers can justify the ranges of these parameters and demonstrate that product quality will not be compromised within the established design space.

This approach also enhances regulatory flexibility. When sufficient product and process understanding has been demonstrated, post-approval changes within the design space may not require additional regulatory submissions. This reduces the burden of compliance and accelerates time to market. Furthermore, a risk-based approach ensures patient safety by minimizing the chances of product variability, contamination, or performance failure. In a global regulatory environment that demands greater transparency, accountability, and evidence-based decision-making, QbD and risk-based development have become essential pillars of modern pharmaceutical development strategy.

2.2 ICH Q8 Guideline: Overview and Implications

2.2.1 Objectives of Q8

2.2.1 Objectives of ICH Q8

The **International Conference on Harmonisation (ICH) Q8 guideline**, formally titled *"Pharmaceutical Development"*, was introduced to guide the industry in adopting a modern, scientific, and risk-based approach to pharmaceutical product development. Before the introduction of ICH Q8, many formulations and manufacturing processes were developed based on empirical knowledge and fixed-process methods. The Q8 guideline brought a major shift by embedding **Quality-by-Design (QbD)** principles into the product development lifecycle. Its objectives are aimed at improving product quality, regulatory flexibility, and operational efficiency in a structured and globally harmonized way.

One of the core objectives of ICH Q8 is to **encourage pharmaceutical developers to establish clear scientific understanding of how raw material properties and process parameters influence the final product's quality**. This is done by linking **critical material attributes (CMAs)** and **critical process parameters (CPPs)** to **critical quality attributes (CQAs)**. CQAs are the physical, chemical, biological, or microbiological properties that must be controlled within defined limits to ensure product safety and efficacy. For example, in a solid oral dosage form, dissolution rate, assay, tablet hardness, and uniformity of content may be considered CQAs. The developer is expected to understand which raw material features (like particle size, moisture content, or polymorphic form) and which process steps (like mixing time or granulation speed) affect these attributes significantly.

To achieve this objective, ICH Q8 promotes the use of scientific tools such as **Design of Experiments (DoE), Risk Assessment,** and **Process Analytical Technology (PAT)**. These tools help in generating data-driven insights rather than relying on fixed recipes. The output of this systematic study is the identification of a **design space**—a multidimensional region that includes ranges of input variables and process parameters where product quality is assured. For instance, if a tablet formulation has been studied across varying binder concentrations (2%–6%) and granulation times (5 to 10 minutes), and results consistently show acceptable CQAs within that range, then this region can be declared as part of the design space.

Importantly, **working within the approved design space does not require post-approval regulatory changes**, offering operational flexibility and enabling manufacturers to respond to minor raw material variability or equipment scale-up without regulatory burden.

Another major objective of ICH Q8 is to **ensure transparency and consistency in regulatory submissions** by expecting applicants to present their development information in a structured, science-based format. This includes detailed rationale for selection of formulation components, explanation of process design, risk management strategies, justification of control points, and all supporting data—submitted within **Module 3 (Quality)** of the **Common Technical Document (CTD)**. When regulatory reviewers are provided with this level of scientific justification, it reduces back-and-forth communication, avoids unnecessary queries, and speeds up the review process. The approach thus benefits both the applicant and the regulatory authority.

ICH Q8 also places a strong emphasis on **product lifecycle management and continuous improvement**. By establishing a solid scientific foundation during development, manufacturers can implement real-time monitoring tools and update their processes based on ongoing manufacturing data, trends, and learnings. This adaptive capability supports long-term process robustness and sustainable compliance. For example, if a granulation step is monitored using PAT and trends indicate slight drift in moisture levels due to seasonal humidity changes, the process can be fine-tuned within the design space without needing to submit a regulatory variation.

In essence, the objectives of ICH Q8 are multifaceted. It aims to bring **science and risk-based thinking** into every step of product development. It promotes **robust process design**, **regulatory flexibility through design space, knowledge sharing through structured documentation**, and **continuous improvement through lifecycle management**. These principles are not limited to new drug applications but are equally applicable to existing products, especially during post-approval changes, scale-up, or technology transfer. Today, ICH Q8 is considered a global standard, and adherence to its objectives is often seen as a hallmark of high-quality and future-ready pharmaceutical development.

2.2 ICH Q8 Guideline: Overview and Implications

2.2.2 Pharmaceutical Development Elements

The ICH Q8 guideline defines **Pharmaceutical Development** as a structured set of activities aimed at designing a product and its manufacturing process to consistently deliver the intended performance, quality, and safety. It outlines several critical elements that must be addressed during product development to ensure that the product meets quality standards throughout its lifecycle. These elements form the scientific basis of the submission and provide evidence of product and process understanding. The guideline emphasizes that development should be based on knowledge of the drug substance, excipients, formulation, manufacturing process, and the link between input variables and critical quality attributes (CQAs).

One of the fundamental elements is **the selection and justification of the formulation design**. This includes choosing appropriate excipients, understanding their functions, and ensuring their compatibility with the drug substance. Developers must also evaluate the **physicochemical characteristics of the active pharmaceutical ingredient (API)** such as solubility, stability, and polymorphic forms, which directly influence the formulation strategy. Another critical element is the **manufacturing process development**, which involves identifying critical process parameters (CPPs) and understanding how they influence product CQAs such as content uniformity, dissolution, and stability. The application of **design of experiments (DoE), risk assessment tools**, and **process analytical technology (PAT)** is encouraged to gain deep insights into process behavior.

The guideline also highlights the importance of defining a **control strategy** that includes raw material specifications, in-process controls, and finished product specifications to ensure quality. Additionally, the concept of a **design space** is introduced, which represents the combination of input variables and process parameters that have been demonstrated to provide quality assurance. Operating within this design space provides manufacturers with flexibility and efficiency in production without needing prior regulatory approval for changes. All these elements are expected to be documented clearly in the **Pharmaceutical Development section of the Common Technical Document (CTD)**, enabling regulatory authorities to assess the robustness of the product and process development.

2.3 Regulatory and Industry Perspectives

2.3.1 FDA and EMA Views

Both the **United States Food and Drug Administration (FDA)** and the **European Medicines Agency (EMA)** strongly support the implementation of QbD principles as outlined in ICH Q8. The FDA has been a pioneer in promoting QbD through its **Pharmaceutical cGMPs for the 21ˢᵗ Century** initiative, which encourages scientific and risk-based approaches to pharmaceutical manufacturing. The agency views QbD not as a regulatory requirement but as a recommended practice that can lead to more flexible and efficient drug development. The FDA also introduced the concept of **regulatory relief within the design space**, meaning that changes within an approved design space do not require prior approval, thereby streamlining post-approval changes.

The EMA also aligns with the ICH Q8 framework and has issued its own guidance documents that emphasize the importance of enhanced product and process understanding. It encourages applicants to include development data that justify formulation decisions, manufacturing process choices, and control strategies. Both agencies expect that submissions reflecting QbD principles will include risk assessments, results from experimental studies, and explanations of how critical attributes are controlled. Importantly, both FDA and EMA consider QbD to be closely linked to lifecycle management and expect companies to demonstrate **continued process verification (CPV)** and opportunities for **continuous improvement**.

2.3.2 Industry Adoption Examples

Many leading pharmaceutical companies have widely adopted QbD across their development pipelines and have reported significant benefits in terms of **cost savings, faster development timelines, and smoother regulatory interactions**. For instance, companies such as Pfizer, Novartis, and AstraZeneca have implemented QbD frameworks for both new chemical entities and generic formulations. One widely known example is the use of QbD by GlaxoSmithKline (GSK) in the development of solid oral dosage forms, where **design of experiments** was used to optimize tablet compression and coating parameters, leading to fewer batch failures and consistent dissolution profiles.

Another notable case is the adoption of **QbD in biopharmaceutical manufacturing**, where companies have applied risk-based approaches to optimize cell culture conditions, purification processes, and formulation stability. In generics, firms like Teva and Sandoz have used QbD to demonstrate bioequivalence more robustly, particularly when applying for biowaivers. These companies report that QbD not only improves internal decision-making but also enhances credibility during regulatory reviews, as it provides comprehensive data that support product quality and process robustness.

The pharmaceutical industry has also observed improvements in **technology transfer and scale-up** when QbD principles are applied early in development. Because QbD provides detailed understanding of material attributes and process sensitivities, transitioning from lab-scale to commercial manufacturing becomes more predictable and efficient. Overall, the industry's experience shows that while implementing QbD requires initial effort and investment, the long-term gains in product quality, regulatory flexibility, and operational excellence are substantial and transformative.

2.4 Practical Applications and Case Studies

2.4.1 Product and Process Development

The application of Quality-by-Design (QbD) in pharmaceutical product and process development has become a benchmark for scientifically sound and regulatory-compliant drug development. In real-world practice, QbD is implemented from the earliest stages of development to understand how formulation components, manufacturing conditions, and equipment variables influence product performance. For instance, when developing an oral tablet, the selection of excipients such as disintegrants, binders, and lubricants is not done arbitrarily. Instead, each excipient is studied for its functional role, compatibility with the active pharmaceutical ingredient (API), and impact on critical quality attributes (CQAs) like hardness, disintegration time, and dissolution rate.

During process development, QbD promotes a systematic exploration of critical process parameters (CPPs) such as blending time, granulation moisture, drying temperature, and compression force. These parameters are studied using tools like risk assessment and design of experiments (DoE). For example, a central composite or Box-Behnken design may be used to identify optimal settings for achieving uniform granule size and acceptable tablet friability. A typical case study could involve optimizing a wet granulation process by adjusting impeller speed and binder concentration to achieve ideal compressibility without affecting dissolution. These relationships are documented to establish a design space, which becomes the foundation for the control strategy and regulatory submission.

Another practical example involves the development of a sustained-release tablet where the ratio of hydrophilic and hydrophobic polymers is varied to control the release profile. By applying QbD tools, developers can map out how these formulation variables influence the drug release kinetics, ensuring a predictable and robust extended-release profile. The insights gained from such experiments reduce development time, minimize the need for post-approval changes, and increase confidence during technology transfer from R&D to manufacturing.

2.4.2 Control Strategy and Lifecycle Approach

A core principle of QbD is the implementation of a **control strategy** that ensures the product remains within quality specifications throughout its lifecycle. A control strategy is a planned set of controls, derived from product and process understanding, that ensures performance consistency and compliance. These controls include **material specifications, in-process checks, process monitoring parameters, and final product specifications.** For example, if the particle size of the API significantly impacts dissolution, then tight control over the particle size distribution will be part of the control strategy. Similarly, if compression force during tablet manufacturing affects both hardness and friability, it will be monitored and controlled in real-time during production.

The QbD-based control strategy is not limited to end-product testing. It is embedded throughout the manufacturing process using tools such as **Process Analytical Technology (PAT)**, which allows for real-time measurement and control of critical parameters. For instance, near-infrared (NIR) spectroscopy may be used to monitor blend uniformity or moisture content in granules during drying. This real-time control leads to greater efficiency, reduced waste, and better assurance of batch quality. The control strategy is documented in the regulatory submission, and working within the approved design space provides flexibility to adjust operations without requiring prior approval.

QbD also aligns with the concept of a **lifecycle approach**, which recognizes that pharmaceutical products may evolve over time due to scale-up, process improvements, or changes in raw material sources. Rather than viewing product quality as static, the lifecycle approach encourages continuous monitoring, trend analysis, and adaptation to new knowledge or technologies. Continued Process Verification (CPV) is an important part of this strategy, where manufacturing data are routinely collected and analyzed to confirm that the process remains under control. For example, if a tablet coating process is being monitored, long-term data trends may reveal a shift in gloss or thickness, prompting a proactive adjustment before any out-of-specification (OOS) result occurs.

In practical settings, companies have implemented lifecycle management systems that integrate QbD with change control, deviation tracking, and knowledge management. This ensures that quality improvements are based on scientific data rather than reactive responses to failure. Case studies from global pharmaceutical companies demonstrate how lifecycle management based on QbD principles has improved compliance, reduced time-to-market for changes, and enhanced overall product robustness.

Review Questions

1. What is the primary aim of Quality-by-Design (QbD) in pharmaceuticals?

To ensure built-in product quality through process understanding and control, rather than relying solely on final product testing.

2. How does QbD differ from traditional development approaches?

Traditional approaches focus on end-product testing, while QbD emphasizes designing quality into the product from the beginning.

3. What does the term "scientific risk-based development" refer to in QbD?

It refers to using data and risk assessment tools to prioritize and control variables that may impact product quality.

4. What is the purpose of a control strategy in QbD?

A control strategy outlines how critical material attributes and process parameters are monitored and controlled to ensure consistent product quality.

5. Define Critical Quality Attributes (CQAs).

CQAs are physical, chemical, biological, or microbiological properties that must be controlled to ensure the final product meets its quality standards.

6. Give two examples of CQAs in a tablet formulation.

Drug content uniformity and dissolution rate.

7. What are Critical Process Parameters (CPPs)?

These are process parameters that have a direct impact on CQAs and must be controlled to ensure product quality.

8. Define the term "design space" as used in QbD.

Design space is the multidimensional combination of input variables and process parameters that have been demonstrated to assure quality.

9. How does the FDA view the concept of design space?

Changes within the approved design space do not require regulatory approval, offering flexibility to manufacturers.

10. What is the Quality Target Product Profile (QTPP)?

It defines the desired product characteristics such as route of administration, dosage form, strength, and quality attributes.

11. How are CQAs identified in a product development process?

By evaluating the impact of material attributes and process parameters on product performance and patient safety.

12. Name a key international guideline that supports QbD implementation.

ICH Q8(R2) – Pharmaceutical Development.

13. What role does ICH Q8 play in QbD?

It provides a harmonized guideline for implementing QbD principles in pharmaceutical development.

14. What is the significance of risk assessment in QbD?

It helps prioritize areas requiring control or deeper understanding by evaluating the probability and severity of failure.

15. Name two risk assessment tools commonly used in QbD.

Failure Mode and Effects Analysis (FMEA) and Fishbone (Ishikawa) diagrams.

16. What is meant by "product and process understanding" in QbD?

A thorough knowledge of how formulation components and manufacturing steps affect product quality.

17. Give an example of a control strategy in tablet manufacturing.

Controlling granule moisture and tablet compression force to ensure consistent hardness and disintegration.

18. How does QbD improve regulatory compliance?

By offering a science-based justification for development decisions and reducing post-approval changes.

19. Which two regulatory agencies actively promote QbD?

The US FDA and the European Medicines Agency (EMA).

20. What does lifecycle management mean in QbD?

It refers to continuous improvement of the product and process throughout its commercial life based on accumulated data.

21. What is meant by a robust process in QbD?

A process that consistently delivers quality products even when there is variability in inputs or environmental conditions.

22. How is QbD applied in formulation development?

By identifying critical material attributes and evaluating their effect on product performance through design of experiments.

23. How does QbD benefit scale-up and technology transfer?

A well-understood and controlled process can be easily scaled or transferred to new sites without compromising quality.

24. What is the benefit of using a Design of Experiments (DoE) in QbD?

DoE allows systematic evaluation of multiple variables and their interactions with fewer experiments.

25. What is a commonly used DoE technique in QbD?

Factorial design, which explores the effect of multiple variables at different levels.

26. How does QbD help reduce product recalls?

By ensuring consistent product quality and reducing the chances of failure due to poor process understanding.

27. What is a material attribute in the context of QbD?

A property of a raw material or excipient that can influence the final product quality.

28. What is meant by process capability in QbD?

The ability of a process to consistently produce within specification limits.

29. Define real-time release testing (RTRT).

RTRT is the ability to evaluate and ensure quality of a product based on process data rather than relying on end-product testing.

30. What is one benefit of real-time release testing?

It enables faster batch release and improves manufacturing efficiency.

31. What is a typical QbD approach to optimizing drug dissolution?

Identifying the key excipients and process variables affecting dissolution and optimizing them using statistical models.

32. What is meant by a "knowledge space"?

The total body of information and understanding accumulated about the product and its manufacturing process.

33. How does QbD support continuous improvement?

By allowing updates to control strategies and processes based on new data without compromising product quality.

34. Give an example of a company implementing QbD in injectables.

Companies like Roche and Novartis have applied QbD to improve consistency and sterility assurance in injectable formulations.

35. How is patient safety enhanced through QbD?

Through better control of product variability, leading to safer and more effective medicines.

36. What is the role of statistical tools in QbD?

They help analyze data, interpret variability, and model the impact of variables on product quality.

37. How is variability managed under QbD?

By identifying critical sources of variability and controlling them within acceptable ranges.

38. Name one example of a CQA for parenteral emulsions.
Droplet size distribution.

39. What kind of software tools are used in QbD?
Design-Expert®, JMP®, Minitab®, and SIMCA®.

40. What is the importance of the "enhanced" QbD approach?
It offers more flexibility in development and manufacturing compared to traditional "minimal" approaches.

41. How does QbD benefit bioequivalence studies?
Better control of variables ensures reproducible performance, improving bioequivalence outcomes.

42. What is a case study example in QbD for oral dosage forms?
Optimizing binder level and granulation time to improve tablet disintegration and hardness.

43. How are CPPs identified?
Through risk assessment and design of experiments to understand their impact on CQAs.

44. What does PAT stand for in QbD?
Process Analytical Technology.

45. How does PAT relate to QbD?
PAT tools enable real-time monitoring and control of critical parameters, supporting QbD implementation.

46. What does the "lifecycle" in QbD refer to?
All stages from development through commercial manufacturing, monitoring, and improvement.

47. How is QbD applied during technology transfer?
It ensures consistent product quality by sharing knowledge on CPPs, CQAs, and control strategies.

48. How is QbD applied in regulatory filings?
It provides a scientific rationale for formulation and process decisions, making submissions more robust.

49. What does the term "enhanced pharmaceutical development" mean?
A development strategy where QbD principles are applied extensively to gain deeper product and process understanding.

50. In QbD, why is robustness testing important?
To evaluate how variations in process parameters affect product quality and ensure performance under normal conditions.

MCQS

What does QbD stand for in pharmaceutical development?

A) Quality before Design

B) Quality by Development

C) Quality by Design

D) Quality beyond Development

The primary goal of QbD is to:

A) Reduce clinical trial phases

B) Build quality into products

C) Increase production volume

D) Eliminate regulatory inspections

QbD focuses on which approach?

A) Trial and error

B) Scientific and risk-based

C) Pure statistical analysis

D) Intuitive judgment

The concept of "Design Space" is defined in:

A) ICH Q10

B) ICH Q8

C) ICH Q7

D) ICH E6

ICH Q8 mainly addresses:

A) Drug labeling

B) Pharmaceutical development

C) Quality control testing

D) Manufacturing site inspection

Which of the following is a key element in QbD?

A) Randomization of experiments

B) Understanding of variability

C) Ignoring process parameters

D) Elimination of validation steps

Risk management tools in QbD include:

A) Ishikawa diagram

B) Kaplan-Meier analysis

C) DNA sequencing

D) Gradient boosting

Which document provides global guidance on QbD?

A) ICH Q8

B) ICH Q1A

C) ICH E3

D) ICH M7

Control Strategy in QbD ensures:

A) Randomized product release

B) Minimal in-process checks

C) Consistent product quality

D) Decreased product life

Critical Quality Attributes (CQAs) refer to:

A) Personnel skills

B) Product characteristics affecting quality

C) Equipment validation

D) Plant location

Design of Experiments (DoE) is primarily used to:

A) Accelerate regulatory approval

B) Systematically study variable effects

C) Minimize marketing timelines

D) Increase drug solubility

Process Analytical Technology (PAT) is important in QbD for:

A) Raw material procurement

B) Real-time monitoring

C) Final batch release only

D) Recruitment of study volunteers

A benefit of applying QbD is:

A) Less documentation

B) Improved process robustness

C) Guaranteed market success

D) Increased manual testing

Quality Target Product Profile (QTPP) defines:

A) Marketing strategy

B) Ideal product attributes

C) Cleaning validation protocols

D) Analytical method validation

Failure Mode and Effects Analysis (FMEA) is used for:

A) Final drug approval

B) Identifying potential risks

C) Hiring manufacturing staff

D) Budget estimation

Critical Process Parameters (CPPs) are variables:
A) That affect equipment size
B) Without impact on product
C) That affect CQAs
D) Related to transport logistics

In QbD, real-time release testing (RTRT) allows:
A) Immediate batch rejection
B) Delayed batch release
C) Release without end-product testing
D) Extended stability studies

ICH Q8 defines "Control Strategy" as:
A) Marketing control plan
B) Risk mitigation report
C) Planned set of controls
D) Crisis management manual

FDA promotes QbD to:
A) Decrease site audits
B) Improve product understanding
C) Eliminate GMP requirements
D) Reduce patent periods

Which of the following is NOT a typical CQA?
A) Dissolution rate
B) Tablet hardness
C) Staff experience
D) Assay value

An example of CPP could be:
A) Operator dress code
B) Drying temperature in granulation
C) Internet connection speed
D) Warehouse ventilation

EMA's perspective on QbD emphasizes:
A) Randomized production
B) Product and process understanding
C) Decreased documentation
D) Rapid patient recruitment

The term "Lifecycle Approach" in QbD refers to:
A) Product recall strategy
B) Continuous improvement from development to commercialization

C) Exclusive pre-approval testing

D) Phase 1 trial only

An industry example of QbD adoption includes:

A) Developing herbal medicines

B) Designing robust generic drugs

C) Launching cosmetic products

D) Retail store management

QTPP is finalized:

A) After marketing approval

B) During initial development

C) During Phase IV studies

D) Only after commercial manufacturing

The concept of risk assessment in QbD includes:

A) Eliminating regulatory audits

B) Identifying and prioritizing potential issues

C) Ignoring minor deviations

D) Post-approval marketing

ICH Q8 guidelines support:

A) Reactive quality assurance

B) Proactive quality design

C) No quality control

D) Increased manual interventions

Process variability understanding leads to:

A) Decreased formulation stability

B) Higher rejection rates

C) Predictable manufacturing performance

D) Lower cost of distribution

Which risk assessment tool uses a cause-and-effect diagram?

A) FMEA

B) Ishikawa diagram

C) DOE

D) SOP analysis

The benefit of QbD from a regulatory view is:

A) Stricter post-approval monitoring

B) Greater product approval flexibility

C) Elimination of clinical trial phases

D) Ignoring validation batches

Answer Key

1. C) Quality by Design
2. B) Build quality into products
3. B) Scientific and risk-based
4. B) ICH Q8
5. B) Pharmaceutical development
6. B) Understanding of variability
7. A) Ishikawa diagram
8. A) ICH Q8
9. C) Consistent product quality
10. B) Product characteristics affecting quality
11. B) Systematically study variable effects
12. B) Real-time monitoring
13. B) Improved process robustness
14. B) Ideal product attributes
15. B) Identifying potential risks
16. C) That affect CQAs
17. C) Release without end-product testing
18. C) Planned set of controls
19. B) Improve product understanding
20. C) Staff experience
21. B) Drying temperature in granulation
22. B) Product and process understanding
23. B) Continuous improvement from development to commercialization
24. B) Designing robust generic drugs
25. B) During initial development
26. B) Identifying and prioritizing potential issues
27. B) Proactive quality design
28. C) Predictable manufacturing performance
29. B) Ishikawa diagram
30. B) Greater product approval flexibility

CHAPTER THREE

Computational Modeling of Drug Disposition

3.1 Introduction to Drug Disposition

3.1.1 Overview of ADME processes

Drug disposition refers to the fate of a drug once it enters the body, and it is governed by four key processes: **Absorption, Distribution, Metabolism, and Excretion (ADME)**. These processes determine the concentration of a drug at its site of action, which in turn influences both its therapeutic effects and toxicity. A clear understanding of ADME is essential in drug development because it helps predict how the drug will behave in different patient populations, dosing regimens, and formulations.

Absorption is the process by which a drug enters the bloodstream from its site of administration. For orally administered drugs, this involves dissolution in the gastrointestinal fluids, permeation across intestinal membranes, and potential degradation or interaction with enzymes and transporters. **Distribution** refers to the movement of the drug throughout the body, including penetration into tissues and binding to plasma proteins. This step is critical in determining the drug's volume of distribution and its availability at the target site. **Metabolism** mainly occurs in the liver and involves enzymatic conversion of the drug into more water-soluble compounds for elimination. Enzymes like cytochrome P450 (CYP) play a major role in metabolic pathways, and variability in their activity can significantly affect drug efficacy and safety. **Excretion**, the final step, involves the removal of the drug and its metabolites from the body, mainly through the kidneys (urine) or bile (feces).

Each of these steps can be influenced by various factors such as age, sex, genetic polymorphisms, disease states, and drug-drug interactions. A drug with poor absorption or rapid metabolism may require a higher dose or special formulation, whereas a drug with a long half-life might be suitable for once-daily dosing. By studying the ADME profile, scientists can design drugs with improved bioavailability, reduced toxicity, and optimal dosing schedules.

3.1.2 Significance of modeling disposition

Modeling drug disposition using computational methods is one of the most powerful advancements in modern drug development. These models allow researchers to simulate and predict the pharmacokinetic behavior of a drug without extensive animal or human testing. Computational modeling supports the interpretation of experimental data, optimization of formulation strategies, and design of efficient clinical trials. It also helps identify potential issues early in development, such as poor absorption or high variability, and provides a scientific basis for decision-making.

One of the major benefits of modeling drug disposition is the ability to predict drug concentrations over time in various tissues, enabling researchers to estimate critical pharmacokinetic parameters such as Cmax (maximum plasma concentration), Tmax (time to reach Cmax), AUC (area under the curve), half-life, clearance, and volume of distribution. These parameters are crucial in understanding the drug's onset, intensity, and duration of action. By using models such as compartmental models or physiologically based pharmacokinetic (PBPK) models, researchers can simulate how the drug will behave in humans based on in vitro and preclinical data.

Modeling is particularly important when studying special populations such as pediatric, geriatric, or renal-impaired patients, where direct clinical data may be limited. It is also used in virtual bioequivalence studies, dose adjustment simulations, and drug-drug interaction predictions. Advanced modeling approaches such as population pharmacokinetics (PopPK) allow the inclusion of inter-individual variability and covariates like age, body weight, and enzyme activity, providing a more realistic prediction of drug behavior in the real-world setting.

Moreover, regulatory agencies such as the FDA and EMA increasingly accept model-based evidence in submissions for first-in-human studies, dosage selection, and biowaivers, recognizing the value of computational models in enhancing scientific understanding and reducing risk. As a result, computational modeling of drug disposition has become an integral tool in streamlining the drug development process, improving patient safety, and accelerating time-to-market.

• 45 •

3.2 Modeling Techniques in ADME

3.2.1 Drug Absorption

The absorption phase of a drug refers to its movement from the site of administration into the systemic circulation. For orally administered drugs, absorption primarily occurs in the gastrointestinal (GI) tract and is influenced by several physicochemical and physiological factors such as solubility, permeability, pH, gastrointestinal transit time, and the presence of transport proteins or enzymes. Understanding the mechanisms of drug absorption is critical for predicting **bioavailability**, which directly affects the onset and intensity of therapeutic action. Computational modeling techniques are used to simulate drug absorption using either compartmental, non-compartmental, or physiologically-based approaches. These models consider both the rate and extent of drug transfer across the intestinal membrane and can help in forecasting the impact of formulation changes, food effects, or drug-drug interactions on oral absorption.

Modern software platforms like **GastroPlus**, **Simcyp**, and **PK-Sim** incorporate detailed models of the human gastrointestinal system and allow simulation of regional absorption, pH-dependent solubility, enzyme degradation, and transporter activity. These tools help developers identify critical absorption-limiting steps and guide formulation development. For instance, a poorly soluble drug may show adequate absorption in fasted state but poor bioavailability in fed state due to solubility shifts, which can be predicted and addressed through simulation models. Absorption modeling is also crucial in **biowaiver** justifications, where in vitro data are used to predict in vivo performance without the need for clinical trials.

3.2.1.1 Passive vs. Active Absorption

Drug absorption across the intestinal epithelium occurs through two main mechanisms: **passive absorption** and **active absorption**, both of which are modeled differently depending on the drug's characteristics.

Passive absorption is the most common and occurs when drug molecules move across the intestinal membrane by simple diffusion, driven by the concentration gradient. It does not require any energy input or involvement of transport proteins. Passive diffusion is usually described using Fick's law, where the rate of absorption is proportional to the drug's concentration, surface area of the membrane, and the permeability coefficient. Lipophilic drugs with low molecular weight and high membrane permeability tend to be absorbed efficiently through this route. In computational models, passive diffusion is usually incorporated as a first-order or linear process, assuming that the absorption rate is directly proportional to the concentration in the GI lumen. These models are straightforward and can be calibrated using permeability data from in vitro models like Caco-2 or PAMPA.

Active absorption, on the other hand, involves specialized carrier proteins embedded in the intestinal epithelium that transport drug molecules against their concentration gradient, often requiring energy in the form of ATP. This mechanism is saturable and subject to competition, inhibition, and genetic variability. Examples of active transporters include PEPT1 (peptide transporter 1), OATPs (organic anion transporting polypeptides), and SLC transporters. Drugs such as levodopa, gabapentin, and valacyclovir utilize active transporters for enhanced absorption. In modeling, active absorption is typically represented by Michaelis-Menten kinetics, where the absorption rate is a nonlinear function of the drug concentration, depending on transporter affinity (Km) and maximum capacity (Vmax).

Differentiating between passive and active absorption is essential in simulation because it determines the drug's behavior under different dosing conditions. For instance, an actively absorbed drug may exhibit saturation at higher doses, leading to non-linear pharmacokinetics. Such scenarios must be accurately represented in PBPK models to ensure reliable predictions. By integrating both passive and active absorption mechanisms into computational models, scientists can design better formulations, predict inter-subject variability, and anticipate challenges during regulatory submission.

3.2.2 Solubility Prediction and Optimization

Solubility is a crucial physicochemical property that significantly influences the oral absorption of drugs. For any orally administered compound to exert its therapeutic effect, it must first dissolve in the aqueous fluids of the gastrointestinal tract. This dissolution is the precondition for the drug to permeate through biological membranes and enter systemic circulation. A drug with high permeability but low solubility is often categorized under Biopharmaceutics Classification System (BCS) Class II, and such compounds face considerable bioavailability limitations unless their solubility is enhanced. In fact, over 40% of marketed drugs and nearly 70% of new chemical entities (NCEs) under development are classified as poorly soluble, creating a substantial bottleneck in formulation development and clinical success.

The early prediction of solubility using computational tools has become a routine and valuable practice in modern pharmaceutical research. In silico solubility prediction involves estimating a compound's aqueous solubility based on its molecular structure and physicochemical properties even before physical synthesis. Several molecular descriptors are key contributors to solubility prediction. These include lipophilicity (log P), which represents the drug's partitioning between lipophilic and aqueous phases; hydrogen bonding capacity, both donor and acceptor; topological polar surface area (TPSA), which influences hydrogen bonding and permeability; molecular weight; and pKa, which governs the ionization state of the drug under various pH conditions. Compounds with high log P values, large molecular weights, and low hydrogen bonding often exhibit poor aqueous solubility.

Various predictive models are used for solubility estimation. Among these, Quantitative Structure–Property Relationship (QSPR) models are the most established. These models correlate structural features (described numerically by molecular descriptors) with experimentally determined solubility data to build mathematical models. Once trained and validated, these models can predict the solubility of new compounds with similar structural properties. Software tools such as ADMET Predictor, GastroPlus, ChemAxon Marvin, and MOE (Molecular Operating Environment) offer robust QSPR models, many of which are enhanced using machine learning techniques like random forest, support vector machines, and neural networks.

Apart from general aqueous solubility, another essential aspect is the pH-dependent solubility profile of ionizable compounds. Since the gastrointestinal tract exhibits a wide pH range (stomach ~1.5 to 3.5, small intestine ~6 to 7.5), the solubility of weak acids and weak bases can vary dramatically across regions. Therefore, pH–solubility curves are generated computationally to assess solubility behavior under dynamic physiological conditions. Tools like Simcyp Simulator and GastroPlus allow simulation of regional solubility, predicting whether the drug will dissolve in the stomach, duodenum, jejunum, or ileum, which in turn helps identify optimal release sites and dosage forms.

When computational tools predict poor solubility, optimization strategies are considered. These strategies aim to modify the drug's physicochemical properties or formulate it in a way that improves its apparent solubility in vivo. One common strategy is salt formation, which is particularly effective for ionizable drugs. The selection of appropriate counter-ions (e.g., sodium, hydrochloride, sulfate, maleate) can increase aqueous solubility by altering the crystal lattice energy and dissolution behavior. In silico tools can simulate the impact of various salt forms on solubility, stability, and precipitation risk upon dilution in physiological fluids.

Another approach is co-crystal engineering, where the active pharmaceutical ingredient (API) is crystallized with a co-former to enhance solubility and stability. Computational software such as CSD-Materials, COSMO-RS, and Schrödinger Suite can be used to screen co-formers based on hydrogen bond complementarity and molecular interaction energy. Particle size reduction, achieved through micronization or nanonization, increases the surface area and hence the dissolution rate. Predictive models help estimate how a decrease in particle size (e.g., from 50 μm to 200 nm) influences solubility and dissolution using the Noyes–Whitney equation and its modifications.

Another widely used technique for improving solubility is the development of solid dispersions, where the drug is dispersed in a hydrophilic polymer matrix such as polyethylene glycol (PEG), polyvinylpyrrolidone (PVP), or hydroxypropyl methylcellulose (HPMC). The dispersion can be crystalline, amorphous, or a combination of both. Amorphous dispersions generally have higher solubility due to the absence of a crystal lattice. However, they are prone to recrystallization, so stability prediction is critical. In silico models simulate the miscibility of drug and polymer based on solubility parameters, glass transition temperatures (Tg), and hydrogen bonding interactions, allowing researchers to identify suitable polymer carriers and optimal drug loading levels before conducting lab trials.

Lipid-based formulations, such as self-emulsifying drug delivery systems (SEDDS), are also frequently used for enhancing the solubility of lipophilic drugs. These systems consist of oils, surfactants, and co-solvents that form fine emulsions or nanoemulsions upon contact with gastrointestinal fluids. Simulation tools can model lipid digestion, drug solubilization in mixed micelles, and precipitation tendencies upon dilution. Parameters such as log P, melting point, and pKa help predict whether the drug will remain solubilized in vivo. Software such as Simcyp, GastroPlus, and PK-Sim can simulate lipid digestion pathways and their impact on drug absorption.

Another modern strategy is the use of prodrugs, where the chemical structure of the parent drug is temporarily modified to improve solubility or permeability. Once administered, enzymatic or chemical conversion regenerates the active drug in the systemic circulation. Computational tools can assess the enzymatic cleavage likelihood, hydrolysis kinetics, and site-specific conversion of such prodrugs.

From a formulation design perspective, solubility prediction also guides dosage form selection. For example, a compound with poor solubility but good permeability may be formulated as a solution-filled capsule, soft gel, or dispersible tablet. Predictive tools help simulate dissolution in various vehicle systems (e.g., buffers, surfactants) and forecast precipitation in the gastrointestinal environment using precipitation time (Tprecip) models.

In summary, computational solubility prediction and optimization provide a scientifically sound and cost-effective path for addressing one of the biggest formulation challenges in pharmaceutical R&D. By screening compounds virtually and simulating formulation outcomes, researchers can avoid late-stage failures and reduce the number of physical experiments required. These tools have become an integral part of preformulation studies, biopharmaceutics classification, and absorption modeling in both small molecule and biologic drug development. As predictive algorithms and databases continue to evolve, the accuracy and scope of solubility optimization using in silico methods will only expand, leading to more rational and successful drug design strategies.

3.2.3 Intestinal Permeation Modeling

Intestinal permeation is one of the most critical steps in the oral absorption process. Once a drug is dissolved in the gastrointestinal fluids, it must traverse the epithelial barrier of the small intestine to enter the portal blood circulation. The efficiency of this permeation directly influences not only the **rate** but also the **extent** of drug absorption. Even for drugs with excellent solubility, poor permeability through the intestinal wall can significantly reduce oral bioavailability. Computational modeling of intestinal permeability helps pharmaceutical scientists understand how a drug will behave in vivo before physical testing, saving time, cost, and resources.

The intestinal epithelium consists primarily of a single layer of enterocytes connected by tight junctions. Most small molecule drugs cross this barrier through transcellular passive diffusion, which is driven by concentration gradients and influenced by the drug's lipophilicity, molecular size, hydrogen bonding capacity, and topological polar surface area (TPSA). Drugs with high log P values (typically between 1 and 3), low molecular weight (less than 500 Da), fewer than five hydrogen bond donors, and a TPSA below 140 Å² tend to exhibit better permeability. These relationships have been quantified in several empirical models and Quantitative Structure–Activity Relationships (QSAR), which use statistical correlations between molecular descriptors and observed permeability data from experimental systems.

Empirical models often rely on in vitro datasets derived from cell-based systems such as Caco-2 monolayers or MDCK cells, which simulate the intestinal barrier. These models calculate apparent permeability (P_app, usually expressed in cm/s) using equations derived from Fick's law of diffusion. For example, a drug with a P_app value greater than 1×10^{-6} cm/s in a Caco-2 model is typically considered highly permeable. These in vitro data can then be integrated into regression equations, neural networks, or machine learning algorithms to predict permeability of structurally similar compounds. Tools like ADMET Predictor, QikProp, and SwissADME use such trained models to generate rapid predictions based on SMILES or molecular files.

On the other hand, mechanistic models simulate drug transport based on physiological structure and known transporter activities. These models account not just for passive diffusion but also for active transport (mediated by influx and efflux proteins such as OATP, PEPT1, and P-glycoprotein) and paracellular transport through tight junctions. Active transport modeling requires knowledge of whether the drug is a substrate for specific proteins, and the kinetic parameters such as Km (Michaelis constant) and Vmax (maximum transport rate) are included when available. Paracellular transport is significant for highly polar and small hydrophilic compounds, and is often modeled using pore-based diffusion approaches.

Advanced simulation platforms such as GastroPlus, Simcyp, and PK-Sim offer Physiologically Based Pharmacokinetic (PBPK) modeling that combines permeability data with dynamic gastrointestinal physiology. These tools can simulate regional absorption across different segments of the GI tract — from the stomach to the colon — considering factors such as surface area, residence time, pH, enzymatic degradation, and transporter expression. They can also model the impact of food intake, which may alter motility, pH, bile secretion, and permeability. For example, drugs that are substrates for bile salt-dependent uptake pathways may show higher absorption in the fed state.

PBPK-based intestinal permeability models are particularly valuable in understanding absorption variability caused by physiological differences among individuals. These differences may include age, gender, disease states like inflammatory bowel disease, or genetic polymorphisms in transporter expression. Additionally, such models help simulate drug-drug interactions, especially when two drugs compete for the same intestinal transporter. For example, co-administration of a P-glycoprotein (P-gp) inhibitor with a P-gp substrate can increase the intestinal absorption of the substrate, leading to higher systemic exposure. These interactions are difficult to predict in vitro but can be evaluated in silico using mechanistic transporter models.

Permeability models also support the Biopharmaceutics Classification System (BCS), which classifies drugs into four categories based on their solubility and permeability. Computational predictions of effective permeability (Peff) values are compared with established thresholds, such as the reference compound metoprolol, which has a human jejunal Peff of around 1.5×10^{-4} cm/s. If a new drug candidate demonstrates similar or higher Peff values in silico, it may be considered BCS Class I or II depending on its solubility. This classification can guide regulatory decisions and waiver opportunities for bioequivalence studies (biowaivers).

To improve the accuracy of intestinal permeation modeling, researchers often combine multiple data sources. For instance, permeability predictions from Caco-2 cell lines may be adjusted using scaling factors to approximate in vivo behavior. Additionally, sensitivity analysis is used to identify which input variables (e.g., pKa, log D, transporter affinity) have the most significant influence on permeability predictions. This helps in refining the model and understanding the level of uncertainty in simulations.

In silico permeability models are not limited to small molecules. They are increasingly being applied to peptides, oligonucleotides, and nanoparticle-based systems, although these compounds often require more complex modeling approaches due to their size, stability, and enzymatic degradation issues. Computational tools are evolving to incorporate such macromolecules, and modern machine learning algorithms are being trained using large permeability datasets from various compound classes..

3.2.3.1 Caco-2, PAMPA models

To experimentally assess and predict intestinal permeability before conducting in vivo studies, two extensively validated in vitro models —

the Caco-2 cell monolayer model and the Parallel Artificial Membrane Permeability Assay (PAMPA) — have become standard tools in preclinical drug development. These models provide highly informative permeability profiles that are particularly valuable during the early screening of drug candidates and are also extensively used to support regulatory filings. The data generated from both models are often directly incorporated into computational absorption models, especially in Physiologically Based Pharmacokinetic (PBPK) platforms like GastroPlus, Simcyp, and PK-Sim, to simulate absorption under varying physiological conditions.

The Caco-2 model is derived from a human epithelial colorectal adenocarcinoma cell line, which, when cultured under appropriate conditions for around 21 days, undergoes differentiation to form confluent monolayers with characteristics closely resembling the absorptive lining of the human small intestine. These cells form well-developed tight junctions and exhibit polarity, with distinct apical and basolateral surfaces. Importantly, they express a broad range of efflux and uptake transporters such as P-glycoprotein (P-gp), Breast Cancer Resistance Protein (BCRP), and Peptide Transporter 1 (PEPT1). Due to this transporter profile, the Caco-2 model offers a robust platform to evaluate both passive diffusion and carrier-mediated absorption, making it the gold standard for permeability assessment.

The apparent permeability coefficient (P_app) is the primary metric obtained from Caco-2 assays. It is calculated using the rate of drug passage from the donor to the receiver compartment across the monolayer, normalized to surface area and initial concentration. The typical P_app range lies between 10^{-6} and 10^{-4} cm/s, where values above 1.0×10^{-6} cm/s are usually considered indicative of adequate human intestinal permeability. Furthermore, by performing bidirectional assays (apical-to-basolateral and vice versa), the efflux ratio can be calculated. An efflux ratio above 2.0 may suggest active efflux, often mediated by P-gp or BCRP. These results are essential in flagging potential drug–drug interactions or bioavailability issues, especially for compounds with narrow therapeutic windows.

Caco-2 data are also used to simulate complex absorption scenarios, such as saturation kinetics, nonlinear transport, and regional variability along the gastrointestinal tract. Additionally, specific inhibitors (e.g., verapamil for P-gp) or inducers can be co-administered in the assay to study transporter-specific interactions. This allows early identification of absorption liabilities, supports transporter-based classification, and aids in QbD-based formulation design. In PBPK modeling, this data feeds into the estimation of intestinal absorption rate constant (Ka) and fraction absorbed (Fa) under fed and fasted states.

In contrast, the PAMPA model is a synthetic, cell-free system designed solely to measure passive transcellular permeability. It employs a simple architecture comprising a donor well and an acceptor well, separated by a lipid-impregnated artificial membrane, typically composed of phospholipids such as lecithin or dipalmitoylphosphatidylcholine (DPPC) in an organic solvent. This setup mimics the lipophilic barrier of intestinal epithelial cells. A test drug is placed in the donor well, and after a specified incubation period, the amount diffused into the acceptor well is quantified. The resulting effective permeability (P_e) is calculated and interpreted similarly to Caco-2 P_app values but is specific to passive transport mechanisms.

The key advantage of PAMPA is its high throughput capability, allowing simultaneous screening of hundreds of compounds with minimal material and time investment. It is especially useful during hit-to-lead optimization and structure–activity relationship (SAR) exploration. Despite its simplicity, PAMPA can be modified to reflect different segments of the GI tract by adjusting the pH of donor and acceptor buffers, thereby generating pH-permeability profiles. This is helpful in identifying the optimal absorption window for pH-sensitive compounds or those formulated with enteric protection. However, since PAMPA does not account for carrier-mediated transport, first-pass metabolism, or mucus diffusion, it cannot predict absorption behavior for hydrophilic or transporter-substrate drugs accurately.

Importantly, these two models are not intended to compete but to complement each other. Caco-2 excels in mimicking biological complexity and active processes, while PAMPA offers a rapid and cost-effective method for estimating passive diffusion. Many drug development programs utilize both systems in tandem to obtain a comprehensive permeability profile. For instance, a drug showing high permeability in both models is a strong candidate for BCS Class I or II, whereas conflicting results (e.g., low PAMPA but high Caco-2 with active uptake) may prompt further transporter investigation.

Furthermore, the data from Caco-2 and PAMPA models are often integrated with computational tools such as QSPR models or PBPK simulators to cross-validate predictions, reduce experimental uncertainty, and guide formulation strategy. These models also support biowaiver applications, where permeability data, combined with solubility and dissolution studies, can justify exemption from in vivo bioequivalence studies for certain drug classes.

In modern pharmaceutical development, the integration of experimental permeability data with in silico modeling represents a scientifically sound and regulatory-acceptable approach to understanding intestinal drug transport. As computational platforms evolve, the relevance of in vitro models like Caco-2 and PAMPA will continue to grow, especially when supported by well-validated datasets and mechanistic interpretations.

3.3 Drug Distribution Models

3.3.1 Compartmental vs. Physiological Models

Drug distribution refers to the reversible transfer of a drug from systemic circulation to various tissues and organs throughout the body. Understanding and modeling drug distribution is critical in pharmaceutical research, as it determines the drug's onset of action, therapeutic concentration at the target site, and potential off-target effects or toxicity. Two primary modeling approaches are used to describe drug distribution: compartmental models and physiological models (also known as physiologically based pharmacokinetic or PBPK models). Both approaches aim to simulate how the drug travels through the body, but they differ significantly in complexity, assumptions, and applications.

Compartmental models are empirical and mathematically simple. In this approach, the human body is represented as one or more hypothetical compartments in which the drug is assumed to distribute uniformly. These models do not correspond to actual anatomical structures but are useful for fitting plasma concentration-time data. The most common types include one-compartment, two-compartment, and multi-compartment models. In a one-compartment model, the drug is assumed to distribute instantaneously throughout the body after administration. In a two-compartment model, the body is divided into a central compartment (usually blood and highly perfused tissues) and a peripheral compartment (poorly perfused tissues). These models are widely used in clinical pharmacokinetic studies to estimate parameters such as volume of distribution (Vd), elimination rate constant (Ke), and clearance (Cl).

Although compartmental models are convenient and require fewer data points, they are limited by their lack of physiological detail. They cannot predict tissue-specific concentrations or account for organ-specific blood flow, binding, or transporter activity. As a result, they are most suitable for initial pharmacokinetic assessments or when only plasma data are available.

In contrast, physiological or PBPK models are mechanistic and based on actual biological structures and functions. These models divide the body into compartments that represent individual organs or tissues such as the liver, kidney, muscle, fat, and brain. Each compartment is defined by its physiological parameters, including organ volume, blood flow rate, tissue-plasma partition coefficients, enzymatic activity, and membrane permeability. PBPK models allow simulation of drug concentration not only in plasma but also in specific tissues over time, offering a detailed understanding of distribution kinetics.

PBPK modeling is highly valuable in predicting drug behavior in special populations (e.g., pediatric, elderly, pregnant, or renally impaired patients), assessing drug-drug interactions, and supporting regulatory decisions. For example, if a drug is highly bound to plasma proteins or accumulates in fatty tissues, a PBPK model can provide insight into how its distribution may vary with changes in body composition or disease states. These models are built using a combination of in vitro data, animal studies, and human physiological databases, and are implemented using software tools like Simcyp, PK-Sim, and GastroPlus.

While PBPK models require more extensive data and expertise to construct and validate, they offer superior predictive power and physiological relevance. Regulatory agencies such as the USFDA and EMA increasingly encourage or accept PBPK modeling in areas like first-in-human dose prediction, formulation bridging, bioequivalence assessment, and pediatric dose extrapolation. As pharmaceutical development moves toward precision medicine, the use of PBPK models is expected to become more prominent, complementing or even replacing traditional compartmental approaches in many areas of drug development.

3.4 Drug Excretion Modeling

3.4.1 Renal Clearance and Biliary Excretion

Drug excretion is the final stage of drug disposition and plays a vital role in determining the duration of drug action and the frequency of dosing. Excretion refers to the irreversible removal of the parent drug or its metabolites from the body. The two most important excretory pathways are renal clearance via the kidneys and biliary excretion via the liver into the gastrointestinal tract. Accurate modeling of these excretion processes is essential for predicting drug accumulation, half-life, dose adjustments in impaired patients, and possible drug interactions. Computational models help simulate excretion kinetics and provide valuable insights for dosage regimen design, especially in populations with variable excretory function, such as the elderly or patients with renal or hepatic disease.

Renal clearance is the predominant excretion route for many drugs, especially those that are water-soluble, have low molecular weight, and are not extensively metabolized. The kidneys eliminate drugs through three main mechanisms: glomerular filtration, tubular secretion, and tubular reabsorption. In computational models, renal clearance (CLr) is calculated based on these processes and is influenced by factors such as plasma protein binding, ionization, urine pH, and renal blood flow. For example, drugs like aminoglycosides and digoxin are eliminated mainly by glomerular filtration, while drugs such as penicillin and probenecid undergo active tubular secretion. Reabsorption, which can be passive or active, often affects weak acids and bases depending on urine pH.

Modeling renal clearance involves using physiological parameters like glomerular filtration rate (GFR), fraction unbound in plasma (fu), and active transport coefficients. In population-based models, these values are adjusted based on individual characteristics like age, sex, weight, and renal function (e.g., creatinine clearance or eGFR). In PBPK models, the kidney is treated as a distinct compartment with its own flow rates and transport processes, allowing prediction of renal elimination under various physiological and pathological conditions. This modeling is critical for dose optimization in patients with renal impairment, where accumulation of renally cleared drugs can lead to toxicity if not adjusted properly.

Biliary excretion is another significant elimination route, particularly for lipophilic drugs and metabolites with high molecular weight, which are actively secreted into bile by hepatocytes and eventually eliminated in feces. Biliary excretion involves uptake transporters on the basolateral side (e.g., OATP, NTCP) and efflux transporters on the canalicular side of hepatocytes (e.g., BSEP, MRP2, P-gp). Drugs such as rifampicin, erythromycin, and some glucuronide conjugates are eliminated by this route. In modeling, biliary clearance is incorporated into liver compartments with active transport kinetics, often described using Michaelis-Menten equations.

PBPK models allow for the integration of bile flow rate, transporter expression levels, and hepatic enzyme activity to simulate the kinetics of biliary elimination. These models are particularly helpful in predicting enterohepatic recirculation, a process in which the drug or metabolite is reabsorbed from the intestine after being excreted into the bile, prolonging its half-life. For example, drugs like ethinylestradiol and chloramphenicol undergo this cycle, which must be considered when predicting their plasma concentration profiles.

Accurate modeling of renal and biliary excretion is crucial in understanding drug elimination patterns, supporting regulatory submissions, and minimizing the risk of toxicity due to impaired clearance. By simulating these processes, researchers can make informed decisions about dose adjustments, drug-drug interactions involving transporter inhibition, and selection of appropriate biomarkers for clearance monitoring.

3.5 Active Transporters and Simulation

Active transporters play a critical role in drug disposition, especially in absorption, distribution, and excretion processes. These membrane-bound proteins facilitate the movement of drug molecules across biological membranes, either by uptake into cells or efflux out of cells, using energy derived from ATP or ion gradients. Their presence in key organs such as the intestine, liver, kidney, and blood-brain barrier significantly influences a drug's bioavailability, tissue penetration, clearance, and potential for drug-drug interactions. In silico modeling of transporter-mediated drug movement is an advanced component of ADME simulation, and it helps in understanding inter-individual variability, predicting pharmacokinetics in special populations, and guiding formulation and dosing strategies.

3.5.1 P-glycoprotein (P-gp)

P-glycoprotein, commonly abbreviated as P-gp and also referred to by its gene name MDR1 or ABCB1, is a well-characterized efflux transporter belonging to the ATP-Binding Cassette (ABC) superfamily. It plays a central role in limiting drug absorption and distribution by actively pumping compounds out of cells against their concentration gradient. This transport process is energy-dependent, relying on ATP hydrolysis, and is considered a protective mechanism in the human body, evolved to defend against xenobiotics and toxic substances. P-gp is highly expressed on the apical surface of enterocytes in the small intestine, where it can significantly affect oral drug bioavailability by returning absorbed drugs back into the gut lumen. It is also found in the canalicular membrane of hepatocytes, where it mediates biliary excretion, in renal proximal tubule cells, facilitating urinary elimination, and in the endothelial cells of the blood-brain barrier, where it prevents certain substances from entering the central nervous system.

Numerous clinically important drugs are known to be P-gp substrates, including digoxin, paclitaxel, loperamide, doxorubicin, fexofenadine, and cyclosporine. The presence of P-gp often results in low and variable bioavailability for these compounds, as well as reduced brain penetration for drugs with therapeutic targets in the central nervous system. For example, loperamide is a potent opioid receptor agonist but does not produce CNS effects under normal circumstances due to efficient exclusion by P-gp at the blood-brain barrier. However, when P-gp is inhibited by drugs like quinidine or verapamil, loperamide can cross into the brain and cause opioid toxicity. Such interactions underscore the importance of characterizing P-gp-mediated efflux during drug development.

To account for P-gp's impact in pharmacokinetic modeling, it is treated as an active transport process characterized by Michaelis-Menten kinetics, involving parameters such as Km (representing the affinity of the substrate for the transporter) and Vmax (the maximum rate of efflux). These kinetic parameters are experimentally determined using in vitro systems like Caco-2 cells, MDCK-MDR1 transfected cell lines, and vesicular transport assays. Once established, the data are incorporated into Physiologically Based Pharmacokinetic (PBPK) models using tools such as Simcyp, GastroPlus, or PK-Sim. These platforms allow simulation of drug concentration-time profiles while factoring in regional P-gp expression levels, luminal drug concentrations, and transport saturation. This enables accurate predictions of the drug's oral absorption, hepatic clearance, brain distribution, and systemic exposure in different populations.

In addition to modeling baseline P-gp activity, these simulation platforms also support drug–drug interaction (DDI) predictions, where the impact of P-gp inhibitors or inducers is evaluated. Many commonly prescribed drugs modulate P-gp expression or activity. For example, ritonavir, used in antiretroviral therapy, is a potent P-gp inhibitor and can increase the bioavailability of co-administered P-gp substrates. On the other hand, rifampin is a known inducer of P-gp, and its chronic use can reduce the efficacy of drugs like digoxin by enhancing their efflux. By inputting the appropriate inhibitory or induction kinetics into PBPK models, these effects can be predicted quantitatively, helping to define safe and effective dosing regimens. This is particularly critical in complex therapeutic settings involving polypharmacy, chronic disease management, or oncology, where narrow therapeutic index drugs and multiple co-medications are often involved.

Moreover, genetic variability in the MDR1 gene encoding P-gp contributes to inter-individual differences in drug disposition. Common single nucleotide polymorphisms (SNPs), such as C3435T, G2677T/A, and C1236T, have been associated with altered P-gp expression and function. For instance, individuals homozygous for the 3435T allele may exhibit lower P-gp activity, resulting in higher systemic exposure to certain substrates. Modern modeling platforms allow simulation of such genotype-based variability, enabling virtual trials in population subgroups, such as extensive vs. poor P-gp expressers. This adds significant value in designing personalized medicine approaches and identifying patients who may be at risk for adverse effects or therapeutic failure due to transporter-related differences.

In pharmaceutical development, P-gp assessment is now a regulatory expectation. Both the US FDA and EMA recommend evaluating whether a drug is a P-gp substrate or modulator during nonclinical development. If positive, interaction studies may be required, or label warnings may be necessary. The combination of in vitro assays and PBPK modeling provides a strong scientific basis to answer these regulatory queries. Additionally, the modeling can explore formulation strategies to overcome P-gp-mediated efflux. For example, the use of lipid-based formulations, P-gp inhibitors, or prodrug approaches can be simulated to determine whether they improve bioavailability and therapeutic outcomes.

3.5.2 Breast Cancer Resistance Protein (BCRP)

Breast Cancer Resistance Protein (BCRP), classified as ABCG2 in the ATP-Binding Cassette (ABC) transporter family, is an important efflux protein that plays a critical role in the pharmacokinetics of many drugs. Like P-glycoprotein, BCRP uses the energy derived from ATP hydrolysis to actively transport a wide variety of substrates across biological membranes, often against their concentration gradient. It is localized primarily on the apical membranes of several barrier tissues, including intestinal enterocytes, canalicular hepatocytes, renal proximal tubule cells, and the endothelial cells of the blood-brain barrier (BBB) and blood-placenta barrier. Its physiological function is largely protective, working to limit systemic absorption of harmful xenobiotics, restrict drug penetration into sensitive organs such as the brain and fetus, and facilitate biliary and urinary excretion of both drugs and their metabolites.

BCRP has a remarkably broad and chemically diverse substrate profile, encompassing numerous clinically relevant drugs such as topotecan, methotrexate, rosuvastatin, sulfasalazine, and various tyrosine kinase inhibitors including imatinib and gefitinib. The presence of BCRP in the gastrointestinal tract means that orally administered BCRP substrates may experience reduced bioavailability due to efflux back into the intestinal lumen, similar to the mechanism seen with P-gp. However, BCRP also exhibits tissue-specific expression patterns and substrate preferences, which makes its role unique in each organ system. For example, in the liver, BCRP contributes to canalicular secretion of certain glucuronide conjugates, while in the kidney, it may complement P-gp in removing drugs into the urine.

Pharmacokinetic modeling of BCRP involves incorporating its kinetic parameters, typically Km (the substrate's affinity for the transporter) and Vmax (the maximal rate of transport), into physiologically based pharmacokinetic (PBPK) models. These models allow simulation of how BCRP influences drug exposure, tissue distribution, and elimination under various physiological conditions. The data for such models are derived from in vitro transport assays using cell lines that overexpress BCRP, such as MDCK-BCRP or LLC-PK1-BCRP cells, as well as membrane vesicle assays and in situ perfusion studies in animals. These platforms provide measurable parameters such as efflux ratio, net flux, and transport inhibition, which are then scaled to predict in vivo behavior.

Incorporating BCRP-mediated transport into PBPK models is especially important in the development of drugs for central nervous system (CNS) conditions, anticancer therapies, and oral medications that exhibit borderline bioavailability. Since BCRP is highly expressed at the blood-brain barrier, many drugs that are BCRP substrates exhibit poor CNS penetration. For example, topotecan, an anticancer agent, is actively removed from the brain by BCRP, limiting its therapeutic utility in brain tumors unless BCRP is inhibited or bypassed through formulation strategies. Similarly, oral bioavailability can be compromised when BCRP efflux is combined with poor solubility or first-pass metabolism. In such cases, co-administration with BCRP inhibitors like elacridar or ketoconazole may be simulated to evaluate whether efflux inhibition leads to a clinically meaningful increase in systemic exposure.

In addition to drug–drug interactions, genetic polymorphisms in the ABCG2 gene have significant impact on transporter function. One of the most studied variants is c.421C>A (Q141K), which leads to a reduced expression or activity of BCRP. Individuals carrying this mutation, especially homozygous A/A genotype, may experience higher plasma levels of BCRP substrates due to reduced efflux. For example, rosuvastatin shows increased systemic exposure in individuals with this variant. Modern PBPK software like Simcyp and GastroPlus now allows simulation of genotype-specific pharmacokinetics, helping developers evaluate dose adjustments and personalized therapy recommendations for genetically defined subpopulations.

Furthermore, BCRP modeling is essential in regulatory science, as authorities like the US FDA, EMA, and PMDA require comprehensive assessment of transporter-mediated drug interactions during new drug applications. In vitro inhibition or induction of BCRP must be evaluated when a compound is intended for chronic use or is co-administered with known substrates or inhibitors. PBPK models offer a mechanistic and quantitative framework to predict these interactions under multiple dosing scenarios, different physiological states, and across diverse population groups. These simulations can also support biowaiver justifications, labeling decisions, and post-approval risk management plans.

Overall, the integration of BCRP into drug disposition modeling has significantly improved the accuracy of pharmacokinetic predictions and has strengthened the rational design of drugs and their delivery systems. By accounting for transporter dynamics, tissue-specific expression, and genetic variability, BCRP modeling enables pharmaceutical scientists to make better-informed decisions, identify absorption and distribution challenges early in development, and reduce the risk of clinical failure due to unpredictable drug exposure. Its role, along with other key transporters, continues to be a cornerstone of modern, model-informed drug development.

3.5.3 Nucleoside Transporters

Nucleoside transporters (NTs) are specialized membrane proteins that regulate the transport of nucleosides and their analogs across cellular membranes. These transporters are of particular importance in the pharmacology of antiviral and anticancer agents, many of which are structurally similar to natural nucleosides and require active transport to reach their intracellular sites of action. Unlike lipophilic small molecules that passively diffuse through lipid bilayers, most nucleoside analogs are hydrophilic and heavily dependent on transporter-mediated uptake for effective absorption, cellular entry, and tissue distribution. As a result, any variation in transporter expression or function can lead to substantial differences in therapeutic efficacy, toxicity, or drug–drug interactions.

There are two major families of nucleoside transporters in humans — Equilibrative Nucleoside Transporters (ENTs) and Concentrative Nucleoside Transporters (CNTs). ENTs, including ENT1 (SLC29A1) and ENT2 (SLC29A2), facilitate bidirectional, passive diffusion of nucleosides across membranes, following their concentration gradients. These transporters are sodium-independent and are expressed in a variety of tissues, including the intestinal epithelium, liver, kidneys, and tumors. In contrast, CNTs such as CNT1 (SLC28A1), CNT2 (SLC28A2), and CNT3

(SLC28A3) mediate active uptake of nucleosides by utilizing the sodium ion gradient, often working against the concentration gradient. Each subtype of CNT shows selectivity for purine or pyrimidine nucleosides. For instance, CNT1 primarily transports pyrimidines, while CNT2 favors purine nucleosides.

Clinically relevant drugs that rely on NTs include zidovudine (AZT), didanosine, cytarabine, fludarabine, gemcitabine, cladribine, and ribavirin. These compounds are used to treat diseases ranging from HIV and hepatitis C to acute myeloid leukemia (AML) and pancreatic cancer. Since these drugs are prodrugs that must first enter cells and undergo phosphorylation to become pharmacologically active, efficient transporter-mediated uptake is essential for their cellular accumulation and cytotoxic activity. A deficiency in transporter function may result in subtherapeutic drug concentrations at the site of action, while excessive uptake may lead to dose-limiting toxicities, particularly in bone marrow and gastrointestinal tissues.

To accurately predict the behavior of such drugs, computational models are developed to simulate nucleoside transporter kinetics under various physiological conditions. These models use kinetic parameters such as Km (affinity of the drug for the transporter) and Vmax (maximum transport rate), often obtained from in vitro studies using transfected cell lines (e.g., HEK293 cells overexpressing ENT1 or CNT2), membrane vesicle assays, or Xenopus oocyte systems. When integrated into Physiologically Based Pharmacokinetic (PBPK) or compartmental models, this data enables simulation of transporter-mediated drug movement across organs such as the intestine (for absorption), kidney (for reabsorption or secretion), liver (for uptake and metabolism), and tumors (for site-specific delivery).

PBPK platforms like Simcyp, GastroPlus, and PK-Sim offer specialized modules for transporter-mediated disposition, allowing researchers to define organ-specific expression levels of nucleoside transporters, simulate concentration-time profiles, and estimate the extent of absorption and distribution of nucleoside analog drugs. For example, the regional expression of ENT1 and CNT1 in the intestinal mucosa can be simulated to predict how efficiently a given drug is absorbed in the duodenum versus the ileum. Similarly, renal CNTs play a crucial role in reabsorption of nucleosides, and their function can influence the systemic clearance and half-life of renally eliminated drugs. In the liver, ENT1 and ENT2 contribute to hepatic uptake, a process that determines how much drug reaches intracellular enzymes for activation or metabolism.

These simulations are especially critical in oncology drug development, where tumor-specific expression of nucleoside transporters determines drug response. Certain cancers, such as acute myeloid leukemia (AML) and pancreatic cancer, show variable expression of ENT1, which affects how much cytarabine or gemcitabine accumulates in malignant cells. In such cases, low ENT1 expression may result in therapeutic failure due to insufficient intracellular drug levels. Computational models can incorporate tumor-specific transporter expression profiles to simulate drug delivery at the tumor site, helping in dose optimization or in designing companion diagnostic tests to stratify patients who are more likely to benefit from the treatment.

Another important application of transporter modeling is in predicting inter-individual variability due to genetic polymorphisms. Single nucleotide polymorphisms (SNPs) in ENT and CNT genes can lead to reduced expression, altered transporter kinetics, or complete loss of function. For instance, polymorphisms in ENT1 (SLC29A1) have been linked to poor response to cytarabine in AML patients. By integrating such genetic variability into PBPK simulations, developers can visualize the impact on plasma concentrations, tissue distribution, and intracellular drug levels, enabling better risk assessment and dose individualization in personalized medicine. Such simulations can also support regulatory submissions by providing a rationale for genetic testing or biomarker development.

Regulatory agencies such as the US FDA and EMA increasingly emphasize the need to study transporter-mediated uptake in new drug applications, especially for nucleoside analog drugs. In vitro assessments of transporter interactions are routinely required during preclinical development. However, by integrating the experimental results into mechanistic simulation frameworks, developers can not only meet regulatory expectations but also use the models for internal decision-making, such as compound selection, formulation planning, and dose justification.

In conclusion, nucleoside transporters are critical determinants of the absorption, distribution, and cellular pharmacology of many antiviral and anticancer agents. Their inclusion in computational disposition models helps improve prediction accuracy, supports regulatory requirements, and enhances our understanding of the factors that influence drug efficacy and safety. With the increasing importance of precision medicine, transporter modeling represents a valuable approach to ensure that the right drug reaches the right patient at the right dose.

3.5.4 hPEPT1 (Human Peptide Transporter 1)

Human Peptide Transporter 1 (hPEPT1) is a proton-dependent uptake transporter primarily expressed on the apical membrane of enterocytes in the small intestine. It plays a major role in the absorption of di- and tri-peptides as well as many peptidomimetic drugs, including beta-lactam antibiotics (e.g., ampicillin, cephalexin), ACE inhibitors (e.g., enalapril), and antiviral agents (e.g., valacyclovir). hPEPT1 has broad substrate specificity and high transport capacity, making it a popular target for prodrug design to enhance oral bioavailability.

From a modeling perspective, hPEPT1 is represented in gastrointestinal absorption models as a saturable uptake pathway with Michaelis-Menten kinetics. Computational models incorporate regional expression data (highest in the jejunum), pH-dependent activity, and transporter parameters to simulate the rate and extent of absorption for hPEPT1 substrates. For example, the oral prodrug valacyclovir uses hPEPT1 to achieve much higher systemic availability than its parent drug acyclovir, and this uptake mechanism can be precisely simulated using tools like GastroPlus and PK-Sim.

Simulation of hPEPT1 is also useful in predicting food effects, since luminal pH and intestinal motility influence transporter activity. Additionally, drug-drug interactions can occur if multiple hPEPT1 substrates or inhibitors are co-administered, potentially altering absorption kinetics. Models can evaluate such scenarios and guide formulation design or dosing recommendations. Understanding the role of hPEPT1 in absorption allows formulation scientists to strategically design prodrugs that leverage this transporter to overcome poor permeability or low solubility.

By integrating hPEPT1 kinetics into PBPK models, researchers can predict how peptidomimetic drugs behave across different populations, optimize dosing regimens, and anticipate variability due to physiological or pathological conditions such as inflammatory bowel disease, which may alter transporter expression. Thus, hPEPT1 modeling is an indispensable tool in the rational design and development of orally administered peptide-like drugs.

3.5.5 ASBT (Apical Sodium-dependent Bile Acid Transporter)

ASBT (Apical Sodium-dependent Bile Acid Transporter) is a sodium-coupled uptake transporter that plays a critical role in the intestinal reabsorption of bile acids. It is highly expressed on the apical surface of enterocytes in the terminal ileum, where it facilitates the active transport of bile acids from the intestinal lumen into the cells. These bile acids are then returned to the liver via the portal vein as part of the enterohepatic circulation. While ASBT primarily functions in bile acid homeostasis, it also has pharmacological relevance for certain lipophilic or bile acid-conjugated drugs, prodrugs, and formulations that exploit bile acid pathways for enhanced absorption.

In computational modeling, ASBT is included as an active uptake mechanism in gastrointestinal absorption models, particularly in the ileal region. Its function is modeled using Michaelis-Menten kinetics, with parameters such as Km (affinity for substrate) and Vmax (maximum transport rate) derived from in vitro transporter assays. These parameters help simulate how efficiently a bile acid-based prodrug, for example, might be absorbed in the presence or absence of competing bile acids.

Pharmaceutical developers are increasingly designing ASBT-targeting prodrugs or drug-bile acid conjugates to exploit this transport route. For instance, certain NSAID prodrugs are conjugated with bile acids to enhance site-specific uptake in the ileum while reducing gastric irritation. ASBT simulations can also predict the impact of diseases like Crohn's disease or ileal resection, where transporter expression or function may be impaired, leading to malabsorption or drug delivery failure.

Furthermore, ASBT inhibitors are under investigation for treating cholestatic liver diseases, and PBPK models can simulate the pharmacokinetics of such compounds by integrating bile acid turnover, enterohepatic cycling, and feedback regulation. These complex models allow researchers to understand the systemic consequences of modifying ASBT function and its downstream effect on drug solubility, metabolism, and excretion. Hence, ASBT modeling is gaining importance in both drug development and formulation strategy when bile acid pathways are pharmacologically or biopharmaceutically relevant.

3.5.6 OCT (Organic Cation Transporters)

Organic Cation Transporters (OCTs) are a family of solute carrier (SLC) transporters responsible for the uptake and distribution of positively charged (cationic) drugs and endogenous compounds across various biological membranes. The most pharmacologically relevant members are:

- OCT1 (SLC22A1) – primarily expressed in hepatocytes (basolateral membrane)
- OCT2 (SLC22A2) – predominant in renal proximal tubule cells (basolateral membrane)
- OCT3 (SLC22A3) – widely expressed in multiple tissues including liver, kidney, and brain

These transporters handle a broad range of substrates such as metformin, cimetidine, amantadine, pindolol, and oxaliplatin. Their role in drug disposition includes hepatic uptake (OCT1), renal clearance (OCT2), and distribution into tissues (OCT3). In silico modeling of OCT-mediated transport is essential in predicting tissue-specific drug concentrations, renal elimination, and drug-drug interactions, especially for drugs that are actively handled by these transporters.

OCTs are modeled in PBPK frameworks using parameters like Km, Vmax, and expression levels in different tissues. These models simulate how variations in transporter activity—due to genetic polymorphisms, disease, or co-medications—can impact drug exposure. For instance, OCT1 polymorphisms are known to affect metformin's hepatic uptake, leading to differences in glucose-lowering efficacy among patients. Similarly, OCT2 plays a key role in the renal secretion of cationic drugs, and its inhibition can lead to elevated plasma concentrations and toxicity.

Regulatory authorities such as USFDA and EMA recommend evaluating OCT-mediated transport during drug development, especially for drugs with narrow therapeutic windows or high renal clearance. In vitro data from HEK293-OCT-transfected cells or vesicular uptake assays are often used as input for computational models, which can then predict the clinical relevance of transporter interactions.

OCT modeling also supports dose adjustment strategies in renal impairment, where transporter function may be altered. When combined with simulations of glomerular filtration and tubular reabsorption, OCT-mediated secretion completes the model of renal clearance for cationic drugs. As such, OCTs are indispensable components of transporter-inclusive PBPK models and play a central role in predicting variability, optimizing dosing, and enhancing drug safety.

3.5.7 OATP (Organic Anion Transporting Polypeptides)

Organic Anion Transporting Polypeptides (OATPs) are a group of important uptake transporters belonging to the SLCO (solute carrier organic anion transporter family). They mediate the influx of a wide range of endogenous and exogenous compounds, including bile acids, steroid conjugates, hormones, toxins, and various drugs. Among these, the most pharmacologically significant are:

- OATP1B1 (SLCO1B1) and OATP1B3 (SLCO1B3), primarily expressed on the basolateral (sinusoidal) membrane of hepatocytes
- OATP2B1, found in enterocytes, liver, and other tissues

OATPs play a critical role in hepatic drug uptake, where they transport drugs from the blood into liver cells for further metabolism and biliary excretion. Drugs such as statins (e.g., atorvastatin, rosuvastatin), bosentan, fexofenadine, rifampicin, and antivirals are substrates for OATP transporters. These transporters are key determinants of hepatic clearance, systemic exposure, and potential drug-drug interactions (DDIs).

In computational modeling, OATP transport kinetics are incorporated using Michaelis-Menten parameters (Km and Vmax) derived from in vitro hepatocyte uptake studies or transfected cell lines. These data are integrated into PBPK models to simulate hepatic drug exposure, particularly for compounds where liver uptake is a rate-limiting step. This is especially important for high-extraction drugs, where transporter activity significantly impacts plasma levels and therapeutic response.

Polymorphisms in OATP1B1, such as the SLCO1B1*5 variant, are known to reduce transporter activity and are associated with increased plasma concentrations and statin-induced myopathy. Modeling such polymorphisms helps predict inter-individual variability and guide personalized dosing strategies. Additionally, many drugs act as inhibitors of OATP transporters, leading to clinically significant DDIs, which can also be predicted and assessed through transporter-based simulations.

Regulatory agencies now expect transporter interaction assessments during drug development. OATP-inclusive PBPK models are accepted to support labeling, dose recommendations, and even to waive clinical DDI studies when simulations demonstrate minimal risk. Thus, OATP modeling is essential in the risk evaluation of hepatic uptake, drug accumulation, and predicting systemic drug levels under various physiological or pathological conditions.

3.5.8 BBB-Choline Transporter

The blood-brain barrier (BBB) is a highly selective barrier formed by brain endothelial cells with tight junctions, limiting the passive diffusion of many drugs into the central nervous system (CNS). To allow essential nutrients into the brain, the BBB expresses a variety of specific uptake transporters, one of which is the Choline Transporter (CHT1). The BBB-choline transporter is a high-affinity, sodium-independent transporter responsible for facilitating the uptake of choline, a precursor for acetylcholine synthesis and an important nutrient for brain function.

This transporter has gained pharmaceutical interest because certain choline-conjugated prodrugs or molecules structurally resembling choline can utilize it to enhance CNS delivery. A few novel CNS-targeted drugs and prodrugs are designed to mimic choline's structure and exploit this transporter for brain-specific drug delivery, especially when the drug's physicochemical properties would otherwise limit BBB permeability.

In computational modeling, the BBB-choline transporter is included in CNS PBPK models as a carrier-mediated influx mechanism at the brain endothelium. Modeling this transporter involves assigning Km and Vmax values, brain blood flow rates, and brain-to-plasma partition coefficients. The transporter's function is especially significant in simulation scenarios where passive diffusion is minimal and active uptake is the primary route for brain entry.

Drug developers can use simulation tools like PK-Sim, Simcyp, or CNS-specific PBPK modules to predict the CNS exposure of choline-like molecules and explore how transporter expression, saturation, or inhibition might affect drug delivery to the brain. Furthermore, disease states such as neurodegenerative disorders or brain ischemia may affect transporter activity, and such conditions can be simulated to predict altered drug disposition in affected patients.

In summary, the BBB-choline transporter modeling supports the rational design of brain-targeted therapies, allows for simulation of drug penetration into the CNS, and provides a tool for optimizing CNS pharmacokinetics, especially for drugs with otherwise poor BBB permeability.

REVIEW QUESTIONS

1. What is meant by drug disposition in pharmacokinetics?
Drug disposition refers to the processes of distribution and elimination of a drug after it enters systemic circulation.

2. Which components of ADME are involved in drug disposition?
Distribution and elimination (metabolism + excretion) are the two key components of disposition.

3. Define computational modeling in the context of drug disposition.
It is the use of mathematical and software-based models to simulate how drugs are distributed, metabolized, and excreted in the body.

4. Name two major types of computational models used in drug disposition.
Compartmental models and physiologically-based pharmacokinetic (PBPK) models.

5. What is the purpose of using computational models in pharmacokinetics?
To predict drug concentrations over time in various tissues and to simulate different clinical scenarios for better dosing strategies.

6. What are compartmental models based on?
They simplify the body into compartments (e.g., central, peripheral) and describe drug movement between them using differential equations.

7. How is a one-compartment model different from a two-compartment model?
A one-compartment model assumes uniform distribution, while a two-compartment model includes distribution between central and peripheral compartments.

8. What is a key limitation of simple compartmental models?
They lack physiological realism and cannot represent tissue-specific differences.

9. What does PBPK stand for?
Physiologically-Based Pharmacokinetic modeling.

10. How does a PBPK model differ from traditional compartmental models?
PBPK models include actual organ-specific parameters like blood flow, organ volume, and enzyme expression.

11. What are the advantages of PBPK modeling?

It allows prediction across populations (e.g., pediatrics, elderly), simulation of drug-drug interactions, and extrapolation from animals to humans.

12. Name one software used for PBPK modeling.

Simcyp®, GastroPlus®, or PK-Sim®.

13. What role does tissue partitioning play in PBPK models?

It helps predict how much drug accumulates in various organs based on tissue affinity.

14. What is the role of blood flow in PBPK models?

It determines how quickly a drug reaches each organ, affecting distribution and clearance rates.

15. Define the volume of distribution (Vd).

Vd is a theoretical volume that relates the amount of drug in the body to its plasma concentration.

16. What does a high Vd indicate?

Extensive distribution of the drug into tissues beyond the plasma.

17. What is clearance (CL) in pharmacokinetics?

Clearance is the volume of plasma completely cleared of drug per unit time, typically expressed in mL/min or L/hr.

18. What is the significance of half-life ($t\frac{1}{2}$) in drug disposition?

It determines how long a drug stays in the body and helps in designing dosing regimens.

19. How can PBPK modeling support drug dosing in children?

It adjusts model parameters like organ size, enzyme activity, and body composition based on age to predict appropriate doses.

20. What kind of data is required for PBPK modeling?

Physiological data (organ size, blood flow), biochemical data (enzyme kinetics), and drug-specific data (solubility, permeability).

21. What are the inputs for a basic PBPK model?

Anatomical, physiological, biochemical, and physicochemical data.

22. How does hepatic metabolism influence drug disposition models?

It determines the rate at which drugs are converted into metabolites, affecting clearance predictions.

23. What is first-pass metabolism?

It is the metabolism of a drug in the liver and gut wall before it reaches systemic circulation.

24. How is renal excretion modeled computationally?

Using glomerular filtration rate, active secretion, and reabsorption parameters.

25. Define bioavailability in pharmacokinetics.

It is the fraction of an administered dose that reaches systemic circulation unchanged.

26. How does the route of administration affect computational modeling?

Different routes (oral, IV, IM) require different absorption and first-pass models.

27. What is a permeability-limited model?

It focuses on the rate at which drugs pass through biological membranes, important for predicting absorption and distribution.

28. What is the role of enzyme kinetics in drug disposition modeling?

Michaelis-Menten parameters (Km and Vmax) help simulate how metabolic saturation affects clearance.

29. How do transporters influence drug disposition?

They control drug entry and exit across cells, affecting absorption, distribution, and excretion.

30. Give an example of an efflux transporter.

P-glycoprotein (P-gp), which pumps drugs out of cells, limiting bioavailability.

31. What is meant by 'virtual patient populations' in modeling?

Simulated individuals created with varying physiological parameters to predict drug response variability.

32. How does inter-individual variability influence model predictions?

It affects the prediction range for drug concentration and efficacy across a population.

33. What is a sensitivity analysis in modeling?

An approach to determine which parameters most influence the model's outputs.

34. What are model diagnostics used for?

To evaluate how well a model predicts observed data using goodness-of-fit, residual plots, etc.

35. Define a prediction-corrected visual predictive check (pcVPC).

A graphical method used to assess the predictive performance of a pharmacokinetic model.

36. How does food intake affect drug disposition modeling?

It alters parameters like gastric emptying time, pH, and enzyme activity, which are adjusted in models.

37. What is a limitation of computational drug disposition models?

They rely heavily on the accuracy of input data and assumptions, which may not always reflect real-world variability.

38. What is the role of simulation in regulatory submissions?

Simulations help justify dose selection, support label claims, and predict outcomes for special populations.

39. What are virtual bioequivalence (VBE) studies?

Simulations used to compare pharmacokinetic profiles of test and reference products without human trials.

40. How is machine learning used in drug disposition modeling?

To identify patterns and predict ADME properties based on large datasets of molecular features.

41. What is compartmental modeling software commonly used in academia?

Phoenix WinNonlin.

42. How is liver enzyme activity incorporated into PBPK models?

Through intrinsic clearance values for specific CYP enzymes, modulated by genetic or drug-induced changes.

43. Why is a model's assumption important?

Incorrect assumptions can lead to inaccurate predictions and unsafe clinical outcomes.

44. How do you validate a drug disposition model?

By comparing simulated results to observed clinical or experimental data.

45. What is model extrapolation?

Using an established model to predict behavior in untested scenarios, such as pediatric or renal-impaired populations.

46. How can models aid in identifying drug-drug interactions?

By simulating enzyme or transporter inhibition/induction and predicting changes in drug levels.

47. What is the role of blood-brain barrier (BBB) modeling?

To assess the likelihood and extent of CNS drug delivery.

48. Why are PBPK models used in generic drug development?

To demonstrate bioequivalence and support biowaivers without the need for in vivo studies.

49. What is a common output of a PBPK simulation?

Plasma drug concentration-time profiles across different compartments.

50. In what scenarios is computational modeling indispensable?

In early drug discovery, pediatric dosing, organ impairment studies, and regulatory justification of dosing strategies.

MCQs

What does ADME stand for in pharmacokinetics?
A) Absorption, Distribution, Metabolism, Excretion
B) Activation, Diffusion, Mutation, Elimination
C) Absorption, Dilution, Modification, Excretion
D) Activation, Distribution, Mutation, Extension

In computational modeling, drug distribution is mainly influenced by:
A) Enzyme affinity
B) Blood flow and tissue permeability
C) Temperature changes
D) Patient diet

A physiologically based pharmacokinetic (PBPK) model is primarily used to:
A) Replace animal studies completely
B) Predict drug behavior based on body physiology
C) Conduct toxicology tests
D) Design clinical trials directly

The main advantage of PBPK modeling is:
A) Reducing drug solubility
B) Simulating tissue-specific drug levels
C) Ignoring drug metabolism
D) Lowering drug potency

Which organ is most crucial for drug metabolism in disposition modeling?
A) Kidney
B) Heart
C) Liver
D) Brain

The term "compartment" in pharmacokinetic modeling refers to:
A) A physical room in the lab
B) A theoretical space representing tissues or fluids
C) A blood vessel
D) A metabolic enzyme

The simplest pharmacokinetic model assumes how many compartments?

A) Two

B) One

C) Three

D) Four

In drug absorption modeling, the rate-limiting step often involves:

A) Metabolism

B) Excretion

C) Membrane permeability

D) Binding to plasma proteins

Which of the following best describes "bioavailability"?

A) Fraction of drug reaching the liver

B) Fraction of drug reaching systemic circulation

C) Fraction of drug eliminated unchanged

D) Fraction of drug distributed to fat tissues

What type of modeling is used when drug concentration is plotted against time?

A) Dynamic modeling

B) Static modeling

C) Kinetic modeling

D) Mathematical modeling

In a PBPK model, which parameter would not typically be needed?

A) Organ volume

B) Blood flow rate

C) Hair color

D) Partition coefficient

The volume of distribution (Vd) describes:

A) Drug elimination speed

B) Drug concentration in plasma only

C) The extent of drug distribution into tissues

D) Rate of metabolism

A higher Vd indicates that the drug:

A) Stays mostly in plasma

B) Distributes extensively into tissues

C) Is rapidly excreted

D) Has a short half-life

Renal excretion modeling focuses mainly on which drug property?

A) Water solubility

B) Lipid solubility

C) Molecular weight only

D) Plasma protein binding

Clearance (CL) is best defined as:

A) Dose per volume

B) Volume of plasma cleared per unit time

C) Half-life of drug

D) Area under the curve (AUC)

Which modeling tool is specifically used for PBPK simulations?

A) Excel

B) GastroPlus™

C) Word

D) Photoshop

The blood-brain barrier (BBB) is modeled mainly to study:

A) Cardiovascular drugs

B) Topical formulations

C) CNS drug delivery

D) Gastrointestinal absorption

Oral bioavailability can be reduced by:

A) Fast metabolism in the liver

B) Slow gastric emptying only

C) High solubility

D) Efficient renal clearance

The half-life ($t\frac{1}{2}$) of a drug is:

A) Time taken to eliminate the drug completely

B) Time taken to eliminate 50% of the drug

C) Time taken for absorption to complete

D) Time taken for drug to distribute

Which term refers to modeling the binding of drug molecules to plasma proteins?

A) Tissue modeling

B) Protein binding modeling

C) Renal clearance modeling

D) Enzymatic modeling

The major enzyme system involved in drug metabolism modeling is:

A) Amylase system

B) Cytochrome P450 system

C) Lipase system

D) Kinase system

Which physiological parameter is most important for modeling lung drug disposition?

A) Blood flow rate

B) Gastric pH

C) Hepatic enzyme activity

D) Gastric emptying time

The concept of "flip-flop" kinetics occurs when:

A) Elimination is faster than absorption

B) Absorption is slower than elimination

C) Excretion rate is very low

D) Drug binds irreversibly to plasma proteins

Molecular weight of a drug is crucial for predicting:

A) Protein binding

B) Distribution

C) Renal filtration

D) Half-life

In modeling oral absorption, which parameter reflects drug dissolution rate?

A) AUC

B) Cmax

C) Ka (absorption rate constant)

D) Ke (elimination rate constant)

A "one-compartment" model assumes:

A) Uniform distribution throughout the body immediately

B) Delayed distribution to tissues

C) Separate plasma and tissue compartments

D) Continuous metabolism during absorption

In a two-compartment model, the initial phase after injection represents:

A) Elimination phase

B) Distribution phase

C) Plateau phase

D) Equilibrium phase

Lipophilic drugs tend to accumulate mainly in:

A) Brain and adipose tissues

B) Plasma water

C) Bone tissue

D) Urine

The predictive success of a PBPK model depends mainly on:

A) Small sample size

B) Accurate physiological parameters

C) Low drug solubility

D) Fast oral absorption

In modeling renal excretion, which factor is least important?

A) Glomerular filtration rate

B) Active tubular secretion

C) Plasma protein binding

D) Taste of the drug

MCQS

Answer Key

1. A) Absorption, Distribution, Metabolism, Excretion
2. B) Blood flow and tissue permeability
3. B) Predict drug behavior based on body physiology
4. B) Simulating tissue-specific drug levels
5. C) Liver
6. B) A theoretical space representing tissues or fluids
7. B) One
8. C) Membrane permeability
9. B) Fraction of drug reaching systemic circulation
10. C) Kinetic modeling
11. C) Hair color
12. C) The extent of drug distribution into tissues
13. B) Distributes extensively into tissues
14. A) Water solubility
15. B) Volume of plasma cleared per unit time
16. B) GastroPlus™
17. C) CNS drug delivery
18. A) Fast metabolism in the liver
19. B) Time taken to eliminate 50% of the drug
20. B) Protein binding modeling
21. B) Cytochrome P450 system

22. A) Blood flow rate
23. B) Absorption is slower than elimination
24. C) Renal filtration
25. C) Ka (absorption rate constant)
26. A) Uniform distribution throughout the body immediately
27. B) Distribution phase
28. A) Brain and adipose tissues
29. B) Accurate physiological parameters
30. D) Taste of the drug

CHAPTER FOUR

Computer-Aided Formulation Development

4.1 Concept of Optimization

4.1.1 Role of Optimization in Formulation

Optimization is a fundamental concept in pharmaceutical formulation development, especially when the goal is to design a product that meets multiple performance criteria such as desired drug release, stability, bioavailability, and patient compliance. In the traditional approach, formulation scientists relied on trial-and-error methods involving sequential experiments that were time-consuming, resource-intensive, and often failed to identify the truly optimal composition or process parameters. With the advent of computer-aided tools and statistical techniques, optimization has become a systematic and efficient strategy that allows for the **quantitative evaluation of multiple variables simultaneously**. It not only accelerates the formulation process but also improves the quality and reproducibility of pharmaceutical products.

In the context of formulation, optimization refers to the process of finding the best possible combination of formulation components and process variables to achieve predefined quality targets. For example, when developing a tablet formulation, parameters such as binder concentration, granulation time, compression force, and disintegrant level can all affect critical quality attributes (CQAs) like hardness, disintegration time, and drug dissolution. The **objective of optimization** is to identify the most suitable values of these variables that ensure the product performs consistently within acceptable limits.

Computer-aided optimization tools, such as **Design-Expert, JMP, Minitab**, and **MODDE**, utilize mathematical models and algorithms to generate response surfaces and contour plots that illustrate how input variables influence the outputs. These tools support **design of experiments (DoE)** approaches, such as **factorial designs, central composite designs**, and **Box-Behnken designs**, which allow researchers to explore the design space effectively and locate the optimum region with minimal experimental runs. Once the data is fitted to a suitable polynomial or non-linear model, optimization is performed using **desirability functions**, where multiple responses are simultaneously maximized or minimized according to the formulation goals.

The role of optimization becomes even more significant under the **Quality-by-Design (QbD)** framework, where it is essential to demonstrate a robust understanding of how formulation variables affect product quality. Optimization ensures that the formulation is not only effective and safe but also manufacturable at scale. Moreover, optimized formulations often show greater robustness to minor changes in raw materials or environmental conditions, reducing batch-to-batch variability and regulatory risk.

In summary, optimization in formulation development is a strategic tool that enhances decision-making, reduces development time, minimizes resource consumption, and ensures the final product consistently meets quality expectations. With the support of computational tools and statistical methodologies, formulation optimization has evolved into a **predictive, data-driven, and scientifically justified process,** forming the backbone of modern pharmaceutical product development.

4.1.2 Design of Experiments (DoE)

Design of Experiments (DoE) is a statistical and mathematical framework widely used in pharmaceutical formulation and process development to study the effect of multiple variables on specific responses systematically. The technique is especially significant because it provides more information per experiment compared to traditional one-variable-at-a-time (OVAT) approaches. In the pharmaceutical domain, where raw materials are costly, and time is limited, DoE offers a way to extract maximum insight with a minimal number of trials. This approach is not just a scientific tool but is an essential element of the Quality-by-Design (QbD) paradigm, as outlined in ICH Q8 guidelines. It helps pharmaceutical scientists and process engineers identify critical material attributes (CMAs) and critical process parameters (CPPs) that influence critical quality attributes (CQAs) like dissolution rate, assay, tablet hardness, friability, and stability.

The basis of DoE lies in planning a set of experiments where multiple input variables, called factors, are varied systematically according to a chosen statistical design. The output responses are then measured and analyzed to evaluate the individual effects of each factor, the interaction effects between two or more factors, and even nonlinear (quadratic) effects where applicable. For instance, in the development of an oral controlled-release tablet, three formulation variables such as polymer concentration (5% to 15% w/w), compression force (4 to 8 kN), and lubricant amount (0.25% to 1% w/w) may all affect the drug release rate at 8 hours. Using DoE, a researcher can evaluate not only how each of these variables independently influences release but also how combinations (such as high polymer and low compression) may produce synergistic or antagonistic effects.

The types of designs used in DoE are selected based on the stage of development and the nature of the problem. In the early screening phase, **full factorial designs** are common. These test all possible combinations of factor levels. For example, a 2^3 full factorial design with three factors at two levels each requires 8 experimental runs and helps identify the main and interaction effects clearly. However, as the number of factors increases, the number of runs increases exponentially. A 2^5 design with five variables would need 32 runs, making it expensive and time-consuming. To overcome this, **fractional factorial designs** are used. These explore only a subset of all combinations and are efficient in screening the most influential variables. A half-fraction 2^{5-1} design, for instance, would require only 16 runs.

Once the key factors are identified, optimization is carried out using **response surface methodology (RSM)**. Two popular RSM designs are **Central Composite Design (CCD)** and **Box-Behnken Design (BBD)**. CCD includes a factorial core, axial (star) points, and center points. For three factors, CCD typically requires 20 experiments. This design is suitable for exploring curvature in the response surface and determining the optimum region. In contrast, BBD uses combinations of three levels without extreme points and generally requires fewer experiments. For three variables, BBD would need 15 runs. Both CCD and BBD allow fitting of second-order (quadratic) models to explore nonlinear responses effectively.

In certain formulation studies, especially when the ingredients must sum to a constant total, **mixture designs** are employed. These are used in semi-solid formulations like gels or liquid formulations such as suspensions, where the proportions of components are constrained. A simplex centroid design or a simplex lattice design can help evaluate the effect of varying component proportions like water, propylene glycol, and surfactant on viscosity and spreadability.

D-optimal designs are flexible designs that are algorithmically generated and used when standard designs cannot be applied due to constraints in formulation ranges or operational limitations. These designs reduce the number of experiments by selecting the most statistically informative points based on a model matrix. For example, in the case of a formulation limited by drug solubility or excipient incompatibility, D-optimal design allows constrained exploration of feasible space.

Once data is generated from these experimental runs, it is analyzed using regression modeling. A typical regression equation may look like:

$$Y = \beta^0 + \beta_1 X_1 + \beta_2 X_2 + \beta_{12} X_1 X_2 + \beta_{11} X_1^2 + \beta_{22} X_2^2$$

Where Y is the response (like % drug release), X_1 and X_2 are input variables (e.g., polymer concentration and compression force), and the β terms are coefficients indicating the strength and direction of effects. Statistical analysis is then conducted using **Analysis of Variance (ANOVA)** to assess whether the model is statistically significant (generally $p < 0.05$) and how well the model fits the data (using R^2 and adjusted R^2 values). Lack-of-fit tests and residual plots are examined to ensure that the model assumptions are valid.

The model is then used to generate **contour plots** and **3D response surface plots**, which help visualize the effect of factor interactions on the response. Using these plots, researchers can identify the "design space" — a multidimensional region within which the formulation meets all required specifications. Optimization tools within DoE software such as **Design-Expert, JMP,** or **Minitab** allow the user to set goals (maximize, minimize, or target) for each response and generate the most desirable combination of factor levels. For example, in optimizing a tablet formulation, the goal may be to maximize drug release at 6 hours, minimize friability below 0.8%, and maintain hardness between 4–6 kg/cm².

DoE implementation is further supported by regulatory authorities. Guidelines such as ICH Q8 encourage the use of statistically designed experiments as part of a risk-based pharmaceutical development strategy. The information generated through DoE not only accelerates development but also provides a strong scientific justification during scale-up and technology transfer. It reduces the likelihood of failure during validation and supports the lifecycle management of products by establishing a robust formulation and process foundation.

Modern DoE tools include user-friendly interfaces that guide the scientist through design selection, input of factor ranges, specification of responses, and real-time visualization of model fitting. These platforms offer detailed diagnostic tools such as Pareto charts, desirability plots, residual plots, and prediction intervals. Moreover, they allow export of model equations, tables, and graphs directly into regulatory documentation.

Case Study Example: Optimization of Sustained Release Matrix Tablet Using Central Composite Design

A pharmaceutical R&D team was assigned the task of developing a sustained-release matrix tablet of a poorly water-soluble antihypertensive drug. The goal was to achieve 80–85% drug release at the end of 12 hours, with acceptable tablet hardness (above 4 kg/cm²) and friability (less than 1%). Initial screening indicated that three formulation factors had the most influence on drug release and tablet integrity: hydroxypropyl methylcellulose (HPMC K100M) concentration (X_1), microcrystalline cellulose (MCC) level (X_2), and magnesium stearate concentration (X_3). The team selected **Central Composite Design (CCD)** to optimize the formulation and study the interaction effects among the variables.

The experimental design included 20 runs covering a wide design space:

- HPMC K100M: 10% to 30% w/w
- MCC: 20% to 40% w/w
- Magnesium stearate: 0.25% to 1% w/w

Each batch was compressed into tablets using a rotary tablet press and evaluated for key responses: percentage drug release at 12 hours (Y_1), tablet hardness (Y_2), and friability (Y_3). The tablets were subjected to dissolution testing in phosphate buffer pH 6.8 using USP Type II apparatus at 50 rpm and 37 °C. Hardness was measured using a Monsanto hardness tester, and friability was tested using a Roche friabilator.

Regression analysis yielded second-order polynomial models for each response. The ANOVA results showed high model significance ($p < 0.001$) and adjusted R^2 values above 0.95, indicating an excellent fit. The HPMC level had the strongest effect on drug release; increasing its concentration slowed the release rate due to gel barrier formation. MCC contributed to tablet hardness and compressibility, while magnesium stearate showed a negative impact on both drug release and hardness due to its hydrophobic nature.

3D surface plots revealed a significant interaction between HPMC and MCC: too low HPMC with high MCC led to faster drug release, while high HPMC with low MCC caused tablet sticking during compression. Optimization was performed using a desirability function with targets: drug release = 83 ± 2%, hardness ≥ 5 kg/cm², friability ≤ 0.8%. The software predicted the optimal formulation with 22% HPMC, 35% MCC, and 0.5% magnesium stearate. This formulation was prepared and evaluated, and experimental results matched the predicted values within 5% error margin.

This DoE-based approach reduced the total number of trials by nearly 60% compared to a traditional trial-and-error method and provided valuable understanding of formulation behavior. Moreover, the design space identified in this study was used during scale-up and validated successfully under process qualification studies.

Case Study Example: Optimization of a Nanoemulsion Drug Delivery System Using D-Optimal Mixture Design

A formulation development team was working on a nanoemulsion system for improving the oral bioavailability of a lipophilic anti-inflammatory drug. The drug had very low aqueous solubility and poor oral absorption (bioavailability <10%), making it a strong candidate for lipid-based delivery. The goal of the study was to develop a self-emulsifying drug delivery system (SEDDS) that would form a nanoemulsion upon contact with gastrointestinal fluids. The targeted globule size was less than 150 nm with low polydispersity index (PDI < 0.25), and the system needed to show over 90% drug release in 30 minutes.

The formulation included three primary excipients: oil (Capryol 90), surfactant (Cremophor EL), and co-surfactant (Transcutol HP). Since the total of these three components must always add up to 100%, the team selected a D-optimal **mixture design** for the study. The design allows efficient exploration of the compositional space under mixture constraints.

The experimental ranges were:

- Capryol 90 (X_1): 20% to 40%
- Cremophor EL (X_2): 30% to 60%
- Transcutol HP (X_3): 10% to 40%

Fifteen formulations were generated by the software (Design-Expert), and each batch was prepared by gentle mixing at 40 °C followed by homogenization using a high-shear homogenizer at 10,000 rpm for 15 minutes. The globule size and PDI were measured using dynamic light scattering (DLS), while in vitro drug release was studied using dialysis bag diffusion in simulated intestinal fluid (pH 6.8) at 37 °C.

Data analysis revealed significant quadratic and interaction effects between the three components. Increasing Capryol improved drug solubilization but also increased globule size. A higher level of Cremophor EL reduced droplet size due to better emulsification, but excessive amounts led to an increase in PDI. Transcutol HP helped reduce interfacial tension and improved drug release, but too high a concentration resulted in system instability. The optimal zone identified by contour plots balanced all three excipients to form a stable nanoemulsion with the desired particle size.

ANOVA showed the models were statistically significant ($p < 0.01$), with high R^2 values (globule size model: $R^2 = 0.964$, drug release model: $R^2 = 0.981$). The software suggested an optimized composition of 28% Capryol 90, 52% Cremophor EL, and 20% Transcutol HP. This batch showed a mean globule size of 122 nm, PDI of 0.21, and 94.8% drug release within 30 minutes. The formulation remained physically stable over 3 months under accelerated conditions (40 °C, 75% RH) without significant change in particle size or drug content.

This case study demonstrated how mixture design in DoE provides a scientific, data-driven approach to optimizing complex formulations like nanoemulsions, where multiple variables interact non-linearly and must obey mixture constraints. It also reduced formulation development time and helped build a robust design space that was later used in scale-up and regulatory documentation. **Case Study Example: Optimization of Oral Antifungal Emulsion Using Box-Behnken Design**

A formulation development project was initiated to design an oral emulsion for a poorly water-soluble antifungal drug intended for pediatric use. The goal was to formulate a stable and palatable emulsion that would deliver the required therapeutic dose in a small volume. The challenges involved included maintaining droplet stability over time, minimizing phase separation, and achieving acceptable taste masking. The desired quality targets included droplet size below 500 nm, low viscosity for ease of administration, and no creaming or sedimentation for at least 30 days under refrigerated and room temperature storage.

The development team selected **Box-Behnken Design (BBD)** under response surface methodology to evaluate the effect of three formulation variables on the final product attributes. The selected independent variables were oil phase volume (X_1), surfactant concentration (X_2), and co-solvent level (X_3). The oil phase used was medium chain triglycerides (MCT oil), the surfactant was polysorbate 80, and the co-solvent was glycerin. The ranges were as follows:

* MCT oil: 10% to 20% v/v
* Polysorbate 80: 1% to 5% w/v
* Glycerin: 5% to 15% v/v

The response variables measured included average droplet size (Y_1), viscosity at 25 °C (Y_2), and stability index based on visual observation of creaming after centrifugation (Y_3). A total of 15 experimental runs were generated using Design-Expert software. The emulsions were prepared using a high-speed homogenizer at 8000 rpm for 10 minutes followed by ultrasonication for 5 minutes to reduce droplet size. The droplet size was measured using a particle size analyzer, and viscosity was determined using a Brookfield viscometer with spindle number 2 at 30 rpm.

The results showed that increasing MCT oil concentration increased droplet size due to the higher oil load and limited emulsifier coverage. On the other hand, increasing the surfactant level significantly reduced droplet size and improved the stability index. However, higher concentrations of surfactant also increased viscosity and caused a bitter taste, which was undesirable for pediatric use. Glycerin had a dual role — it enhanced mouthfeel and contributed to taste masking, but beyond 12%, it increased viscosity excessively and slowed down drug release.

The model was statistically validated through ANOVA, showing high significance ($p < 0.005$) and R^2 values above 0.92 for all three responses. The 3D response surface plots and overlay contour plots helped identify the optimal region where all formulation requirements were met. The software-suggested optimized formulation contained 14% MCT oil, 3.2% polysorbate 80, and 9% glycerin. The predicted responses were: droplet size = 346 nm, viscosity = 195 cP, and stability index = 95%. Experimental verification showed close agreement with predicted values, confirming model reliability.

The optimized emulsion was physically stable for three months under both refrigerated (2–8 °C) and ambient (25 °C / 60% RH) storage. There was no visible creaming, cracking, or phase separation. Taste masking was confirmed through a sensory panel using a 5-point hedonic scale, and the final formulation scored above 4.0 for overall palatability. This case study showed how DoE, specifically Box-Behnken Design, can be used successfully in optimizing complex liquid and emulsion dosage forms where multiple variables interact non-linearly. The design also minimized development cost and supported risk-based justification during regulatory review.

Parameter	Details
Formulation Objective	Develop sustained-release tablet with optimized drug release
DoE Type	Central Composite Design (CCD)
Independent Variables	HPMC K100M (10–30% w/w), MCC (20–40% w/w), Magnesium Stearate (0.25–1%)
Responses Measured	% Drug Release at 12 h, Tablet Hardness (kg/cm²), Friability (%)
Experimental Design Size	3 Factors, Quadratic Model
Number of Trials	20 runs
R² Values (Adjusted)	Drug Release: 0.97, Hardness: 0.94, Friability: 0.91
ANOVA Significance (p-value)	All models p < 0.001
Software Used	Design-Expert
Significant Findings	HPMC slowed release; MCC increased hardness; lubricant reduced hardness
Optimal Formulation	22% HPMC, 35% MCC, 0.5% lubricant
Final Results	83% release at 12 h, Hardness ~5.2 kg/cm², Friability 0.75%

Table 1: DoE Case Study – Sustained Release Matrix Tablets

Parameter	Details
Formulation Objective	Enhance oral bioavailability using nanoemulsion
DoE Type	D-Optimal Mixture Design
Independent Variables	Capryol 90 (20–40%), Cremophor EL (30–60%), Transcutol HP (10–40%)
Responses Measured	Droplet Size (nm), PDI, % Drug Release (30 min)
Experimental Design Size	3 Components with Mixture Constraints
Number of Trials	15 runs
R² Values (Adjusted)	Droplet Size: 0.964, Drug Release: 0.981, PDI: 0.928
ANOVA Significance (p-value)	All models p < 0.005
Software Used	Design-Expert
Significant Findings	High oil increased droplet size; surfactant reduced PDI and improved stability
Optimal Formulation	28% Capryol 90, 52% Cremophor EL, 20% Transcutol HP
Final Results	122 nm droplet size, PDI 0.21, 94.8% drug release

Table 2: DoE Case Study – Nanoemulsion Drug Delivery System

Parameter	Details
Formulation Objective	Develop palatable, stable emulsion for pediatric oral use
DoE Type	Box-Behnken Design (BBD)
Independent Variables	MCT Oil (10–20%), Polysorbate 80 (1–5%), Glycerin (5–15%)
Responses Measured	Droplet Size (nm), Viscosity (cP), Stability Index (%)
Experimental Design Size	3 Factors, Quadratic Model (BBD)
Number of Trials	15 runs
R^2 Values (Adjusted)	Droplet Size: 0.922, Viscosity: 0.935, Stability: 0.915
ANOVA Significance (p-value)	All models $p < 0.005$
Software Used	Design-Expert
Significant Findings	Oil increased size; surfactant improved stability; glycerin aided taste masking
Optimal Formulation	14% MCT oil, 3.2% surfactant, 9% glycerin
Final Results	346 nm droplet size, 195 cP viscosity, 95% stability index, good palatability

Table 3: DoE Case Study – Oral Antifungal Emulsion

4.2 Optimization Parameters and Technology

4.2.1 Independent and Dependent Variables

In pharmaceutical formulation optimization, the classification of variables into **independent** and **dependent** is foundational for designing meaningful experiments and interpreting results. These variables are the core components of any model developed through Design of Experiments (DoE) or response surface methodology (RSM).

Independent variables, also known as **factors or input variables**, are those that are purposefully varied by the formulation scientist to study their effect on the formulation or process. These can include material-related variables like **drug-to-polymer ratio, excipient concentration, surfactant type**, or **binder level**, as well as process-related variables such as **mixing time, granulation speed, drying temperature**, and **compression force**. Independent variables are selected based on prior knowledge, pre-formulation studies, risk assessments, and scientific understanding of the formulation design space.

On the other hand, **dependent variables**, also known as **responses or output variables**, are the outcomes that are measured during or after experimentation to assess the effect of the independent variables. These responses are linked to **critical quality attributes (CQAs)** such as **drug content uniformity, disintegration time, tablet hardness, friability, dissolution rate, particle size**, or **zeta potential**. The goal of optimization is to adjust the independent variables so that these dependent responses are brought within desired limits or specifications.

To illustrate, in the development of a fast-dissolving tablet, independent variables might include **superdisintegrant concentration** and **compression pressure**, while dependent variables would be **disintegration time** and **percent drug released at 10 minutes**. Establishing a reliable model that connects the inputs and outputs helps researchers understand the influence of each variable and make decisions that lead to a robust and optimized product.

4.2.2 Responses and Desirability

In the context of computer-aided optimization, **responses** are the outcomes of interest that are mathematically analyzed to assess product quality or performance. Most formulations involve multiple responses that need to be optimized simultaneously. However, these responses often have competing requirements—for instance, increasing tablet hardness may lead to slower disintegration. This necessitates a method to balance different goals in a scientifically sound manner.

The **desirability function approach** is one of the most widely used methods in pharmaceutical optimization to achieve this balance. Each response is transformed into a **desirability value ranging from 0 (completely undesirable) to 1 (fully desirable)**. The desirability function allows for customization—some responses may need to be **maximized** (e.g., percent drug release), some **minimized** (e.g., disintegration time), and others **targeted** to a specific value (e.g., tablet weight).

For example, if a response such as **tablet hardness** must lie between 4 and 7 kg/cm², a target of 5.5 kg/cm² might be chosen. The desirability function will then assign higher desirability values to results closer to this target. When multiple responses are involved, the individual desirability scores are combined (usually through geometric mean) into a **composite desirability index**, which is then maximized using numerical optimization techniques.

Software tools such as **Design-Expert**, **JMP**, and **Minitab** support multi-response optimization through desirability functions and generate **overlay contour plots** and **optimization reports**. These tools allow scientists to explore the trade-offs between responses and select the formulation that best meets all quality requirements.

In summary, identifying the right **independent and dependent variables** and applying **desirability-based multi-response optimization** provides a scientific and systematic pathway to robust formulation development. It enhances understanding of formulation behavior, supports QbD principles, and ensures reproducibility, regulatory compliance, and product success.

4.3 Formulation Design Using Computers

4.3.1 Development of Emulsions

Emulsions are biphasic dosage forms consisting of two immiscible liquids—typically oil and water—where one is dispersed as small droplets within the other. These systems are widely used in pharmaceutical formulations for oral, topical, parenteral, and ophthalmic drug delivery. The development of emulsions involves selecting suitable components, understanding phase behaviour, and optimizing critical formulation and processing parameters to ensure physical stability, drug release, and therapeutic efficacy.

In recent years, **computer-aided formulation development** has significantly improved the design and optimization of emulsions. Using statistical tools and simulation software, formulators can minimize trial-and-error experimentation, predict droplet behaviour, and develop stable emulsions with desired characteristics.

Types of Emulsions

Emulsions are broadly classified into:

- **Oil-in-Water (O/W)** emulsions – oil droplets dispersed in water.

  ○ Example: Oral and parenteral emulsions (e.g., Intralipid®).

- **Water-in-Oil (W/O)** emulsions – water droplets dispersed in oil.

  ○ Example: Topical formulations for dry skin.

- **Multiple Emulsions (W/O/W or O/W/O)** – complex systems for controlled drug release.

  ○ Used in vaccines and sustained release topical agents.

Key Components of Emulsion Systems

1. **Oil Phase**

   ○ Common oils: soybean oil, mineral oil, castor oil, isopropyl myristate.

- Selected based on solubility of the drug and compatibility with the target site.
- Example: Soybean oil (refractive index ~1.47; density ~0.92 g/cm^3).

2. **Aqueous Phase**

- Typically purified water or buffer solution (pH 4–7 depending on drug stability).
- For parenteral emulsions, isotonicity is adjusted using sodium chloride or dextrose.

3. **Surfactants (Emulsifying Agents)**

- Reduce interfacial tension and stabilize droplets.
- Hydrophilic-Lipophilic Balance (HLB) values guide the choice:

    - For O/W: HLB 8–18 (e.g., Tween 80, HLB ~15).
    - For W/O: HLB 3–6 (e.g., Span 80, HLB ~4.3).

4. **Co-surfactants**

- Enhance stability and reduce required surfactant concentration.
- Common examples: ethanol, propylene glycol, lecithin.

5. **Preservatives and Stabilizers**

- For microbial protection (e.g., methylparaben 0.1%) and viscosity control (e.g., carbomers or xanthan gum).

Formulation Parameters Influencing Emulsion Quality

1. **Droplet Size and Distribution**

- Ideal droplet size: 100–1000 nm for nanoemulsions, 1–5 μm for conventional emulsions.
- Narrow polydispersity index (PDI < 0.3) indicates uniform droplets.

2. **Zeta Potential**

- Charge on droplet surface affects physical stability.
- Zeta potential > |30| mV typically indicates stable emulsions due to repulsive forces.

3. **Viscosity and Rheological Properties**

- Critical for topical applications.
- Measured using rotational viscometers (target range: 1000–10,000 cP depending on dosage form).

4. **pH and Osmolality**

- Important for parenteral and ophthalmic emulsions.
- Adjusted to pH 7.4 for IV emulsions and ~300 mOsm/kg for isotonicity.

Computer-Aided Design in Emulsion Development

The use of **Design of Experiments (DoE)** and **software modelling tools** such as *Design-Expert®, Minitab®, and JMP®* allows systematic optimization of emulsion formulation and processing variables.

Independent Variables (Input Factors):

- Oil phase concentration (e.g., 10% to 40%)
- Surfactant concentration (e.g., 1% to 5%)
- Homogenization speed (e.g., 5000–15,000 rpm)
- Mixing time (e.g., 2 to 10 minutes)
- Aqueous phase pH (e.g., 4 to 7)

Dependent Variables (Responses):

- Droplet size (nm or μm)
- Polydispersity index (PDI)
- Drug loading (%)
- Emulsion stability (measured as % creaming or phase separation over 30 days)

Example DoE Setup:

A **3^2 factorial design** can be used with two variables—surfactant concentration (X1) and oil content (X2)—each at three levels (low, medium, high). This design yields 9 experimental runs and allows the analysis of both main effects and interaction effects on emulsion characteristics like droplet size and PDI.

Stability Testing of Emulsions

Emulsions are subjected to **accelerated and real-time stability testing**:

- **Centrifugation (3000 rpm for 30 min)**: Checks phase separation.
- **Freeze-thaw cycles (–20°C to 40°C)**: 3 cycles to test stability under extreme conditions.
- **Storage at 25°C/60% RH and 40°C/75% RH**: Over 3–6 months.
- **Visual Inspection**: For creaming, coalescence, cracking, or phase inversion.

Applications of Emulsions in Drug Delivery

- **Parenteral Nutrition**: Lipid emulsions like *Intralipid®* deliver essential fatty acids.
- **Topical Formulations**: O/W emulsions for moisturizing; W/O emulsions for protective applications.
- **Oral Delivery**: Emulsions enhance bioavailability of poorly water-soluble drugs (e.g., cyclosporine in *Neoral®*).
- **Ophthalmic Emulsions**: E.g., *Restasis®* for dry eye treatment using castor oil-based emulsion.

4.3.2 Microemulsion Drug Carriers

4.3.2.1 Introduction to Microemulsions

Microemulsions are thermodynamically stable, optically transparent, and isotropic liquid systems that are composed of oil, water, surfactant, and usually a co-surfactant. The size of droplets in microemulsions typically ranges between 10 and 100 nanometres. Unlike coarse emulsions, microemulsions form spontaneously when the right ratios of components are mixed due to their ultra-low interfacial tension, without the need for external energy. This property is attributed to the synergistic action of surfactants and co-surfactants, which lower the interfacial tension between the oil and water phases and allow for the self-assembly of nano-sized droplets. Microemulsions have been extensively used in pharmaceutical formulation, particularly to enhance the solubility and bioavailability of poorly water-soluble drugs. Because of their nanometric droplet size and large interfacial area, microemulsions offer improved drug absorption, faster onset of action, and in some cases, controlled or targeted delivery, which makes them an ideal choice for various routes of administration including oral, topical, ocular, nasal, and parenteral.

4.3.2.2 Components of Microemulsions

Microemulsions are classified primarily based on the nature of the continuous phase. In oil-in-water (O/W) microemulsions, oil droplets are dispersed within a continuous aqueous phase and are ideal for oral and parenteral delivery of hydrophobic drugs. Water-in-oil (W/O) microemulsions, in contrast, consist of water droplets dispersed in a continuous oil phase and are often used in topical formulations. Bicontinuous microemulsions represent an intermediate structure where both oil and water form interconnecting domains, stabilized by the surfactant-co-surfactant interface, and provide a flexible platform for drug delivery. The choice between these types depends on the solubility characteristics of the drug, route of administration, and desired pharmacokinetic profile.

4.3.2.3 Types of Microemulsions

Microemulsions can be classified based on the dispersed and continuous phases:

- **Oil-in-water (o/w) microemulsion:** Oil droplets dispersed in a continuous aqueous phase; suitable for **oral and parenteral delivery** of lipophilic drugs.
- **Water-in-oil (w/o) microemulsion:** Water droplets dispersed in an oil phase; used for **topical and transdermal systems.**
- **Bicontinuous microemulsion:** Interconnected domains of oil and water stabilized by surfactants; provides flexibility in drug loading.

Each system offers distinct advantages depending on the **route of administration, drug solubility,** and **targeted bioavailability.**

4.3.2.4 Advantages in Drug Delivery

Microemulsions offer multiple advantages over conventional dosage forms:

- **Enhanced solubility and bioavailability**: Especially for hydrophobic drugs like **cyclosporine A, itraconazole**, and **fenofibrate**.
- **Improved drug absorption**: Due to nanosized droplets and better mucosal penetration.
- **Ease of preparation**: Thermodynamic stability allows simple mixing of components without need for high energy input.
- **Versatility in routes**: Suitable for **oral, topical, ocular, nasal**, and **parenteral** routes.
- **Controlled drug release**: Can sustain or delay release depending on composition.

4.3.2.5 Computer-Aided Design of Microemulsions

Modern microemulsion systems are increasingly designed using **computer-aided techniques** like **Design of Experiments (DoE)** and **statistical modeling tools**. Software such as **Design-Expert, JMP**, and **Minitab** enables researchers to systematically vary key formulation factors (oil, surfactant, co-surfactant, water ratios) and study their effects on responses like **droplet size, polydispersity index (PDI), drug loading**, and **in-vitro drug release**.

- **Independent variables**: Oil concentration (e.g., 10–30%), surfactant-to-co-surfactant ratio (1:1 to 3:1), aqueous phase (40–70%), stirring speed (500–1500 rpm).
- **Responses evaluated**: Mean globule size (10–100 nm), zeta potential (± 20 to ± 40 mV), drug release at 1 and 6 hours (%), and viscosity (10–200 cP).

A **pseudo-ternary phase diagram** is often constructed with the help of software tools to identify the **microemulsion region**, helping in the selection of an optimal composition range.

4.3.2.6 Evaluation Parameters

To confirm the suitability and stability of microemulsions, several evaluation techniques are performed:

- **Droplet Size and PDI**: Measured by Dynamic Light Scattering (DLS), optimal systems have a size <100 nm and PDI < 0.3.
- **Zeta Potential**: Indicator of stability; values > ± 30 mV indicate electrostatic stabilization.

- **Drug Content and Loading**: Quantified using HPLC/UV-visible spectroscopy; loading efficiency usually ranges from **70–95%**.
- **Thermodynamic Stability Tests**: Include **heating-cooling cycles, centrifugation (3000–5000 rpm for 30 min)**, and **freeze-thaw cycles**, to ensure robustness.

In-vitro Drug Release: Using **Franz diffusion cells** or **dialysis bag method**, with release media simulating physiological pH (1.2 or 6.8). Kinetic models like **Higuchi, Korsmeyer-Peppas,** or **first-order** help interpret the release mechanism

4.3.2.7 Examples of Microemulsion-Based Drug Products

Drug	Route	System	Key Outcome
Cyclosporine A	Oral	O/W microemulsion	Enhanced absorption, marketed as **Neoral®**
Ketoconazole	Topical	W/O microemulsion	Deep skin penetration, improved efficacy
Diazepam	Nasal	Bicontinuous system	Rapid CNS delivery in seizure management
Flurbiprofen	Ocular	O/W microemulsion	Sustained release, reduced irritation

Table 4: Microemulsion-Based Drug Products

4.3.2.8 Limitations and Challenges
While microemulsions offer many advantages, challenges include:

- **Irritation potential** due to high surfactant concentrations.
- **Drug precipitation** upon dilution, especially in oral formulations.
- **Regulatory complexity** due to classification as complex systems.
- **Physical instability** over long storage periods if not optimized properly.

Nanoparticles and Vesicular Systems
Introduction to Nanoparticles and Vesicular Systems in Formulation
Nanoparticles and vesicular systems have emerged as highly sophisticated and promising carriers in the field of drug delivery due to their ability to overcome several challenges associated with conventional formulations. These systems are defined based on their structure,

composition, and method of drug encapsulation. Nanoparticles are solid colloidal particles ranging in size typically from 1 to 1000 nanometres. They can be composed of polymers, lipids, metals, or other biodegradable materials, and are often used to entrap, encapsulate, or adsorb drugs on their surface. On the other hand, vesicular systems are bilayered or multilayered structures that are formed by amphiphilic molecules such as phospholipids or surfactants, creating a closed spherical vesicle with an internal aqueous core. Common vesicular systems include liposomes, niosomes, ethosomes, and transferosomes. While nanoparticles are usually solid matrix systems, vesicular carriers have a hollow structure capable of housing both hydrophilic and lipophilic drugs depending on their composition and arrangement.

The classification of these systems is generally based on material type and structural behaviour. Polymeric nanoparticles can be further categorized as nanospheres, where the drug is uniformly dispersed within the polymer matrix, and nanocapsules, which possess a core-shell structure. Lipid-based nanoparticles include solid lipid nanoparticles and nanostructured lipid carriers, offering high stability and biocompatibility. In contrast, vesicular systems are mostly differentiated by their membrane-forming agents and their target site within the body. For example, liposomes are made of natural or synthetic phospholipids, whereas niosomes use non-ionic surfactants. These structural variations allow significant flexibility in designing drug delivery systems based on the nature of the drug and therapeutic requirement.

The significance of nanoparticles and vesicular systems lies in their ability to provide site-specific and controlled release of drugs. These carriers can protect the drug from premature degradation in the systemic circulation, enhance its solubility, and facilitate better penetration across biological membranes. One of the most vital advantages of nanocarriers is their ability to pass through physiological barriers such as the blood-brain barrier and gastrointestinal mucosa. Additionally, by functionalizing their surface with targeting ligands, they can achieve receptor-mediated uptake by specific cells, such as cancerous or inflamed cells. This reduces systemic side effects and enhances therapeutic efficacy. Furthermore, sustained or controlled drug release from these carriers can maintain a constant plasma drug concentration for extended durations, improving patient compliance and therapeutic outcomes.

In modern pharmaceutical technology, these systems have found applications in cancer therapy, vaccine delivery, neurological disorders, and infectious disease management. With advances in molecular biology, materials science, and computational drug design, nanoparticles and vesicular systems are continuously being improved for better safety, scalability, and clinical performance. Their growing importance in personalized medicine, gene delivery, and immunotherapy highlights the need for detailed understanding and computer-aided formulation strategies to harness their full potential.

Types of Nanocarriers

Nanocarriers are highly advanced drug delivery systems designed to transport drugs in a protected and targeted manner. The two major categories of nanocarriers commonly explored in pharmaceutical formulation are polymeric nanoparticles and lipid-based nanoparticles. These systems provide improved pharmacokinetics, site-specific drug delivery, and better patient outcomes in both acute and chronic diseases. Their formulation design depends on various factors such as the nature of the drug, route of administration, release profile desired, and the target site of action. Among these, polymer-based and lipid-based nanocarriers have gained the most attention due to their versatility and proven biocompatibility in many therapeutic applications.

Polymeric Nanoparticles

Polymeric nanoparticles are solid colloidal particles made from natural, semi-synthetic, or synthetic polymers. These polymers form a matrix or shell structure that holds the drug either by entrapment, adsorption, or conjugation. The commonly used polymers in pharmaceutical formulations include poly(lactic-co-glycolic acid) or PLGA, chitosan, Eudragit, polycaprolactone (PCL), and poly(methyl methacrylate) or PMMA. PLGA is a well-known biodegradable and biocompatible polymer approved by regulatory agencies for controlled drug release. It undergoes hydrolytic degradation into lactic acid and glycolic acid, which are naturally metabolised in the body. Chitosan, a natural polysaccharide derived from chitin, is used for mucoadhesive drug delivery and provides good stability and permeability enhancement. Eudragit, a synthetic polymer, is often used for pH-controlled release, especially in gastrointestinal targeting.

Polymeric nanoparticles offer the advantage of sustained and controlled drug release, which helps maintain therapeutic drug levels over extended periods. This is particularly useful for drugs with a short half-life, narrow therapeutic index, or high frequency of dosing. For example, PLGA nanoparticles have been successfully used for encapsulating anticancer drugs, peptides, and proteins to provide extended release and reduce systemic toxicity. The formulation process typically involves methods such as solvent evaporation, nanoprecipitation, emulsification-diffusion, and ionic gelation depending on the polymer properties and drug solubility. These nanoparticles also provide high encapsulation efficiency and can be surface-modified with targeting ligands or PEGylation to enhance their circulation time and biodistribution.

Solid Lipid Nanoparticles (SLNs) and Nanostructured Lipid Carriers (NLCs)

Solid lipid nanoparticles (SLNs) are submicron colloidal carriers composed of solid lipids that remain solid at both room and body temperatures. These lipids include glyceryl behenate, glyceryl monostearate, stearic acid, and cetyl palmitate, which are commonly used in pharmaceutical and cosmetic products. SLNs are stabilized using surfactants such as polysorbates, lecithin, or poloxamers. These nanoparticles combine the advantages of traditional lipid-based systems and solid matrix carriers, providing a stable, non-toxic platform for drug delivery. They are particularly suited for lipophilic drugs and provide protection against chemical degradation, light sensitivity, and hydrolysis.

Nanostructured lipid carriers (NLCs) were developed to overcome the limitations of SLNs, such as limited drug loading and drug expulsion during storage. NLCs are composed of a mixture of solid and liquid lipids, which results in an imperfect crystal structure. This disordered matrix provides more space for drug accommodation, thereby improving drug loading capacity and minimizing leakage. NLCs show improved stability, lower particle aggregation, and better release profiles compared to SLNs.

Formulation of SLNs and NLCs usually involves high-pressure homogenization, microemulsion techniques, or ultrasonication. Key factors such as lipid composition, surfactant concentration, processing temperature, and homogenization cycles need to be optimized for desired particle size, stability, and entrapment efficiency. SLNs and NLCs have been explored for intravenous, oral, topical, and ocular delivery of various drugs including anticancer agents, anti-inflammatory drugs, antivirals, and vaccines. However, challenges such as polymorphic transitions, crystallization behaviour, and long-term physical stability require careful selection of lipid and formulation parameters.

Computer-Aided Design and Optimization of Nanocarriers

Developing effective nanoparticle and vesicular formulations requires the careful selection and optimization of numerous parameters, including **particle size, surface charge (zeta potential), polydispersity index (PDI), encapsulation efficiency,** and **drug release kinetics.** These parameters are often interdependent and influenced by multiple formulation and process variables. Here, **computer-aided formulation tools** become indispensable.

Design of Experiments (DoE) is frequently employed to evaluate the effect of variables such as **drug-to-lipid ratio, type and concentration of surfactant, stirring speed, solvent system**, and **temperature.** Response surface methodology (RSM), a common DoE approach, helps identify the optimal conditions for preparing nanoparticles with minimal size and maximum encapsulation efficiency. For example, in the development of PLGA nanoparticles for a poorly soluble anticancer drug, RSM might be used to simultaneously optimize **particle size (<200 nm)** and **drug loading (>80%).**

Simulation and modelling tools also assist in **predicting drug release** profiles, estimating **stability under various conditions**, and visualizing **nanoparticle-drug interactions.** Software platforms like **GastroPlus™, Simcyp™, and MATLAB** are widely applied for simulating **pharmacokinetic behavior**, especially in nanoformulations intended for **oral, ocular, or parenteral delivery.**

Applications in Drug Delivery and Therapeutics

Nanoparticles and vesicular systems are widely used in **oncology, neurology, infectious disease,** and **dermatology. Liposomes** loaded with anticancer drugs like doxorubicin (e.g., Doxil®) have significantly reduced cardiotoxicity compared to free drug forms. **Niosomes** have shown improved bioavailability in oral delivery of poorly absorbed drugs like **insulin** and **levodopa.** In brain-targeted delivery, **polymeric nanoparticles** help transport drugs across the **blood-brain barrier (BBB)** by utilizing **surface-modified ligands** that allow receptor-mediated endocytosis.

For skin and mucosal applications, **ethosomes** and **transferosomes** provide enhanced penetration due to their **deformable lipid membranes,** allowing drugs like corticosteroids, antivirals, and antifungals to be delivered effectively through the stratum corneum. Furthermore, **solid lipid nanoparticles** are gaining attention in **ocular delivery** systems for diseases like glaucoma and uveitis, where prolonged residence time is desired.

Challenges and Future Prospects

Despite their benefits, nanoparticle and vesicular drug delivery systems face several challenges including **physical instability, aggregation, burst release, scale-up difficulties**, and **regulatory complexities**. However, with the integration of **artificial intelligence (AI)** and **machine learning (ML)** into formulation software, it is becoming possible to **predict optimal formulations** faster, analyze **multi-variable datasets**, and develop **personalized drug delivery systems**. Current trends are moving toward **stimuli-responsive nanoparticles, multi-drug-loaded vesicles**, and **hybrid systems** that combine different nanotechnologies to achieve **precision medicine**.

Metallic and Inorganic Nanoparticles

Metallic and inorganic nanoparticles are a distinct category of nanoscale drug carriers that are prepared using metal-based or non-organic materials. These systems have attracted significant attention in pharmaceutical research due to their unique physical and chemical properties such as large surface area-to-volume ratio, tunable size, optical properties, and surface modifiability. Unlike polymeric or lipid-based carriers, metallic nanoparticles are generally more rigid and offer better control over shape and structure. Some common metals used in the preparation of these nanoparticles include silver, gold, zinc oxide, titanium dioxide, and iron oxide, while inorganic materials such as silica and calcium phosphate are used for creating non-metallic inorganic nanoparticles. These nanosystems are primarily applied in the fields of targeted drug delivery, diagnostics, photothermal therapy, and biosensing, especially in cancer and infectious disease management.

Silver nanoparticles (AgNPs) are among the most widely studied metallic nanocarriers due to their well-known antimicrobial properties. They can be synthesized using chemical reduction, green synthesis with plant extracts, or photochemical methods. Silver nanoparticles can inhibit bacterial growth by damaging bacterial cell membranes, interacting with thiol groups in enzymes, and generating reactive oxygen species. In drug delivery systems, silver nanoparticles are used either alone for antimicrobial coatings or in combination with antibiotics to enhance the effect against resistant strains. However, the risk of cytotoxicity and accumulation in the liver and kidneys remains a major concern in their clinical application, and thus dose optimization and toxicity evaluation are mandatory during formulation development.

Gold nanoparticles (AuNPs) are especially useful due to their biocompatibility, ease of synthesis, and surface functionalization with ligands, antibodies, or drugs. Gold nanoparticles can be produced in various shapes such as spheres, rods, or shells, and their optical properties are exploited in imaging, biosensors, and photothermal cancer therapy. In drug delivery, gold nanoparticles serve as carriers for anticancer drugs like doxorubicin or paclitaxel, and can also be conjugated with targeting moieties like folic acid or monoclonal antibodies to achieve tumor-specific accumulation. Their size can be controlled from 1 to 100 nanometers, and surface plasmon resonance properties make them suitable for hyperthermia treatments where localized heating destroys cancer cells. Moreover, gold nanoparticles are used in gene delivery and in diagnostic kits for detecting biomarkers due to their signal-enhancing capabilities in lateral flow assays.

Silica nanoparticles, particularly mesoporous silica nanoparticles (MSNs), represent an important class of inorganic carriers. They have a porous structure with high surface area, tunable pore size, and excellent thermal stability, making them suitable for loading a variety of drugs including poorly water-soluble compounds. Drugs can be encapsulated within the pores or adsorbed on the surface, and the release can be modified by coating the particles with polymers or targeting ligands. The mesoporous nature allows controlled release and protection of sensitive drugs from environmental degradation. In cancer therapy, MSNs can be functionalized with targeting ligands such as peptides or aptamers to increase site-specific delivery and reduce systemic toxicity. Additionally, silica nanoparticles are used in imaging applications when loaded with contrast agents for MRI or fluorescent dyes for optical imaging.

In addition to silver, gold, and silica, other inorganic nanoparticles like iron oxide nanoparticles (Fe3O4) are used for magnetic drug targeting and imaging. These nanoparticles can be guided to specific locations in the body using external magnetic fields and are also employed as contrast agents in magnetic resonance imaging. Calcium phosphate nanoparticles are biodegradable and can be used for bone-targeted delivery due to their natural affinity for hydroxyapatite in bone tissue. Titanium dioxide nanoparticles are being explored for their photocatalytic properties in photodynamic therapy and dental applications.

Despite their advantages, the use of metallic and inorganic nanoparticles in pharmaceuticals must be carefully evaluated for biocompatibility, biodistribution, clearance pathways, and long-term toxicity. Computational modelling and in-silico prediction tools are often integrated during their development to simulate interactions with biological systems. The pharmacokinetics and pharmacodynamics of drugs loaded in these carriers can be significantly influenced by the size, surface charge, and route of administration. Regulatory considerations for these systems are stringent due to potential risks of accumulation and unknown interactions with proteins or DNA. Therefore, proper surface modification, coating with polyethylene glycol (PEG), or conjugation with biocompatible polymers is often required to reduce immunogenicity and improve circulation time.

Vesicular Systems

Vesicular systems are microscopic or nanoscopic carriers made of one or more concentric bilayer membranes surrounding an aqueous core. These systems are highly effective in delivering drugs in a controlled and targeted manner, especially for drugs that are poorly water-soluble or require protection from degradation. The bilayer structure of vesicles mimics biological membranes, making them biocompatible and useful in enhancing drug absorption, stability, and bioavailability. Vesicular carriers are suitable for both systemic and topical drug delivery, and computer-aided formulation design helps in optimizing their composition, size, entrapment efficiency, and release characteristics. The three most commonly used vesicular systems in pharmaceutical formulation include liposomes, niosomes, and advanced flexible vesicles such as ethosomes and transferosomes.

Liposomes

Liposomes are spherical vesicles composed of one or more phospholipid bilayers enclosing an aqueous core. These bilayers are typically made of natural or synthetic phospholipids such as phosphatidylcholine, phosphatidylethanolamine, or phosphatidylserine, which assemble spontaneously in aqueous environments due to their amphiphilic nature. Liposomes can encapsulate both hydrophilic and lipophilic drugs. Hydrophilic drugs are trapped inside the aqueous core, while lipophilic drugs partition into the lipid bilayer. This dual encapsulation ability makes liposomes versatile carriers for a wide range of therapeutic agents including anticancer drugs, antifungals, antibiotics, and vaccines.

The preparation of liposomes involves methods such as thin film hydration, reverse-phase evaporation, ethanol injection, and extrusion techniques. Parameters such as lipid composition, cholesterol content, hydration temperature, and sonication time influence the size, lamellarity, and drug entrapment efficiency. Cholesterol is often added to the lipid bilayer to improve membrane rigidity and reduce leakage. Computer modeling helps in predicting the optimal lipid-to-drug ratio, encapsulation efficiency, and release kinetics. Liposomal formulations have shown significant clinical success. For example, liposomal doxorubicin (marketed as Doxil) is used in cancer therapy with reduced cardiotoxicity compared to free drug. However, liposomes have some limitations such as high production cost, limited physical stability, and susceptibility to oxidation and hydrolysis.

Niosomes

Niosomes are structurally similar to liposomes but are composed of non-ionic surfactants instead of phospholipids. These surfactants form bilayer vesicles capable of encapsulating drugs within their aqueous core or hydrophobic region. Common surfactants used in niosome formulation include Span 60, Tween 80, and Brij. Niosomes also include stabilizing agents like cholesterol to maintain bilayer integrity and prevent aggregation or leakage. Compared to liposomes, niosomes are more stable against oxidation, have a longer shelf-life, and are relatively cheaper to manufacture due to the use of synthetic surfactants.

Niosomes offer multiple advantages in drug delivery, especially for topical, transdermal, and oral routes. Their vesicular nature allows sustained drug release, site-specific targeting, and improved bioavailability. They are especially useful for poorly water-soluble drugs or for agents that require a controlled release profile. The method of preparation involves thin film hydration, ether injection, or microfluidization. Variables such as surfactant-to-cholesterol ratio, hydration time, and temperature must be optimized using design of experiments (DoE) approaches to achieve desirable vesicle size, zeta potential, and entrapment efficiency. Applications of niosomes include the delivery of anticancer drugs, vaccines, insulin, and skin care actives. Their lower cost and chemical stability make them suitable for large-scale pharmaceutical and cosmetic formulations.

Ethosomes and Transferosomes

Ethosomes and transferosomes are novel vesicular carriers designed primarily to enhance transdermal drug delivery. These systems are characterized by their flexible structure and enhanced skin permeation ability. Ethosomes consist of phospholipids and a high concentration of ethanol, which imparts softness and deformability to the vesicle membrane. The ethanol disrupts the stratum corneum lipid organization, allowing deeper penetration into the skin layers. Ethosomes are particularly effective in delivering both hydrophilic and lipophilic drugs through the skin barrier, including corticosteroids, antiviral agents, and antifungals.

Transferosomes are ultra-deformable vesicles that contain phospholipids, an edge activator such as sodium cholate or Span 80, and water. The edge activator destabilizes the lipid bilayer, making the vesicles highly flexible and able to squeeze through the narrow intercellular spaces of the stratum corneum. Transferosomes are driven by the osmotic gradient created by skin hydration and are capable of penetrating intact skin without causing damage. Their applications include transdermal delivery of analgesics, anti-inflammatory drugs, and hormones like insulin or testosterone. The preparation of ethosomes and transferosomes requires precise control over surfactant concentration, lipid ratio, and processing conditions, which can be optimized using computer-aided formulation tools.

In conclusion, vesicular systems such as liposomes, niosomes, ethosomes, and transferosomes offer significant advancements in modern drug delivery. Their ability to encapsulate a wide range of therapeutic agents, provide sustained or targeted release, and overcome biological barriers makes them indispensable in pharmaceutical formulation development. With the aid of computer modeling, their design parameters can be systematically optimized, ensuring reproducibility, scalability, and improved therapeutic efficacy.

Computer-Aided Formulation and Optimization

The development of nanoparticles and vesicular systems often involves a complex interplay between formulation variables and desired responses. This complexity requires a systematic and data-driven approach to formulation design, which is made possible through computer-aided techniques such as Design of Experiments (DoE). DoE is a statistical and mathematical tool that allows formulators to evaluate the effect of multiple formulation and process parameters simultaneously, identify critical factors, and optimize the overall formulation for desired outcomes. In the context of nanoparticle formulation, DoE is particularly valuable in reducing the number of experimental trials, saving time and cost, while increasing the robustness and reproducibility of the formulation. Software platforms such as Design-Expert, JMP, and Minitab are commonly used to perform factorial designs, response surface methodology (RSM), Box-Behnken designs, and central composite designs, enabling prediction and validation of optimal conditions.

4.3.3.4.1 DoE in Nanoparticle Formulation

In nanoparticle formulation, various independent variables—also known as factors—are carefully chosen based on preliminary studies or existing scientific literature. These variables can be classified as formulation variables, such as the polymer-to-drug ratio or lipid concentration, and process variables, such as stirring speed, homogenization pressure, solvent type, and emulsification time. For example, in polymeric nanoparticle systems made using PLGA or chitosan, the polymer-to-drug ratio influences drug encapsulation efficiency and release kinetics, while stirring speed during emulsification controls the droplet size, which ultimately affects particle size and polydispersity index (PDI). Similarly, in lipid-based nanoparticles such as SLNs or NLCs, the type and amount of lipid and surfactant, as well as the cooling rate, impact the stability and morphology of the particles.

The responses or dependent variables are the measurable outcomes that reflect the performance and quality of the final formulation. In nanoparticle formulation, the most commonly studied responses include particle size, polydispersity index (PDI), zeta potential, drug loading capacity, and entrapment efficiency. Particle size, typically measured using dynamic light scattering, is a critical parameter affecting drug release rate, cellular uptake, and bioavailability. A smaller particle size generally enhances absorption and tissue penetration, whereas a narrow PDI (typically <0.3) indicates a uniform size distribution, essential for consistency and stability. Entrapment efficiency, defined as the percentage of drug successfully encapsulated within the nanoparticle, depends on both formulation and process variables and is crucial for achieving sustained or targeted drug delivery.

A common application of DoE in nanoparticle development is using a 3-factor, 3-level Box-Behnken design to study the effect of three variables such as polymer concentration, surfactant concentration, and stirring speed on three responses like particle size, PDI, and entrapment efficiency. The software generates a series of experimental runs with different combinations of the chosen variables. The results are then fitted into a quadratic model, which helps to identify significant main effects, interactions, and quadratic effects. From these models, three-dimensional response surface plots can be generated to visualize how changes in variables affect the responses. Finally, a desirability function is used to simultaneously optimize all responses by identifying the formulation conditions that give the most favorable outcomes for all parameters.

For instance, in the case of curcumin-loaded PLGA nanoparticles, a DoE approach may reveal that a higher PLGA-to-drug ratio increases entrapment efficiency but also increases particle size. The optimal point may be a compromise that achieves both high entrapment and acceptable particle size. Similarly, in SLNs prepared using glyceryl monostearate and Tween 80, DoE may show that increasing lipid concentration decreases particle size up to a certain point but may later cause aggregation, affecting PDI adversely. By using statistical desirability functions, an optimized set of variables can be selected that provides the best balance between particle size, PDI, and drug entrapment.

Software Tools and Models

In the modern approach to nanoparticle and vesicular system development, computer-based software tools and mathematical modeling have become indispensable in optimizing formulation design and predicting in vivo performance. These tools allow researchers to simulate drug behavior, understand formulation effects, and reduce the need for exhaustive experimental trials. The use of advanced computational platforms significantly improves the efficiency of the formulation process and enables rational design of delivery systems with enhanced accuracy and reproducibility.

Design-Expert and **JMP** are two widely used software programs for statistical design and analysis of experiments. Both platforms support a variety of design types such as full factorial, central composite, Box-Behnken, and mixture designs. They allow the user to input formulation and process variables, define desired outcomes, and generate predictive mathematical models based on experimental results. Once data are entered, these tools use regression analysis and analysis of variance (ANOVA) to identify significant factors, interactions, and quadratic effects. The output includes statistical models, response surface plots, and desirability functions that help in identifying optimal formulation conditions. In nanoparticle systems, these tools can be applied to correlate input variables like polymer concentration, emulsifier levels, and sonication time with critical quality attributes such as particle size, polydispersity index (PDI), entrapment efficiency, and zeta potential.

Another advanced software platform used in drug delivery modeling is **GastroPlus™**, developed by Simulations Plus. GastroPlus is a physiologically based pharmacokinetic (PBPK) simulation software that predicts the absorption, distribution, metabolism, and excretion (ADME) of drugs based on their physicochemical properties and dosage form characteristics. In nanoparticle-based drug delivery, GastroPlus can simulate how particle size, surface charge, and release kinetics influence bioavailability and systemic drug exposure. It integrates in vitro data from dissolution or release studies and uses them to estimate the in vivo pharmacokinetic profile in both animals and humans. For instance, it can predict how lipid-based nanoparticles may enhance lymphatic transport or how vesicular systems like ethosomes improve dermal and transdermal penetration of active molecules. This predictive capability is especially important for poorly soluble or highly variable drugs, where formulation plays a crucial role in therapeutic outcome.

These software tools also support **stability modeling**, which is vital for ensuring the shelf-life and robustness of nanoparticle systems. Statistical tools in Design-Expert or JMP can be used to assess the impact of storage conditions such as temperature and humidity on drug degradation, particle size growth, and physical instability like aggregation or phase separation. Accelerated stability data can be input into the models to project real-time shelf-life using regression equations. Moreover, simulation tools can help in understanding how variables like surfactant concentration or lipid crystallinity affect long-term stability of systems like solid lipid nanoparticles and nanostructured lipid carriers.

Another advantage of using software tools in formulation design is the ability to develop **in silico prototypes**, or virtual formulations, before performing any physical experiments. This significantly reduces development costs, especially in the early stages of research. Once validated, these models become valuable tools in scale-up and regulatory submissions, as they demonstrate a science-based approach to formulation development and risk minimization.

Evaluation Parameters for Nanocarriers

The evaluation of nanoparticle and vesicular systems is essential for ensuring their quality, performance, and stability before progressing to preclinical or clinical stages. Several physicochemical and functional parameters are routinely assessed to determine the suitability of these nanocarriers for drug delivery applications. These parameters help in characterizing the carrier system, predicting its biological behavior, and optimizing formulation variables to achieve the desired therapeutic outcome.

Particle size and distribution are among the most critical evaluation parameters for nanocarriers, as they directly influence drug release, stability, biodistribution, and cellular uptake. The particle size of nanoparticles typically ranges from 10 nm to 1000 nm, while vesicular systems such as liposomes and niosomes also fall within a similar range depending on preparation methods. The most common technique for measuring particle size is **Dynamic Light Scattering (DLS)**, also known as photon correlation spectroscopy. DLS estimates the hydrodynamic diameter by measuring fluctuations in the intensity of light scattered by particles suspended in a liquid. The output includes **average particle size** (Z-average) and **Polydispersity Index (PDI)**, which reflects the uniformity of the size distribution. A PDI value less than 0.2 indicates a narrow and homogenous distribution, which is desirable for reproducible drug delivery behavior.

Zeta potential is another vital parameter used to evaluate the surface charge and colloidal stability of nanoparticles. It is measured in millivolts (mV) using **electrophoretic light scattering**. Zeta potential reflects the degree of electrostatic repulsion between particles in suspension. Higher absolute values (either positive or negative) generally indicate better stability by preventing aggregation due to repulsive forces. For most pharmaceutical nanocarriers, a zeta potential above ±30 mV is considered optimal for long-term physical stability. Additionally, surface charge influences biological interactions, such as mucoadhesion, cellular uptake, and protein adsorption (opsonization), which in turn affect biodistribution and clearance.

Encapsulation efficiency (EE%) and **drug loading (DL%)** are crucial for evaluating how effectively the drug is incorporated into the carrier system. Encapsulation efficiency refers to the percentage of drug that is successfully entrapped within the nanocarrier compared to the initial amount used in the formulation process. It is calculated using the formula:

EE% = (Amount of drug encapsulated / Total drug added) × 100.

Drug loading, on the other hand, indicates the weight percentage of drug present in the total formulation (drug plus carrier material):

DL% = (Amount of drug encapsulated / Total weight of nanoparticles) × 100.

These parameters are typically determined using techniques such as **ultracentrifugation, dialysis,** or **gel filtration**, followed by drug quantification using **UV spectrophotometry, HPLC,** or **fluorimetry.** High EE% and optimal DL% are desirable for reducing the frequency of administration and minimizing side effects due to excipient overload.

In-vitro drug release profiling is essential for understanding the release kinetics and behavior of the drug from the nanoparticle system under physiological conditions. It provides insight into whether the drug is released in a controlled, sustained, or burst manner. Common methods for conducting in-vitro release studies include the **dialysis bag technique, franz diffusion cell,** and **USP dissolution apparatus.** The release data obtained is then subjected to **kinetic modeling** to determine the release mechanism. Mathematical models such as **zero-order, first-order, Higuchi, Korsmeyer–Peppas,** and **Hixson–Crowell** equations are commonly applied. The **correlation coefficient (R^2)** is used to assess the best-fitting model, helping researchers predict in-vivo performance and therapeutic consistency.

In conclusion, thorough evaluation of these parameters ensures the reproducibility, efficacy, and safety of nanoparticulate drug delivery systems. By understanding and optimizing these critical quality attributes, formulators can design nanocarriers with superior pharmacokinetic and pharmacodynamic profiles tailored for specific therapeutic applications.

Applications in Drug Delivery

Nanoparticles and vesicular drug delivery systems have shown remarkable promise in transforming the landscape of pharmaceutical formulations. Their small size, modifiable surfaces, and ability to encapsulate both hydrophilic and hydrophobic drugs make them ideal candidates for overcoming many limitations of conventional dosage forms. These nanocarriers have been applied in various specialized therapeutic areas, including **tumor targeting, central nervous system (CNS) drug delivery, ocular therapy, vaccine delivery,** and **infectious disease management.** Moreover, several **FDA-approved nanoformulations** have already demonstrated significant clinical benefits, paving the way for widespread integration into modern therapeutics.

One of the most notable applications of nanoparticle-based systems is **tumor-targeted drug delivery.** Traditional chemotherapy drugs often suffer from lack of specificity, leading to serious side effects on healthy tissues. Nanoparticles can exploit the **enhanced permeability and retention (EPR) effect,** where they accumulate preferentially in tumor tissues due to leaky vasculature and poor lymphatic drainage. For example,

liposomal formulations of doxorubicin, such as **Doxil®**, encapsulate the anticancer drug within a PEGylated liposome, allowing prolonged circulation time, reduced cardiotoxicity, and targeted delivery to tumor sites. Similarly, **Abraxane®**, an albumin-bound nanoparticle formulation of paclitaxel, enables improved solubility and greater tumor accumulation without the need for toxic solvents like Cremophor EL.

Another vital area of application is **CNS drug delivery**, which is often restricted by the blood-brain barrier (BBB). Nanocarriers can be engineered with specific ligands (e.g., transferrin, lactoferrin) or surface charges that facilitate **receptor-mediated transcytosis** or **adsorptive-mediated endocytosis**, thereby enhancing penetration across the BBB. Drugs for **neurodegenerative diseases** (like Parkinson's and Alzheimer's), **brain tumors**, and **central infections** have been successfully delivered using lipid-based nanoparticles, polymeric nanocarriers, and nanoemulsions. These systems protect the active pharmaceutical ingredients from enzymatic degradation and allow controlled release, reducing the dosing frequency and improving therapeutic outcomes.

In **ocular drug delivery**, nanoparticles and vesicular systems such as **liposomes, niosomes, and nanomicelles** play a crucial role in overcoming barriers like tear dilution, corneal impermeability, and nasolacrimal drainage. They prolong the residence time on the ocular surface and enable penetration into deeper ocular tissues. Drugs used for **glaucoma, conjunctivitis, uveitis,** and **retinal disorders** have shown enhanced efficacy when delivered using nanocarrier systems, especially when combined with mucoadhesive polymers or in-situ gelling formulations.

Anticancer drug delivery remains the most extensively studied and clinically validated domain for nanotechnology. Various nanoformulations of chemotherapeutic agents like **docetaxel, paclitaxel, doxorubicin, cisplatin,** and **camptothecin** have demonstrated improved pharmacokinetics, reduced systemic toxicity, and better patient compliance. Moreover, combination therapies incorporating drugs and siRNA or imaging agents into a single nanoparticle offer both **theranostic** capabilities and synergistic treatment effects, especially in **multidrug-resistant (MDR)** cancers.

In **antiretroviral therapy**, especially for **HIV**, nanoparticulate systems help in targeting infected macrophages and lymph nodes, which act as reservoirs for the virus. **Long-acting nanoformulations** of drugs like **ritonavir, lopinavir,** and **tenofovir** can sustain drug release for days or weeks, thereby improving adherence and reducing dosing frequency. These systems also reduce systemic exposure, thereby minimizing adverse effects like hepatotoxicity or nephrotoxicity.

The use of nanocarriers in **vaccine delivery** has gained significant attention, particularly in the development of **mRNA vaccines** and **subunit vaccines**. Lipid nanoparticles (LNPs) have been used successfully to encapsulate and deliver mRNA in COVID-19 vaccines such as **Pfizer-BioNTech's Comirnaty®** and **Moderna's Spikevax®**. These LNPs protect the mRNA from degradation, facilitate uptake by dendritic cells, and enable efficient antigen presentation, leading to robust immune responses. Similarly, **niosomes and immunoliposomes** are being explored for delivery of antigens, adjuvants, and DNA vaccines in cancer immunotherapy and infectious diseases.

The regulatory landscape is gradually adapting to these novel formulations. **FDA-approved nanomedicines**, such as **Doxil® (PEGylated liposomal doxorubicin)**, **Abraxane® (albumin-bound paclitaxel)**, **Marqibo® (liposomal vincristine)**, and **Onpattro® (siRNA lipid complex for hereditary transthyretin amyloidosis)**, have proven their safety, efficacy, and therapeutic advantage over traditional formulations. These approvals validate the practical success of nanoparticle-based drug delivery systems and have set a benchmark for future innovations.

4.4 Screening and Factorial Designs

4.4.1 Full and Fractional Factorial Design

In pharmaceutical formulation and process development, the number of variables (or factors) that influence product quality can be quite large. To manage this complexity, **screening designs** and **factorial designs** are applied using computer-aided tools to identify **significant factors** that impact **critical quality attributes (CQAs)**. Among the most widely used are **full factorial designs** and **fractional factorial designs**, which are foundational in **Design of Experiments (DoE)**. These designs offer a structured, statistically reliable way to study multiple variables simultaneously, enabling researchers to obtain deeper insights with fewer experiments compared to traditional one-variable-at-a-time methods.

A **full factorial design** is a type of experimental design where all possible combinations of factor levels are tested. For example, in a 2^n full factorial design, where 'n' is the number of factors and each factor is studied at two levels (e.g., low and high), all 2^n combinations are included. In the case of 3 factors, this results in $2^3 = 8$ experiments. Full factorial designs are powerful because they allow the estimation of **main effects** (individual impact of each factor) and **interaction effects** (how the combined variation of two or more factors influences the response). This is particularly important in formulations where, for instance, the interaction between a binder and disintegrant may drastically influence disintegration time or hardness.

However, as the number of factors increases, full factorial designs become impractical due to the exponential rise in the number of required runs. For example, a 2^5 full factorial design requires 32 experiments, which may be too resource-intensive during early screening phases.

To address this, **fractional factorial designs** are used. These designs evaluate only a **subset (fraction)** of the total possible combinations, yet still provide meaningful insights about the most influential factors. For example, a 2^{5-1} fractional factorial design uses only 16 runs instead of 32, reducing workload while still capturing **main effects and selected interactions**. The trade-off is that some higher-order interactions may be confounded (i.e., indistinguishable from others), but this is generally acceptable in early-phase screening when the goal is to identify the most critical variables for further detailed study.

Computer software like **Design-Expert, JMP, and Minitab** allows researchers to easily generate full and fractional factorial designs, analyze data, and interpret results through **ANOVA, Pareto charts, half-normal plots**, and **interaction plots**. These visual tools make it easier to pinpoint which variables significantly affect the response, thereby guiding further optimization.

In summary, **full factorial designs** are comprehensive and suitable when the number of factors is small or when interaction effects are of primary interest. In contrast, **fractional factorial designs** are highly efficient and ideal for initial screening to narrow down the variables that matter most. Both designs are integral to modern, computer-aided formulation development and support the goals of **efficiency, scientific justification, and regulatory compliance.**

4.4.2 Plackett-Burman and Taguchi Methods

In the early stages of pharmaceutical formulation and process development, it is essential to identify which factors significantly influence the product's quality attributes. When the number of potential variables is high, screening designs like the **Plackett-Burman design** and **Taguchi method** are widely used. These techniques allow for efficient assessment of multiple factors with a minimal number of experiments, reducing both cost and time. Modern computer-aided formulation tools incorporate these designs to help scientists systematically plan, execute, and analyze screening studies.

Plackett-Burman Design

The **Plackett-Burman design (PBD)** is a type of **two-level screening design** used to identify the most significant variables out of a large set, while assuming that **interactions between factors are negligible**. This design is particularly useful in formulation studies where the goal is not to optimize but to **filter out the non-influential variables**, so that attention can be focused on the critical few.

PBD matrices are available for specific run numbers such as 12, 16, 20, etc., and can evaluate up to $(N - 1)$ variables in N experimental runs. For example, a 12-run PBD can evaluate up to 11 variables. Each factor is tested at two levels, typically coded as **high (+1)** and **low (−1)**. After running the experiments and recording the responses (e.g., dissolution rate, particle size, hardness), statistical tools such as **Pareto charts, main effects plots, and ANOVA** are used to identify which variables significantly affect the response.

PBDs are commonly used to screen:

- Types and concentrations of excipients (e.g., binders, disintegrants, surfactants)
- Processing parameters (e.g., mixing time, drying temperature)
- Equipment settings (e.g., spray rate, nozzle size)

Because it ignores interaction effects, the Plackett-Burman design is best used as a **first-pass tool** before more detailed optimization using factorial or response surface designs. Its integration into computer-aided tools such as **Design-Expert** or **JMP** allows quick model construction, analysis, and visualization.

Taguchi Method

The **Taguchi method**, developed by Dr. Genichi Taguchi, is another widely used approach in pharmaceutical research for improving product quality by making it **robust against variation**. It focuses on **designing experiments using orthogonal arrays** to study the effect of multiple variables with fewer experiments than a full factorial design. While Taguchi methods are sometimes used for screening, their primary purpose is **robust design optimization** rather than just identifying significant factors.

The strength of the Taguchi method lies in its focus on **signal-to-noise (S/N) ratios**, which quantify how much a particular variable affects the variability of a response. This allows researchers not just to target a specific performance level, but also to **minimize variability** due to uncontrollable factors (known as "noise"). For example, in a tablet formulation, Taguchi design can help identify the optimal level of a disintegrant that ensures rapid disintegration even when there is minor batch-to-batch variability in raw materials.

The Taguchi method typically uses standard orthogonal arrays such as **L4, L9, L16, L25**, where "L" denotes the number of experiments. These arrays ensure that all factor levels are balanced and uncorrelated, allowing for independent assessment of each variable's effect.

Applications of the Taguchi method in formulation include:

- Optimizing granulation parameters in wet granulation
- Improving film-coating uniformity
- Minimizing tablet weight variability
- Enhancing emulsion or suspension stability

Modern DoE software platforms provide built-in templates for Taguchi designs and support S/N ratio analysis, main effect plots, and interaction plots. These capabilities make Taguchi methods accessible and effective even for researchers with limited statistical background.

In conclusion, both **Plackett-Burman** and **Taguchi** methods are powerful tools in computer-aided formulation development:

- **PBD** is ideal for quick identification of key factors among many.
- **Taguchi** is better suited for robust optimization and variation control.

When used appropriately and supported by computer-aided tools, these methods help streamline development, reduce experimentation, and contribute to the creation of high-quality, reliable pharmaceutical products.

4.5 Legal Protection of Computer Innovations

4.5.1 Patents in Software-Based Formulation

As the pharmaceutical industry increasingly adopts **computer-aided tools** for drug design and formulation development, the need to legally protect innovations involving **software algorithms, digital platforms, and simulation-based methods** has become critical. One of the primary legal mechanisms for securing such innovations is through **patents**. However, obtaining patents for **software-based inventions**—especially those applied to pharmaceutical formulation—requires careful navigation of both **technological and legal standards**, as not all software is automatically patentable.

In general, for any invention to be patentable, it must meet the basic criteria of being **novel**, **non-obvious**, and **industrially applicable**. In the case of **software-based pharmaceutical formulation systems**, patentability often hinges on whether the invention involves a **technical advancement or practical application**, rather than being a mere mathematical method or abstract idea. For example, a claim for a general algorithm that calculates the HLB value of surfactants may not be patentable on its own. However, a **computer-implemented system that integrates formulation parameters, predicts emulsion stability, and optimizes surfactant ratios based on real-time data** might be considered patentable because it solves a concrete technical problem in a specific industrial context.

In jurisdictions like the **United States, European Union, India**, and **Japan**, the approach to software patents varies:

* In the **U.S.**, software-related inventions are generally patentable if they are tied to a **specific technological process or produce a concrete result**, as per the **Alice v. CLS Bank** decision.
* The **European Patent Office (EPO)** allows software patents if the invention has a **technical character or solves a technical problem**.
* **India** is more restrictive, generally disallowing software patents unless they are part of a **hardware-based invention or result in tangible technical effects**.

In the pharmaceutical context, patents have been successfully granted for:

- **Simulation models that predict drug absorption, distribution, and metabolism**
- **Computer systems that optimize formulation using artificial intelligence or machine learning**
- **Digital platforms that integrate experimental data with mathematical modeling to design drug delivery systems**
- **Software that automates the construction of design spaces under QbD**

A good example might be a patented **AI-based formulation engine** that recommends the best excipient combination for a poorly soluble drug by learning from a large database of previous formulations. Such systems, when described with sufficient detail in terms of their architecture, algorithms, and specific application, are more likely to be eligible for patent protection.

To draft a strong patent application for a **software-based formulation system**, it is essential to:

- Clearly define the **problem being solved** in the pharmaceutical domain.
- Describe the **technical architecture**, algorithms used, and **step-by-step functionality**.
- Demonstrate **novelty** over existing formulation tools or statistical software.
- Show how the invention contributes to improved **efficiency, accuracy, or quality control** in formulation development.

Patent protection for these types of innovations can provide **commercial exclusivity**, **strategic advantage**, and **attract investment**, especially for companies specializing in **digital pharmaceutical technologies**. In addition, it offers legal tools to prevent unauthorized use, duplication, or commercialization by competitors.

In conclusion, as software becomes deeply embedded in pharmaceutical formulation processes, the legal framework for **protecting such digital innovations through patents** is becoming increasingly relevant. Pharmaceutical scientists, IP professionals, and regulatory strategists must collaborate to ensure that valuable software inventions are properly documented, legally protected, and strategically utilized in global drug development.

4.5.2 Copyrights and Proprietary Algorithms

In the context of computer-aided formulation and pharmaceutical software development, **copyright protection** and the use of **proprietary algorithms** play a crucial role in securing intellectual property rights, especially when the invention does not meet the strict criteria for patentability. While patents protect inventions that are novel and have industrial application, copyrights are used to protect the **expression of ideas**, such as **source code, graphical user interfaces (GUIs), databases, documentation,** and **user manuals** associated with formulation software or digital drug design tools. In India, the **Copyright Act, 1957**, as amended, provides automatic protection to original literary works, which includes computer programs. This protection arises the moment the software or source code is written and fixed in a tangible form like a digital file, even without registration.

In pharmaceutical formulation, companies and research institutions often develop their own **in-house software platforms** for tasks like excipient screening, optimization using artificial neural networks, or drug release modeling. These platforms may contain **original source code**, designed algorithms, and unique graphical structures that are protectable under copyright law. For example, a formulation simulation software that graphically displays the influence of polymer ratio and pH on drug release kinetics may include original programming that is subject to copyright. What is protected here is not the underlying scientific theory, but the specific **way in which the software expresses and executes that theory** through code, design, and interface.

Alongside copyright protection, **proprietary algorithms** are used to maintain the confidentiality and commercial value of the computational logic that powers these formulation tools. These algorithms often involve complex calculations, machine learning processes, or artificial intelligence-based models that take in experimental data and provide output in the form of optimal formulations or predicted dissolution profiles. For instance, a company may develop a proprietary algorithm that predicts in vitro–in vivo correlation (IVIVC) using nonlinear regression and population-based modeling. Such algorithms may not be easily patentable if they are mathematical in nature, but they can be protected by **keeping the algorithm confidential** and licensing the software as a **closed-source product**.

Proprietary algorithms are typically safeguarded through **contractual means** such as non-disclosure agreements (NDAs), user license agreements, and restrictive terms of use. These legal tools prevent end users from copying, modifying, reverse-engineering, or distributing the software. In addition, encryption and software obfuscation techniques are applied to make the underlying code difficult to decipher. In India and globally, the use of **Digital Rights Management (DRM)** systems further enhances the control that creators maintain over how their software is accessed and used.

From an industry perspective, companies prefer to keep powerful formulation algorithms as **trade secrets** rather than seeking patents or publishing them, because this offers **indefinite protection** as long as secrecy is maintained. Unlike patents, which expire after 20 years, trade secrets can offer longer competitive advantage if properly handled. However, this approach demands robust internal policies on access control, developer contracts, and data security.

In the academic setting, software tools developed for formulation research may be copyrighted and shared under **open-source licenses** or restricted for internal institutional use only. When research institutions collaborate with industry partners, careful agreements are drafted to define the **ownership, licensing, and revenue-sharing** terms for jointly developed algorithms or software.

Therefore, in modern pharmaceutical formulation practice, especially when computers and digital tools are involved, **copyright law and proprietary protection strategies** are critical to safeguard the significant intellectual and commercial value generated by software innovations. They provide a strong legal foundation for companies and researchers to develop, distribute, and profit from their computational tools, while ensuring that their original work remains protected from unauthorized use or duplication.

4.6.1 Ethical issues in data privacy and algorithms

As the pharmaceutical industry increasingly relies on computer-based systems for research and development, several ethical concerns have emerged—particularly surrounding data privacy and the use of algorithms. These concerns are especially significant in areas where human data is involved, such as patient records, clinical trial data, pharmacogenomics, and electronic health records. The use of algorithms, including machine learning and artificial intelligence, to process this data must be guided by ethical principles to ensure transparency, fairness, accountability, and respect for individual privacy.

In computer-aided drug formulation and clinical trial simulation, large datasets are often collected, shared, and processed to predict outcomes or guide decision-making. This data may include sensitive health information, patient demographics, biomarker profiles, and treatment responses. If such information is not handled properly, it may lead to breaches of confidentiality or misuse of personal data. In India, while the Information Technology Act, 2000 provides a basic legal framework for data protection, there is growing demand for stronger, dedicated legislation similar to the General Data Protection Regulation (GDPR) implemented in the European Union.

The core ethical issue lies in ensuring that data is collected and processed with informed consent, used only for the stated purpose, and stored in secure systems that prevent unauthorized access. In many cases, algorithms used to model clinical or formulation outcomes are trained on historical data that may carry hidden biases—whether related to age, gender, ethnicity, or disease stage. If not corrected, these biases can lead to skewed predictions or discriminatory outcomes. For example, an algorithm trained predominantly on adult data may not perform reliably for pediatric formulations, leading to flawed decisions in pediatric drug design.

Another serious ethical concern is the opacity of certain algorithms, particularly those based on artificial intelligence and deep learning. These models often function as "black boxes," making decisions that are difficult to explain or interpret. In a regulated field like pharmaceuticals, where product quality and patient safety are non-negotiable, this lack of transparency can become problematic. Regulatory bodies expect clear justifications for formulation decisions, dosage recommendations, and clinical trial designs. If such decisions are guided by opaque algorithms, it becomes difficult to hold developers accountable in case of failure or adverse events.

There is also the risk of algorithmic manipulation, where data may be selectively included or excluded to influence predictions in a desired direction. This becomes ethically unacceptable, especially in drug development, where commercial pressures may lead to intentional or unintentional biasing of data inputs. Moreover, if proprietary algorithms are deployed without external validation, they may produce results that favor one outcome while ignoring others, affecting scientific objectivity.

To mitigate these issues, institutions and companies must adopt strong governance policies for data ethics. These include regular audits of algorithms, inclusion of diverse and representative datasets, use of explainable AI techniques, and strict data anonymization protocols. Ethical review boards and data safety monitoring committees must also be involved not only in clinical research but also in early formulation simulations when patient data is used.

In summary, the ethical use of data and algorithms in pharmaceutical computing is not just a regulatory requirement—it is a moral obligation. It ensures that the benefits of technology do not come at the cost of individual rights or scientific integrity. As computing becomes more deeply embedded in pharmaceutical R&D, ethical vigilance must grow alongside technological progress.

4.6.2 GxP compliance and audit trails

In the pharmaceutical industry, the use of computerized systems in formulation development, clinical trials, and quality control must comply with a set of regulatory standards known collectively as **GxP**. The term GxP refers to "Good x Practices", where "x" may stand for laboratory (GLP), clinical (GCP), or manufacturing (GMP) practices. These standards are enforced by regulatory agencies such as the USFDA, EMA, and CDSCO to ensure that pharmaceutical products are safe, effective, and consistently produced under controlled conditions. When computers are used to manage data, calculate formulation parameters, or automate decision-making, the system must be validated and maintained in compliance with GxP principles.

One of the essential elements of GxP compliance in computerized systems is the presence of **audit trails**. An audit trail is a secure, time-stamped, computer-generated log that records all critical actions, changes, or deletions made to data within the system. It provides a transparent history of who did what, when, and why—ensuring **data integrity**, **traceability**, and **accountability**. Audit trails are especially important in software used for tasks such as dose optimization, excipient selection, or in vitro–in vivo correlation modeling, where even small alterations in input values can significantly affect the final outcome.

In GxP-compliant systems, audit trails must be tamper-proof and easily retrievable for review during inspections or internal quality checks. For example, if a formulation scientist adjusts the polymer concentration in a microemulsion model, the system should record the username, timestamp, and nature of the change. Similarly, if a clinical trial database is modified to correct a data entry error, the original value, corrected value, and justification for change must be captured and stored. Regulatory guidelines such as **21 CFR Part 11 (U.S.)** and **Annex 11 (EU)** explicitly require such features in systems handling electronic records and signatures.

Computerized systems must also support **access controls**, user-level permissions, and **data backup mechanisms** to ensure only authorized individuals can perform sensitive tasks. Furthermore, periodic system validations and user training are essential to maintain GxP readiness. Validation involves confirming that the software performs its intended functions accurately and consistently under real-world conditions. Documentation of validation protocols, test scripts, and results becomes part of the compliance package.

Lack of proper audit trails or non-compliance with GxP requirements can lead to regulatory action, including warning letters, product recalls, or even license suspension. Therefore, pharmaceutical companies must establish robust **Standard Operating Procedures (SOPs)** for system usage, maintenance, and audit trail review. Internal audits should periodically verify that audit trails are active, complete, and reviewed routinely by qualified personnel.

In essence, GxP compliance and audit trails form the ethical and regulatory backbone of computer-aided pharmaceutical operations. They ensure not only product quality but also trust in digital data and accountability in scientific decisions. As digital transformation accelerates in the pharmaceutical sector, integrating these controls into all levels of software design and usage is no longer optional—it is a regulatory and ethical necessity.:

4.7 Computers in Market Analysis

4.7.1 Demand forecasting tools

In the pharmaceutical industry, accurate demand forecasting is essential to ensure timely production, supply chain efficiency, inventory control, and ultimately, patient access to medicines. Demand forecasting helps predict the **future market need for a particular drug** based on various data inputs such as past sales trends, seasonal variations, disease prevalence, demographic factors, and prescription behavior. With the help of computers and advanced analytics software, demand forecasting has evolved from basic spreadsheet calculations to complex predictive models driven by real-time data and machine learning algorithms.

Modern demand forecasting tools used in the pharmaceutical sector include platforms like **SAP Integrated Business Planning (IBP), Oracle Demantra, SAS Forecast Server, and Forecast Pro.** These tools enable companies to handle vast amounts of historical and market data, analyze consumption patterns, and generate forecasts at national, regional, or even hospital levels. Computers allow for the integration of **structured data** (e.g., prescription records, inventory reports) with **unstructured data** (e.g., market news, social media trends, health alerts) to provide a holistic view of market behavior.

In practice, demand forecasting tools are used to support **new product launches, sales and operations planning (S&OP), tender bidding**, and **budget allocation**. For example, in the case of a seasonal influenza vaccine, forecasting tools analyze data from past flu seasons, current infection rates, and public health advisories to estimate the demand for the upcoming season. In another example, when a generic drug is launched post-patent expiry, forecasting models estimate expected market share based on competitor behavior, pricing, and prescribing habits.

These tools also offer features like **what-if scenario analysis**, where users can simulate how external events (such as policy changes or competitor entry) may impact demand. Additionally, **collaborative forecasting modules** allow input from sales, marketing, and supply chain teams, promoting cross-functional planning. Computers not only speed up the process but also improve the accuracy, flexibility, and transparency of forecasting activities, which are vital in a regulated and highly competitive environment like pharma.

4.7.2 Predictive analytics in pharma marketing

Predictive analytics is a powerful computer-based technique that uses **statistical modeling, machine learning, and data mining** to predict future outcomes based on historical and current data. In pharmaceutical marketing, predictive analytics has become an indispensable tool for designing **targeted marketing campaigns, forecasting product uptake**, and **identifying high-potential healthcare professionals (HCPs), regions, or patient segments.** These models help marketers shift from reactive to proactive decision-making, thereby improving return on investment (ROI) and customer engagement.

Pharmaceutical companies deploy predictive analytics platforms such as **IBM SPSS Modeler, SAS Advanced Analytics, Microsoft Azure ML, and R-based custom solutions** to process large datasets gathered from multiple sources including **electronic medical records (EMRs), prescription databases, social media, call center logs, and CRM systems.** By analyzing patterns within this data, companies can identify which physicians are most likely to prescribe a new drug, which regions may have unmet clinical needs, or which promotional channels are most effective for a particular product.

For instance, in the launch of a new oncology drug, predictive analytics may reveal that oncologists in metro cities are early adopters while uptake in tier-2 cities lags due to awareness gaps. This insight allows marketing teams to customize their messaging and resource allocation. Similarly, models can be built to score and rank physicians based on their likelihood of switching to a competitor's product, enabling **targeted retention strategies.**

Predictive analytics also supports **patient adherence programs**, where algorithms can predict which patients are likely to stop medication based on refill history, socioeconomic data, and previous behavior. Interventions can then be planned through SMS reminders, telephonic follow-ups, or patient counseling.

Moreover, predictive tools help in **pricing strategy, competitor tracking, sentiment analysis**, and **market access planning**, making them versatile assets across commercial functions. With the integration of **AI and natural language processing (NLP)**, newer systems can analyze public health data, news feeds, and even doctor-patient conversations (where permitted) to detect emerging trends or risks that could affect market performance.

Review questions

1. What is computer-aided formulation development?
It refers to the use of computer software and statistical tools to design, optimize, and analyze pharmaceutical formulations more systematically and efficiently.

2. Why is computer-aided formulation important in pharmacy?
It minimizes trial-and-error experiments, saves time and cost, improves quality, and accelerates product development.

3. Name two commonly used software tools in formulation development.
Design-Expert® and Minitab®.

4. What is optimization in the context of formulation?
Optimization refers to adjusting formulation and process variables to achieve the best possible product quality attributes.

5. Define Design of Experiments (DoE).
DoE is a structured method to study the effect of multiple input variables on output responses in a systematic way.

6. Give an example of an independent variable in formulation.
Polymer concentration in a sustained-release tablet.

7. Give an example of a dependent variable in formulation studies.
Drug release percentage after 6 hours.

8. What is the advantage of using DoE over traditional methods?
DoE studies multiple factors simultaneously and identifies interactions, leading to better understanding and faster optimization.

9. What is a factorial design?
A factorial design is a type of DoE where all possible combinations of factor levels are studied.

10. What is the difference between full and fractional factorial designs?
Full factorial studies all combinations; fractional factorial studies only a fraction to reduce the number of experiments.

11. Define response surface methodology (RSM).
RSM is a statistical technique used to optimize processes by modeling the relationships between input factors and responses.

12. What is a contour plot used for?
To visualize how two variables simultaneously affect a response in RSM.

13. What is a desirability function in optimization?
It transforms multiple responses into a single score to find the most

desirable formulation.

14. Give an example of a formulation parameter optimized using computers.

Emulsifier concentration in an oil-in-water emulsion.

15. What is a pseudo-ternary phase diagram?

It is a graphical tool used to identify microemulsion regions by plotting ratios of oil, surfactant/co-surfactant, and water.

16. What type of formulations use pseudo-ternary phase diagrams?

Microemulsions.

17. Define droplet size in emulsions.

It is the average diameter of dispersed droplets, measured in nanometers or micrometers.

18. Why is droplet size important in emulsions?

Smaller droplet sizes enhance stability, drug release, and absorption.

19. What is polydispersity index (PDI)?

PDI measures the uniformity of droplet size distribution; values closer to 0 indicate uniform droplets.

20. What is a typical PDI value for a stable nanoemulsion?

Below 0.3.

21. What does zeta potential measure?

It measures the electrical charge on particle surfaces, indicating emulsion stability.

22. What zeta potential value indicates a stable emulsion?

Greater than +30 mV or less than −30 mV.

23. What is homogenization speed's role in emulsion development?

Higher speeds reduce droplet size, improving emulsion stability.

24. Name two types of vesicular systems used in drug delivery.

Liposomes and niosomes.

25. What is a liposome?

A vesicle made of phospholipid bilayers encapsulating hydrophilic and lipophilic drugs.

26. What is a niosome?

A vesicle formed using non-ionic surfactants, offering better stability and cost-effectiveness compared to liposomes.

27. What are solid lipid nanoparticles (SLNs)?

They are submicron colloidal carriers made from solid lipids, used for controlled drug delivery.

28. What is a nanostructured lipid carrier (NLC)?

An improved version of SLNs that combines solid and liquid lipids for better drug loading and stability.

29. What are the main advantages of nanoparticles in drug delivery?

Enhanced bioavailability, targeted delivery, and sustained release.

30. What is entrapment efficiency?

It is the percentage of drug successfully incorporated into the carrier system.

31. How is drug loading different from entrapment efficiency?

Drug loading refers to the amount of drug relative to the total carrier weight.

32. Name a metallic nanoparticle used in medicine.

Silver nanoparticles.

33. What is the use of gold nanoparticles in pharmaceuticals?

They are used for targeted drug delivery and cancer therapy.

34. What are ethosomes?

Soft vesicles enriched with ethanol for enhanced skin penetration.

35. What are transferosomes?

Ultra-deformable vesicles designed for transdermal drug delivery.

36. What is one advantage of ethosomes over liposomes?

Ethosomes penetrate deeper into the skin due to ethanol fluidization.

37. Name one evaluation method for particle size analysis.

Dynamic Light Scattering (DLS).

38. Why is in-vitro release study important?

It predicts how a drug will release over time from its formulation.

39. What type of kinetic models are used in release studies?

Zero-order, first-order, Higuchi, and Korsmeyer-Peppas models.

40. What is a control strategy in QbD formulation development?

A planned set of controls derived from process understanding to ensure consistent quality.

41. What does ICH Q8 emphasize regarding formulation?

Systematic product and process design based on scientific understanding and risk management.

42. Give one example of an FDA-approved nanoformulation.

Doxil® (liposomal doxorubicin).

43. What is the primary goal of computer simulations in drug delivery design?

To predict formulation behavior and optimize parameters before conducting actual experiments.

44. What is GastroPlus™ used for?

For simulating drug absorption, dissolution, and pharmacokinetics.

45. Why are phase diagrams important in formulation?

They help identify stable compositions in multi-component systems.

46. What is meant by the term "design space" in QbD?

It is the multidimensional combination of input variables that assures product quality.

47. Name a real-world application of microemulsions in pharma.

Topical delivery of antifungal drugs like ketoconazole.

48. What is a key challenge in nanoformulation development?

Physical and chemical instability, such as aggregation or degradation.

49. What is the impact of surfactant selection on emulsion properties?

It affects droplet size, stability, drug release, and skin irritation potential.

50. Why is computer-aided formulation development considered essential today?

Because it accelerates innovation, improves success rates, reduces development costs, and ensures regulatory compliance.

MCQS

What does optimization in formulation mainly aim for?
A) Minimizing taste
B) Enhancing product performance
C) Increasing manufacturing time
D) Reducing shelf-life
Design of Experiments (DoE) helps to:
A) Randomize clinical trials
B) Systematically study variable effects
C) Replace clinical testing
D) Estimate market price
In computer-aided formulation, independent variables are also called:
A) Responses
B) Output factors
C) Input factors
D) Endpoints
Which is a dependent variable in formulation optimization?
A) Stirring speed
B) Drug entrapment efficiency
C) Polymer grade
D) Solvent selection
A pseudo-ternary phase diagram is used in the design of:
A) Capsules
B) Microemulsions
C) Tablets
D) Powders
Which software is widely used for DoE in pharmaceutical development?
A) Photoshop
B) Design-Expert®
C) Excel
D) Microsoft Word
What does PDI (Polydispersity Index) measure in a formulation?
A) Density
B) Uniformity of particle size
C) Color
D) pH stability

A high zeta potential generally indicates:

A) Instability

B) Good stability

C) Large droplet size

D) Low drug loading

What happens if a surfactant concentration is too high in an emulsion?

A) Smaller droplets always form

B) Risk of irritation increases

C) Drug absorption stops

D) Viscosity drops sharply

Solid lipid nanoparticles (SLNs) are stabilized mainly by:

A) Lipophilic drugs

B) High temperature

C) Surfactants

D) Sugars

Microemulsions differ from emulsions because they are:

A) Always unstable

B) Thermodynamically stable

C) Only water-based

D) Crystalline solids

Vesicular carriers like liposomes are made of:

A) Proteins

B) Sugars

C) Phospholipids

D) Metals

In microemulsion formulation, a co-surfactant helps to:

A) Increase viscosity

B) Expand the microemulsion region

C) Create larger droplets

D) Freeze the formulation

What is the typical droplet size range in a nanoemulsion?

A) 1–10 mm

B) 10–100 nm

C) 1–5 µm

D) 10–20 µm

Which factor strongly influences emulsion creaming?

A) Molecular weight

B) Viscosity difference

C) Surfactant pH

D) Stirrer color

Higher homogenization speed during emulsification usually:

A) Increases droplet size

B) Decreases droplet size

C) Changes viscosity only

D) Prevents drug solubilization

Zeta potential is usually expressed in:

A) Volts

B) Millivolts

C) Hertz

D) Newtons

In computer-aided design, dependent variables are also referred to as:

A) Responses

B) Inputs

C) Constants

D) Backgrounds

The "desirability function" in optimization combines:

A) Two input variables

B) Multiple responses into a single score

C) Drug solubility only

D) Water and oil phases

What is the advantage of nanoparticles in drug delivery?

A) Reduced manufacturing cost

B) Controlled and targeted release

C) Easier taste masking

D) Lower regulatory approval need

Emulsion stability on storage can be tested by:

A) Short freezing only

B) Centrifugation tests

C) Adding more oil

D) Decreasing surfactant dose

Liposomes can encapsulate:

A) Only hydrophilic drugs

B) Only lipophilic drugs

C) Both hydrophilic and lipophilic drugs

D) Only peptides

Which tool helps in predicting GI absorption using simulations?

A) GastroPlus™

B) AutoCAD

C) ChemDraw

D) Illustrator

A drug formulation with a PDI value of 0.6 indicates:

A) Very uniform size

B) Very broad size distribution

C) Good zeta potential

D) Low drug release

Transferosomes are used mainly for:

A) Oral delivery

B) Parenteral delivery

C) Enhanced transdermal delivery

D) Eye drop formulations

Dynamic Light Scattering (DLS) is used to measure:

A) Drug content

B) Particle size

C) Zeta potential

D) Droplet viscosity

Solid lipid nanoparticles are typically stabilized by:

A) Strong acids

B) Water-immiscible oils

C) Surfactants

D) Sugars

The type of surfactant needed for O/W emulsions generally has:

A) High HLB value

B) Low HLB value

C) No HLB importance

D) Variable HLB

Which parameter is important for predicting stability of vesicles?

A) Oil type

B) Particle color

C) Zeta potential

D) Solvent purity

A key feature of computer-aided formulation is:

A) Trial-and-error guessing

B) Systematic experimental design

C) Reduced data recording

D) Elimination of all experiments

Answer Key:

1. B
2. B
3. C
4. B
5. B
6. B
7. B
8. B
9. B
10. C
11. B
12. C
13. B
14. B
15. B
16. B
17. B
18. A
19. B
20. B
21. B
22. C
23. A
24. B
25. C
26. B
27. C
28. A
29. C
30. B

Computer-Aided Biopharmaceutical Characterization

5.1 Gastrointestinal Absorption Simulation

5.1.1 Modeling GI Physiology

Modeling gastrointestinal (GI) physiology is a foundational aspect of computer-aided biopharmaceutical characterization, especially for predicting the absorption of orally administered drugs. The human GI tract is a complex system composed of several regions—stomach, duodenum, jejunum, ileum, and colon—each with distinct anatomical, biochemical, and physiological characteristics. Drug absorption is influenced by multiple regional factors such as pH variation, fluid volume, surface area, enzyme activity, motility, transit time, and the presence of transporters or metabolic enzymes. By simulating these elements using computational models, scientists can better predict oral bioavailability, optimize drug formulation, and anticipate food effects or variability between individuals.

Computerized platforms such as GastroPlus, Simcyp Simulator, and PK-Sim use detailed physiologically based pharmacokinetic (PBPK) models to replicate GI physiology and predict drug absorption behavior. These platforms incorporate quantitative data for each GI segment, such as average length, pH, fluid content, bile salt concentration, permeability, and enzymatic degradation potential. For example, the stomach typically has a low pH (1–3 in the fasted state), which may degrade acid-labile drugs or delay dissolution of enteric-coated formulations. In contrast, the small intestine has a higher pH (5–7.5), rich enzymatic activity, and a large surface area due to villi and microvilli, making it the primary site for absorption.

The models also simulate gastrointestinal transit times, which influence how long a drug remains in each segment. Fasted-state gastric emptying is typically around 15–30 minutes, whereas fed-state emptying can extend to over 2 hours, significantly affecting the onset of drug absorption. Motility patterns and fluid dynamics, such as those driven by peristalsis or segmentation, are also integrated into the model to replicate real physiological movement. Moreover, the influence of bile salts, which enhance solubilization of lipophilic drugs, is considered in the small intestine segments.

Advanced models take into account the presence of active transporters (like PEPT1, OATP, and P-glycoprotein) and metabolizing enzymes (like CYP3A4) located along the intestinal wall. These affect both the extent and rate of drug absorption. For example, first-pass metabolism in enterocytes may significantly reduce the systemic availability of certain drugs like midazolam or cyclosporine. By integrating these features, models provide more realistic predictions than traditional empirical approaches.

Computational simulations of GI physiology are also customized for different age groups, disease conditions, and ethnic populations. Pediatric and geriatric models adjust for age-related differences in gastric pH, transit time, enzyme expression, and mucosal permeability. Disease-specific models account for altered GI conditions in states such as Crohn's disease, diarrhea, or gastric bypass surgery.

Overall, modeling GI physiology with computational tools provides a virtual laboratory where numerous absorption scenarios can be tested without performing time-consuming or expensive in vivo studies. This not only reduces development costs but also enhances formulation design, supports regulatory decisions, and enables rational selection of dosage forms and release profiles. As regulatory bodies increasingly recognize the predictive value of these models, GI physiology simulation is becoming a standard practice in early drug development and biopharmaceutical assessment.

5.1.2 Software Platforms for Absorption (GastroPlus, Simcyp)

In modern pharmaceutical research, computer-aided tools have become indispensable for simulating gastrointestinal absorption, especially during preclinical and early clinical stages of drug development. Two of the most widely adopted platforms in this area are GastroPlus and Simcyp Simulator. These software tools use physiologically based pharmacokinetic (PBPK) modeling frameworks to predict the absorption, distribution, metabolism, and excretion (ADME) of drugs based on their physicochemical properties and interaction with human physiology. They are designed to integrate multiple data sources—in vitro, in vivo, and in silico—into a unified model to simulate oral drug absorption under various physiological and pathological conditions.

GastroPlus, developed by Simulations Plus, is one of the most advanced tools for oral absorption simulation and dosage form design. It features an Advanced Compartmental Absorption and Transit (ACAT) model, which divides the gastrointestinal tract into multiple compartments corresponding to real anatomical segments such as the stomach, duodenum, jejunum, ileum, and colon. Each segment is parameterized for pH, fluid volume, surface area, transit time, and enzyme/transporter expression. GastroPlus also integrates drug-specific data such as solubility, pKa, log P, particle size, permeability, and dissolution profile. Using this information, the software predicts regional absorption, bioavailability, Cmax, Tmax, and the effect of food on drug exposure.

GastroPlus is also widely used to simulate in vitro–in vivo correlation (IVIVC), develop biowaivers, and assess formulation performance under fed and fasted conditions. It supports different formulation types including immediate-release, controlled-release, suspensions, and lipid-based systems. Moreover, the software can simulate special populations like pediatrics, geriatrics, and patients with GI disorders, allowing researchers to anticipate variability and guide clinical trial design.

On the other hand, Simcyp Simulator, developed by Certara, offers a more comprehensive whole-body PBPK modeling platform, including advanced absorption models under the Simcyp ADAM (Advanced Dissolution, Absorption, and Metabolism) model. While GastroPlus is widely used in formulation development, Simcyp is more commonly applied in drug-drug interaction (DDI) prediction, population pharmacokinetics, and first-in-human (FIH) dose selection. Its absorption module considers pre-systemic metabolism, intestinal enzyme/transporter activity, and formulation dissolution behavior, making it suitable for predicting complex absorption profiles, particularly for drugs undergoing extensive intestinal metabolism or efflux.

Simcyp's strength lies in its ability to simulate virtual populations using demographic and physiological variability. For example, users can create a virtual cohort of 100 patients aged 65+ with reduced gastric acid and slower transit time to predict how a controlled-release formulation will perform in the elderly. Simcyp also allows the simulation of drug absorption across different ethnic groups, disease conditions, and co-medications, making it highly valuable for regulatory submissions and clinical study planning.

Both GastroPlus and Simcyp are validated, peer-reviewed, and widely accepted by regulatory agencies including the USFDA, EMA, and PMDA. They have been successfully used in waiving in vivo studies, designing biopredictive dissolution methods, and supporting bioequivalence justifications. These platforms have significantly reduced the reliance on animal models, shortened development timelines, and minimized clinical trial risk by enabling mechanistic, science-based decisions in formulation design and drug absorption prediction.

In summary, GastroPlus and Simcyp serve as the digital backbone of absorption modeling, offering simulation power, flexibility, and regulatory confidence for pharmaceutical scientists working in formulation, biopharmaceutics, and clinical pharmacokinetics. Their adoption has transformed the way drug developers approach oral drug delivery, enabling a shift toward predictive, model-informed development strategies.

5.2 Theoretical and Mathematical Foundations

5.2.1 Diffusion, Dissolution, Partitioning

A clear understanding of diffusion, dissolution, and partitioning is essential in biopharmaceutical characterization because these fundamental processes govern how a drug moves from its dosage form into the body, and ultimately into systemic circulation. These physicochemical principles provide the mathematical basis for simulating drug absorption using computer-aided models, and are integrated into every level of predictive software used in formulation and pharmacokinetics.

Diffusion is the process by which drug molecules move from a region of high concentration to one of lower concentration. It is described mathematically by Fick's first law of diffusion, which states that the rate of diffusion across a membrane is proportional to the concentration gradient and the diffusion coefficient of the molecule. In the context of drug absorption, diffusion plays a key role as the drug crosses biological membranes, particularly the intestinal epithelium. The diffusion coefficient (D) depends on factors such as molecular size, solvent viscosity, and temperature. Computer models use these parameters to estimate how quickly a drug molecule can move through aqueous environments or lipid bilayers in the gastrointestinal tract.

Dissolution, on the other hand, refers to the process by which a solid drug dissolves in a liquid medium, usually gastrointestinal fluids in the case of oral formulations. This process is described by the Noyes–Whitney equation, which expresses the dissolution rate as a function of the surface area of the solid, diffusion coefficient of the solute, saturation solubility, and thickness of the diffusion layer. The dissolution rate is often the rate-limiting step for absorption of poorly soluble drugs, especially those classified under Biopharmaceutics Classification System (BCS) Class II and IV. For such compounds, enhancing the dissolution through micronization, solid dispersion, or surfactant addition becomes critical. Computer-aided models incorporate the Noyes–Whitney equation or its modifications to predict the dissolution profile of a drug under various pH and physiological conditions.

Partitioning describes how a drug distributes itself between two immiscible phases, typically a lipid phase (like a biological membrane) and an aqueous phase (such as intestinal fluid or blood plasma). This behavior is quantified using the partition coefficient (P) or its logarithmic value log P, which is a measure of a drug's lipophilicity. The higher the log P, the more lipophilic the compound, which generally favors membrane permeability but may reduce solubility in aqueous environments. For ionizable drugs, the distribution coefficient (log D), which considers the drug's ionization state at a particular pH, is more relevant. This is important because the pH of different GI segments affects the degree of ionization and thus the effective partitioning of the drug.

In silico absorption models integrate these concepts to simulate the dynamic environment of the gastrointestinal tract. For instance, software like GastroPlus uses diffusion and dissolution equations to model how a tablet releases drug in the stomach and intestine, and uses partitioning data to simulate how much of that drug will permeate the epithelial barrier and enter the bloodstream. These models allow for precise prediction of Cmax, Tmax, AUC, and bioavailability by accounting for the physicochemical properties of the drug alongside physiological conditions.

Altogether, the mathematical foundations of diffusion, dissolution, and partitioning form the core framework for predictive modeling in drug absorption. These principles help pharmaceutical scientists in formulation design, dosage form selection, and risk assessment, especially when supported by computer simulations that can predict in vivo behavior without needing extensive experimental trials.

5.3 Model Construction and Validation

5.3.1 Model Building Workflow

The process of constructing a reliable computational model for drug absorption or biopharmaceutical prediction follows a systematic and structured workflow. The objective of this model-building workflow is to simulate how a drug behaves inside the human body, particularly in the gastrointestinal (GI) tract, and to predict key pharmacokinetic outcomes such as bioavailability, Cmax, Tmax, and extent of absorption. This is achieved by combining drug-specific physicochemical properties with human physiological parameters within a mathematical framework. The workflow involves multiple stages, from data collection to simulation and validation.

The first step in model construction is the gathering of input data, which includes both drug-specific parameters and physiological system parameters. Drug-specific inputs include molecular weight, pKa, log P, solubility, permeability, particle size, dosage form characteristics, and dissolution profile. These may be obtained from in vitro studies, experimental measurements, or quantitative structure–activity relationships (QSAR). System-related parameters include GI segment pH, fluid volume, enzyme and transporter expression levels, and regional surface area, which are usually built into PBPK modeling platforms like GastroPlus, Simcyp, or PK-Sim.

The second stage is model selection and compartment definition. In this stage, the developer decides whether to use a simple compartmental absorption model or a more detailed physiologically based pharmacokinetic (PBPK) model. PBPK models divide the GI tract into multiple compartments (e.g., stomach, duodenum, jejunum, ileum, colon), each with its own unique parameters. The drug's journey through each compartment is modeled by equations describing dissolution, degradation, metabolism, and transport across membranes.

Once the structure is set, the next step is mathematical modeling, where equations like Fick's Law for diffusion, Noyes–Whitney equation for dissolution, and Michaelis–Menten kinetics for transporter interactions are integrated into the software environment. These equations are parameterized using the previously gathered data to calculate concentration-time profiles across GI compartments.

Following model setup, parameter estimation is done using available experimental or clinical data. If there are missing parameters, software tools can use fitting algorithms or Monte Carlo simulations to estimate likely values based on population variability. At this point, sensitivity analysis is often performed to assess which parameters most significantly affect the outputs, helping prioritize further experimental work if required.

The next and most critical step is model validation. The model's predictions are compared with observed in vivo data from preclinical studies or clinical trials. Key outputs such as plasma concentration-time curves, AUC, and bioavailability are compared. If the model accurately replicates the experimental data within acceptable error margins, it is considered valid. Otherwise, the model must be refined, which may include adjusting parameters, modifying equations, or incorporating additional biological processes.

Finally, once validated, the model is ready for application. It can be used to simulate food effects, bioequivalence scenarios, formulation changes, pediatric or geriatric population predictions, and even to justify biowaivers. The entire workflow must be well-documented, with all assumptions, equations, and parameters clearly stated to ensure transparency and reproducibility.

Thus, the model building workflow is a cyclical and iterative process, involving data input, system modeling, simulation, validation, and refinement. Computer-aided modeling platforms guide scientists through this structured approach, reducing guesswork and ensuring that formulation and pharmacokinetic predictions are grounded in mechanistic, quantitative science.

5.3.2 Internal vs. External Validation

Once a computational model for drug absorption or biopharmaceutical prediction is constructed, its reliability and credibility must be verified through a process called validation. Validation ensures that the model can predict real-world outcomes accurately and consistently. In pharmaceutical modeling, two key types of validation are recognized: internal validation and external validation. Both play essential but distinct roles in establishing the strength of a model and are commonly required in regulatory submissions and quality assessments.

Internal validation refers to the process of checking how well the model fits the data that were used during its development. In this approach, the same experimental or clinical data that helped build the model are used to assess its performance. For example, if a model was developed using dissolution and permeability data from a specific drug in healthy adult volunteers, internal validation would involve comparing the predicted plasma concentration-time profile against the actual observed data from the same study. The goal is to confirm that the model equations and parameters are behaving as expected and that there is no overfitting or mathematical inconsistency.

Common methods for internal validation include:

- Goodness-of-fit plots (predicted vs. observed concentrations)
- Residual analysis (to detect bias or systematic errors)
- Statistical measures like root mean square error (RMSE), mean absolute error (MAE), and coefficient of determination (R^2)
- Sensitivity analysis to evaluate how small changes in input affect the output

While internal validation is necessary, it has limitations. It does not guarantee that the model will perform well outside the conditions in which it was built. A model may show excellent internal fit but fail when applied to a different population or formulation.

This is where external validation becomes essential. External validation evaluates the model's predictive performance using new, independent data that were not involved in model construction. For instance, if a model built using adult data is tested using clinical data from a pediatric population or a new formulation, the process is considered external validation. This step demonstrates the model's generalizability and robustness, which is critical for real-world applications such as predicting food effects, bioequivalence outcomes, or dosage adjustments in special populations.

External validation is often conducted during:

- Formulation bridging studies
- Cross-population extrapolations (e.g., adult to pediatric)
- Scenario-based simulations (e.g., predicting fed vs. fasted state performance)
- Virtual bioequivalence trials

Models that pass external validation are considered predictive and regulatory acceptable, especially in model-informed drug development

(MIDD). Regulatory agencies such as the USFDA and EMA increasingly emphasize external validation as part of submissions involving physiologically based pharmacokinetic (PBPK) modeling.

In summary, internal validation ensures the model works well with known data, while external validation proves that it can reliably predict new and independent outcomes. A scientifically credible model must demonstrate good performance in both validation types to be confidently used for decision-making in pharmaceutical development.

5.4 Parameter Sensitivity Analysis

5.4.1 Impact of Physicochemical Changes

Parameter sensitivity analysis is a powerful computational technique used to understand how changes in specific input parameters influence the output of a biopharmaceutical model. In the context of oral drug absorption, one of the most critical areas of sensitivity analysis is the evaluation of how physicochemical properties of a drug substance—such as solubility, pKa, log P, molecular weight, and particle size—affect absorption, bioavailability, and overall pharmacokinetic performance. This type of analysis allows formulation scientists and pharmacokineticists to identify critical formulation parameters (CFPs) and risk factors early in development, thereby supporting rational decision-making.

When developing a formulation, even minor changes in a drug's solubility profile can dramatically affect its dissolution rate and subsequent absorption, especially in Biopharmaceutics Classification System (BCS) Class II drugs that are poorly soluble but highly permeable. Using sensitivity analysis, one can simulate various solubility scenarios under different pH conditions and assess how they impact Cmax (peak plasma concentration), Tmax (time to reach peak), and AUC (area under the curve). These simulations help determine whether solubility enhancement techniques—such as solid dispersions, micronization, or salt formation—are required to achieve adequate bioavailability.

Similarly, changes in pKa can influence a drug's ionization profile in different regions of the gastrointestinal tract, affecting its ability to permeate biological membranes. For weakly basic drugs, increased ionization in the acidic stomach may reduce permeability, while ionization behavior in the small intestine can determine the main site of absorption. Sensitivity analysis allows the modeling of different ionization states and the resulting partition coefficients (log D) to simulate the absorption window and predict site-specific uptake.

Log P, which represents the drug's lipophilicity, is another critical parameter. A drug with a high log P value may have better membrane permeability but lower aqueous solubility, while a low log P value may suggest poor permeability despite adequate solubility. By adjusting log P in a sensitivity simulation, one can evaluate the trade-off between solubility and permeability, and explore whether permeability enhancers or lipid-based formulations are necessary.

Other physicochemical factors like particle size and drug polymorphism also influence the rate of dissolution. A decrease in particle size increases the surface area, thereby enhancing dissolution and absorption. Sensitivity analysis can quantify the impact of various particle size distributions on drug exposure, helping in the selection of optimal milling or micronization techniques.

These analyses are performed using software platforms like GastroPlus, Simcyp, and PK-Sim, which allow the user to modify one parameter at a time (local sensitivity analysis) or multiple parameters simultaneously (global sensitivity analysis). The results are typically presented as tornado plots, spider plots, or percentile ranking charts, which visually highlight the most sensitive parameters.

In summary, parameter sensitivity analysis of physicochemical properties is not only a theoretical exercise—it directly supports formulation optimization, risk assessment, and regulatory justification. By identifying which properties have the greatest influence on drug performance, scientists can prioritize development activities, design robust formulations, and reduce the risk of late-stage failure.

5.4.2 Scenario Analysis

Scenario analysis is an advanced component of parameter sensitivity assessment in computer-aided biopharmaceutical modeling. It involves simulating multiple hypothetical conditions or "what-if" cases to evaluate how different physiological, formulation, or dosing scenarios can influence the pharmacokinetic outcomes of a drug. Unlike simple one-variable sensitivity analysis, which tests the impact of changing a single input parameter, scenario analysis evaluates the combined influence of multiple variables to mimic real-world situations such as fed vs. fasted state, disease conditions, age-related changes, different formulations, or dose strengths.

In pharmaceutical development, scenario analysis helps in predicting how a drug will perform under variable clinical and environmental conditions. For example, a single oral drug may be administered to both adults and pediatric patients, in both fed and fasted states, using different strengths or formulations (e.g., tablet vs. suspension). Each of these conditions introduces variability in parameters such as gastric pH, gastrointestinal transit time, bile salt concentration, fluid volume, and enzyme/transporter expression levels. With the help of simulation platforms like GastroPlus or Simcyp, these variations can be modeled and compared side by side to evaluate their influence on drug absorption, Cmax, Tmax, and overall bioavailability.

A common application of scenario analysis is the simulation of fed vs. fasted state absorption. In the fasted state, gastric emptying is faster and stomach pH is lower, while in the fed state, the pH rises, gastric emptying slows down, and bile secretion increases. These changes can significantly affect drugs that are pH-sensitive, poorly soluble, or food-dependent. Scenario analysis allows the developer to predict whether a drug may show positive, negative, or no food effect, helping to determine appropriate labeling instructions and study designs.

Another frequent scenario simulated is the effect of gastrointestinal disease states, such as Crohn's disease, ulcerative colitis, or post-gastrectomy conditions. These conditions alter GI tract structure and function, affecting drug dissolution, transit, permeability, and metabolism. For instance, in patients with reduced intestinal surface area or faster colonic transit, the absorption window for extended-release formulations may shift or narrow, potentially leading to subtherapeutic exposure. Simulating such cases during formulation development provides early insights into how the product may behave in special populations.

Scenario analysis is also used to assess formulation modifications, such as switching from a conventional immediate-release tablet to a sustained-release or lipid-based system. By adjusting parameters like release kinetics, excipient properties, or capsule disintegration time, the model can predict how these changes influence the pharmacokinetic profile and therapeutic performance of the drug. This is especially useful when making post-approval changes or performing bridging studies.

Simulation of dose variation scenarios—including under-dosing, overdosing, or multiple dosing regimens—is another key use of scenario analysis. These simulations help define the therapeutic window, accumulation potential, and time to steady-state, all of which are crucial for dosage optimization and safety assessments.

Ultimately, scenario analysis enhances the decision-making process in drug development by allowing teams to anticipate risks, evaluate alternatives, and make scientifically sound choices without needing extensive clinical trials. It supports regulatory communication, improves formulation robustness, and helps identify patient-specific dosing strategies, aligning with the principles of model-informed drug development (MIDD) and precision medicine.

5.5 Virtual Trials

5.5.1 Virtual Patient Population

Virtual trials represent a transformative approach in pharmaceutical development, where computer-generated simulations are used to model the pharmacokinetics, pharmacodynamics, and clinical outcomes of a drug across a virtual patient population. These populations are mathematically constructed to reflect the real-world variability seen in humans, including differences in age, gender, body weight, genetic makeup, disease status, organ function, and enzyme/transporter expression. This approach allows drug developers to explore how different types of patients may respond to a drug—without exposing real individuals to risk in the early phases of development.

A virtual patient population is created using software platforms like Simcyp, GastroPlus Population Simulator, or PK-Sim, which include extensive built-in demographic and physiological databases. These databases are derived from clinical literature, national health surveys, and pharmacokinetic studies. They cover a wide range of subgroups, including pediatric, geriatric, hepatic-impaired, renally-impaired, pregnant women, and ethnically diverse populations. Each virtual individual is assigned a unique set of physiological parameters, such as gastric pH, liver blood flow, body surface area, glomerular filtration rate (GFR), and expression levels of CYP enzymes or drug transporters.

In simulation, a drug is administered to these virtual subjects, and their absorption, distribution, metabolism, and excretion (ADME) profiles are calculated using physiologically based pharmacokinetic (PBPK) models. The outcome provides a population-level prediction of key pharmacokinetic parameters like Cmax, Tmax, AUC, clearance, and volume of distribution. The variability observed in these simulations mirrors what would be expected in actual clinical settings, thus offering a reliable prediction of inter-subject variability.

For example, when developing a new antihypertensive tablet, a developer can simulate its behavior in a virtual population of 500 elderly patients with varying degrees of renal impairment. The model will account for the lower GFR, altered protein binding, and potential changes in transporter activity associated with age and kidney function. This helps in predicting whether dose adjustment is needed for these patients even before starting real-world trials.

Virtual patient populations also allow testing of different dosing regimens, formulation types, and food intake conditions. In cases where clinical trials in certain groups (like pediatrics or pregnant women) are ethically or logistically difficult, virtual populations provide a scientifically sound basis for making dose recommendations and supporting regulatory submissions. These simulations can also identify outliers or high-risk patients who may experience exaggerated drug exposure or adverse effects due to physiological extremes.

Another important application is in bioequivalence and bridging studies, where virtual populations are used to simulate the performance of a generic formulation compared to a reference product under fasting and fed conditions. If the simulations predict similar pharmacokinetic behavior within acceptable bioequivalence limits, they may help justify biowaiver requests and reduce the need for full-scale in vivo studies.

In summary, modeling with virtual patient populations has become a cornerstone of model-informed drug development (MIDD). It allows researchers to make data-driven decisions early, reduce dependency on animal or human testing, and support precision medicine approaches. These virtual simulations improve clinical trial design, minimize failure risk, and accelerate time to market—all while ensuring patient safety and regulatory compliance.

5.5.2 Predicting Clinical Outcomes

One of the most powerful applications of computer-aided biopharmaceutical characterization and virtual trials is the prediction of clinical outcomes based on in silico simulations. These predictions are made by integrating drug-specific properties with physiological and disease-related parameters within mechanistic models to estimate how a drug will behave in human subjects. This approach enables researchers to foresee therapeutic responses, variability among patients, safety margins, and potential efficacy before initiating or completing real-world clinical trials.

Predicting clinical outcomes begins with a validated pharmacokinetic and pharmacodynamic model that is built using preclinical, in vitro, and early clinical data. Once the model is constructed, virtual patient populations are created to simulate a range of dosing scenarios. These simulations help forecast important clinical parameters such as time to reach maximum concentration, total drug exposure over time, and drug concentration at the site of action. In pharmacodynamic simulations, the model extends further to estimate the onset, magnitude, and duration of therapeutic or adverse effects based on drug concentration-response relationships.

For example, in the case of an anti-diabetic drug, predictive models can simulate how different patient groups with varying insulin sensitivity, renal clearance, and body mass index will respond to different doses. These simulations help estimate the proportion of patients likely to achieve target blood glucose levels or the percentage at risk of hypoglycemia. Similarly, in oncology, computer models may predict tumor shrinkage dynamics or time to progression using drug-specific cytotoxicity and patient-specific tumor growth kinetics.

These outcome predictions are particularly valuable in special populations, such as pediatric, geriatric, hepatic-impaired, or pregnant patients, where ethical or logistical constraints make direct clinical testing difficult. They are also useful in predicting long-term outcomes when only short-term clinical data are available, for example by simulating the effect of chronic dosing on disease progression, cumulative toxicity, or therapeutic resistance.

In regulatory science, predicting clinical outcomes through virtual trials supports model-informed drug development and decision-making. Regulatory agencies accept these simulations as supplementary evidence in dose selection, clinical trial design, and bridging studies. For instance, when a formulation is changed post-approval, simulations can be used to demonstrate that the clinical performance remains equivalent, potentially avoiding the need for repeat clinical trials.

Moreover, these predictions guide internal development decisions, such as identifying optimal dose ranges, designing adaptive trial protocols, or prioritizing drug candidates based on expected clinical performance. Advanced modeling also enables simulation of competitive scenarios, such as comparing the new drug's expected response rate or safety profile against existing market products.

Overall, predicting clinical outcomes through virtual trials reduces uncertainty, supports ethical and cost-effective development, and enhances confidence in formulation and dosing decisions well before real patient data become available. This approach is not just a theoretical exercise—it is increasingly embedded into the regulatory and scientific framework of modern pharmaceutical development.

5.6 Fed vs. Fasted State Simulations

5.6.1 Biopharmaceutics Classification System (BCS) Impact

The influence of food on oral drug absorption is a critical consideration during drug development and regulatory evaluation. Simulating fed versus fasted state conditions helps predict how food intake affects drug bioavailability, and this is strongly guided by the principles of the Biopharmaceutics Classification System (BCS). The BCS classifies drugs based on their solubility and intestinal permeability into four categories, each with distinct implications for food-drug interactions.

For BCS Class I drugs (high solubility, high permeability), the presence of food usually has minimal impact on bioavailability. These drugs dissolve easily and are rapidly absorbed, regardless of gastric conditions. Computer simulations using tools like GastroPlus or Simcyp typically predict similar plasma concentration-time profiles under both fasted and fed states for such drugs, making them good candidates for biowaivers.

For BCS Class II drugs (low solubility, high permeability), food can significantly impact absorption. In the fed state, the presence of bile salts, lipids, and delayed gastric emptying can enhance solubility and prolong the absorption window, leading to higher bioavailability. This positive food effect can be beneficial, but it also adds variability. Simulations allow developers to evaluate how different food compositions (high-fat, standard meals) influence the dissolution rate and systemic exposure. For these drugs, model-based strategies help optimize formulation approaches like lipid-based systems or amorphous solid dispersions to reduce food dependency.

BCS Class III drugs (high solubility, low permeability) are generally not limited by dissolution, but their absorption can be affected by changes in intestinal motility, pH, and transporter activity in fed conditions. Simulation helps predict whether food-induced delays in transit time may improve absorption by extending drug contact time with the intestinal wall.

BCS Class IV drugs (low solubility, low permeability) are the most complex to simulate. They may show erratic absorption, and food effects are often unpredictable. For these molecules, fed vs. fasted state simulations are critical to guide formulation selection and dosing recommendations. Simulated profiles provide early insights into variability and risk, supporting the design of clinical food-effect studies.

In summary, integrating BCS classification with simulation models enables a predictive, systematic approach to evaluating food effects. This reduces reliance on post hoc clinical observations and supports biowaiver decisions, formulation design, and risk assessments during regulatory submissions.

5.6.2 Case-Based Comparison

Case-based simulation comparisons between fed and fasted states provide practical insights into how specific drugs respond to food intake, aiding formulation scientists and clinical pharmacologists in decision-making. These comparisons are commonly performed using software like GastroPlus, where drug-specific data are combined with fed and fasted physiological parameters to generate absorption profiles under both conditions.

For example, in the case of **griseofulvin**, a poorly soluble BCS Class II drug, simulations reveal that its absorption improves significantly in the fed state due to enhanced solubilization by bile salts and delayed gastric emptying. By adjusting meal composition in the model, developers can predict the optimal food type or fat content required to maximize bioavailability. This supports label recommendations that griseofulvin should be taken with a high-fat meal.

In contrast, **paracetamol**, a BCS Class I drug, shows minimal difference between fasted and fed states. Simulated plasma profiles under both conditions overlap closely, indicating consistent absorption. This justifies a label statement that the drug may be taken with or without food.

Another case is **itraconazole**, a weakly basic, lipophilic antifungal agent. Simulations show a strong positive food effect due to higher gastric pH and improved dissolution in the fed state. When itraconazole is administered as a capsule, the fed state enhances systemic exposure significantly. However, the oral solution form shows less dependence on food. Such case-based simulations help justify formulation-specific recommendations.

A more complex scenario can be seen in **gabapentin**, a BCS Class III drug absorbed via a saturable transporter. Simulations show that food delays its absorption (increased Tmax) but may not change total exposure (AUC), which aligns with clinical findings. The case helps differentiate between changes in absorption rate and extent—both of which may have clinical relevance.

These comparative simulations provide regulators and developers with visual, quantitative data to support claims of food effects or the absence thereof. They also assist in designing **fed and fasted bioequivalence studies**, determining the need for food-effect studies in special populations, and crafting patient counseling statements.

Ultimately, case-based fed vs. fasted simulations enhance confidence in drug labeling, reduce clinical trial burden, and support the broader goals of model-informed drug development.

5.7 *In Vitro–In Vivo Correlation (IVIVC) and In Vitro Dissolution*

5.7.1 Level A, B, and C Correlation Models

In vitro–in vivo correlation (IVIVC) is a predictive mathematical model that describes the relationship between an in vitro property of a dosage form—typically drug dissolution—and the in vivo response, most commonly plasma drug concentration or amount absorbed. Establishing a reliable IVIVC allows pharmaceutical developers to reduce the number of in vivo bioequivalence studies needed during product development and post-approval changes. Regulatory authorities such as the USFDA and EMA recognize several types of IVIVC, classified as Level A, Level B, and Level C, based on the strength and detail of the correlation.

Level A correlation is the most informative and preferred type of IVIVC. It represents a point-to-point relationship between in vitro dissolution and the in vivo input rate (e.g., absorption or plasma concentration) of the drug. Typically, a deconvolution approach is used to estimate the in vivo absorption profile from plasma data, which is then directly compared to the in vitro dissolution profile. A successful Level A correlation implies that the entire dissolution curve can predict the entire plasma concentration–time profile, allowing for confident prediction of in vivo performance based solely on in vitro data. This model is particularly useful in extended-release formulations and is often used to justify biowaivers for formulation changes.

Level B correlation is based on statistical moment analysis. It compares the mean in vitro dissolution time with the mean in vivo residence time or mean absorption time. Unlike Level A, Level B does not provide a point-to-point relationship, and multiple in vivo profiles can theoretically result in the same statistical moments. As a result, Level B correlations are less commonly used for regulatory decision-making because they do not offer a precise predictive value, although they can still support general trends in formulation performance.

Level C correlation is the simplest form of IVIVC. It establishes a single-point relationship between one dissolution parameter (e.g., time to 50% dissolution, T50%) and one pharmacokinetic parameter (e.g., Cmax or AUC). While easy to develop, Level C correlations are considered weak because they provide limited predictive capability. They are most useful in the early stages of development for screening formulations or when only a small number of in vivo studies are available. Multiple Level C correlations can sometimes be combined to strengthen predictability, but they still fall short of the robustness of Level A models.

Each level of IVIVC requires careful experimental planning and validation. Dissolution methods used to generate in vitro data must be discriminatory and biorelevant, meaning they should reflect the conditions in the gastrointestinal tract. Similarly, in vivo data used for correlation should be from well-designed studies with consistent dosing, sampling, and analytical methods.

In modern development, computer-aided tools like GastroPlus, Phoenix WinNonlin, and Simcyp are used to develop, test, and validate IVIVC models efficiently. These tools support both deconvolution-based and convolution-based approaches, automate model fitting, and provide statistical outputs for model evaluation. Establishing a validated IVIVC allows for the simulation of in vivo performance under different formulation or manufacturing conditions, reducing the need for repeated clinical testing and supporting regulatory flexibility in post-approval changes.

In summary, Level A offers a detailed and regulatory-preferred correlation, Level B provides general statistical relationships, and Level C gives limited but useful insight. The selection and application of an IVIVC model depend on the formulation type, available data, and intended regulatory use.

5.7.2 Software Tools for IVIVC Development

The development of an in vitro–in vivo correlation (IVIVC) model requires the integration of dissolution data, pharmacokinetic data, and mathematical modeling, which is best accomplished using specialized software tools. These tools streamline the complex calculations involved in deconvolution, regression, model fitting, and validation, allowing scientists to construct robust and predictive IVIVC models. With advancements in computational modeling and regulatory acceptance of model-informed approaches, software tools have become essential components in both early and late stages of formulation development.

One of the most widely used tools for IVIVC development is Phoenix WinNonlin by Certara. It offers a comprehensive module specifically designed for IVIVC studies. Using this software, users can perform Wagner-Nelson or Loo-Riegelman deconvolution, fit the correlation between in vitro dissolution and in vivo absorption, and generate Level A, B, or C

IVIVC models. The software provides graphical outputs such as observed versus predicted concentration-time profiles, residual plots, and model validation reports. Importantly, Phoenix allows users to perform internal and external validation, calculate percent prediction error (%PE), and assess model acceptance based on regulatory guidelines. This makes it particularly suitable for preparing IVIVC data for submission to regulatory agencies like USFDA or EMA.

Another popular platform is GastroPlus by Simulations Plus. Although primarily known for its advanced PBPK and absorption modeling, GastroPlus also includes powerful IVIVC modules. It allows users to input in vitro dissolution profiles, link them to simulated in vivo absorption profiles, and evaluate the resulting pharmacokinetic behavior using built-in prediction engines. GastroPlus supports convolution-based IVIVC, which is especially useful when multiple formulation strengths are evaluated or when working with extended-release products. The software can simulate virtual bioequivalence studies, helping developers explore formulation changes and predict the need for clinical studies.

Simcyp Simulator, while more focused on whole-body PBPK modeling, can also contribute to IVIVC through its ADAM (Advanced Dissolution, Absorption, and Metabolism) model. It allows developers to test how different dissolution scenarios translate to in vivo absorption, although it is more often used for mechanistic modeling rather than regulatory-focused IVIVC filing.

Other useful tools include DDSolver, a free Excel add-in developed by the Chinese Academy of Sciences. It provides support for model-independent and model-dependent IVIVC analysis, including deconvolution and correlation assessment. Although less sophisticated than Phoenix or GastroPlus, it is user-friendly and suitable for academic research or initial formulation screening.

Many organizations also use MATLAB or R to develop custom IVIVC models, particularly when the formulation type or dataset does not align with the constraints of commercial software. These platforms provide greater flexibility in algorithm design and statistical analysis but require advanced programming skills and validation of the custom scripts.

Across all platforms, the key capabilities for IVIVC modeling include:

- Deconvolution and convolution functions
- Regression modeling for correlation development

- Visual and statistical diagnostics for model assessment
- Prediction of plasma profiles from in vitro data
- Validation tools (internal and external)
- Scenario simulation (e.g., formulation changes, strength scaling)

In conclusion, software tools like Phoenix WinNonlin and GastroPlus play a pivotal role in the development, validation, and regulatory submission of IVIVC models. They enable accurate, efficient, and transparent modeling of drug performance, reduce the need for redundant in vivo studies, and support the wider adoption of model-informed drug development (MIDD) practices in pharmaceutical research.

5.8 Biowaiver Considerations
5.8.1 WHO and USFDA Guidelines

Biowaivers are regulatory approvals that allow a pharmaceutical product to be approved without the need for in vivo bioequivalence (BE) studies, based on strong in vitro and theoretical evidence. The concept is primarily applied to generic drugs and post-approval changes in formulation. International regulatory agencies such as the World Health Organization (WHO) and the United States Food and Drug Administration (USFDA) have developed specific guidelines outlining the conditions under which a biowaiver may be granted, especially using the Biopharmaceutics Classification System (BCS) as a foundation.

According to both WHO and USFDA, biowaivers are most applicable to BCS Class I drugs, which have high solubility and high permeability, and, under certain conditions, to BCS Class III drugs that are highly soluble but have low permeability. For Class I drugs, if the product demonstrates rapid and similar in vitro dissolution in multiple media (typically pH 1.2, 4.5, and 6.8), a biowaiver can be considered. For Class III drugs, in addition to rapid dissolution, excipients must be qualitatively and quantitatively similar to those in the reference product because permeability is already a limiting factor.

The WHO guidelines on biowaivers, particularly outlined in the "WHO Prequalification Programme" and "WHO Technical Report Series," provide biowaiver acceptance criteria with a focus on global health products, especially generics. WHO accepts BCS-based biowaivers for Class I and III drugs, particularly for immediate-release solid oral dosage forms, provided that dissolution studies show rapid (>85% in 30 minutes) and similar dissolution between test and reference products in all three media.

The USFDA guidance, titled *"Waiver of In Vivo Bioavailability and Bioequivalence Studies for Immediate-Release Solid Oral Dosage Forms Based on a Biopharmaceutics Classification System,"* is more detailed and includes criteria for solubility, permeability, dissolution, and excipient risk assessment. It also outlines the need for validated and standardized in vitro methods, and the use of f2 similarity factor to compare dissolution profiles. USFDA guidance accepts biowaivers for post-approval changes as well, provided that formulation and manufacturing site changes do not significantly affect the bioavailability.

Both WHO and USFDA emphasize the importance of batch-to-batch consistency, manufacturing controls, and product stability, as well as a full justification for any biowaiver request. The use of modeling and simulation tools to support such justifications is encouraged and increasingly accepted as part of model-informed drug development.

5.8.2 In Silico Justification of Waiver

With the advancement of computational tools and modeling techniques, in silico simulations are now being used to strengthen or even form the basis of biowaiver justifications. These simulations typically combine in vitro dissolution data with physiologically based pharmacokinetic (PBPK) modeling to predict how a drug will perform in vivo. If the in silico model reliably demonstrates that the test formulation behaves similarly to the reference under a variety of physiological conditions, a regulatory authority may consider this evidence sufficient to grant a biowaiver.

Software platforms like GastroPlus, Simcyp, and PK-Sim are commonly used for such simulations. The process usually starts by inputting drug-specific parameters such as solubility, permeability, pKa, log P, particle size, and dissolution data from the final formulation. These inputs are combined with physiological data to simulate plasma concentration-time profiles for both test and reference formulations. If the predicted profiles match within regulatory limits for Cmax, AUC, and Tmax, the model is said to support biowaiver justification.

In silico approaches are particularly useful when slight changes in formulation or manufacturing site raise regulatory concerns, but in vivo studies are not feasible or ethical. For example, when switching between different strengths of the same product with dose-proportional pharmacokinetics and similar dissolution behavior, simulations can demonstrate that systemic exposure will remain unaffected. Similarly, in pediatric formulations, where clinical testing is difficult, PBPK models adjusted for age-related physiological changes can provide predictive evidence.

To be accepted by regulatory bodies, the in silico models must be:

- Mechanistically sound and based on validated principles
- Built using reliable and transparent data
- Properly validated using available clinical or literature data
- Accompanied by sensitivity and variability analyses

Regulators also expect a detailed report including model assumptions, parameter sources, simulation results, and justification for decisions. If the model shows high predictive accuracy for known formulations, it may then be used confidently to support a waiver for new strengths, minor formulation changes, or even new generic versions.

In summary, the combination of robust regulatory guidelines (from WHO, USFDA) and validated in silico tools offers a powerful pathway for securing biowaivers, accelerating drug development, and reducing unnecessary human testing. This aligns with global efforts to promote efficient, ethical, and scientifically sound pharmaceutical innovation.

Review questions

1. What is computer-aided formulation development?
It refers to the use of computer software and statistical tools to design, optimize, and analyze pharmaceutical formulations more systematically and efficiently.

2. Why is computer-aided formulation important in pharmacy?
It minimizes trial-and-error experiments, saves time and cost, improves quality, and accelerates product development.

3. Name two commonly used software tools in formulation development.
Design-Expert® and Minitab®.

4. What is optimization in the context of formulation?
Optimization refers to adjusting formulation and process variables to achieve the best possible product quality attributes.

5. Define Design of Experiments (DoE).
DoE is a structured method to study the effect of multiple input variables on output responses in a systematic way.

6. Give an example of an independent variable in formulation.
Polymer concentration in a sustained-release tablet.

7. Give an example of a dependent variable in formulation studies.
Drug release percentage after 6 hours.

8. What is the advantage of using DoE over traditional methods?
DoE studies multiple factors simultaneously and identifies interactions, leading to better understanding and faster optimization.

9. What is a factorial design?
A factorial design is a type of DoE where all possible combinations of factor levels are studied.

10. What is the difference between full and fractional factorial designs?
Full factorial studies all combinations; fractional factorial studies only a

fraction to reduce the number of experiments.

11. Define response surface methodology (RSM).

RSM is a statistical technique used to optimize processes by modeling the relationships between input factors and responses.

12. What is a contour plot used for?

To visualize how two variables simultaneously affect a response in RSM.

13. What is a desirability function in optimization?

It transforms multiple responses into a single score to find the most desirable formulation.

14. Give an example of a formulation parameter optimized using computers.

Emulsifier concentration in an oil-in-water emulsion.

15. What is a pseudo-ternary phase diagram?

It is a graphical tool used to identify microemulsion regions by plotting ratios of oil, surfactant/co-surfactant, and water.

16. What type of formulations use pseudo-ternary phase diagrams?

Microemulsions.

17. Define droplet size in emulsions.

It is the average diameter of dispersed droplets, measured in nanometers or micrometers.

18. Why is droplet size important in emulsions?

Smaller droplet sizes enhance stability, drug release, and absorption.

19. What is polydispersity index (PDI)?

PDI measures the uniformity of droplet size distribution; values closer to 0 indicate uniform droplets.

20. What is a typical PDI value for a stable nanoemulsion?

Below 0.3.

21. What does zeta potential measure?

It measures the electrical charge on particle surfaces, indicating emulsion stability.

22. What zeta potential value indicates a stable emulsion?

Greater than +30 mV or less than −30 mV.

23. What is homogenization speed's role in emulsion development?

Higher speeds reduce droplet size, improving emulsion stability.

24. Name two types of vesicular systems used in drug delivery.

Liposomes and niosomes.

25. What is a liposome?

A vesicle made of phospholipid bilayers encapsulating hydrophilic and lipophilic drugs.

26. What is a niosome?

A vesicle formed using non-ionic surfactants, offering better stability and cost-effectiveness compared to liposomes.

27. What are solid lipid nanoparticles (SLNs)?

They are submicron colloidal carriers made from solid lipids, used for controlled drug delivery.

28. What is a nanostructured lipid carrier (NLC)?

An improved version of SLNs that combines solid and liquid lipids for better drug loading and stability.

29. What are the main advantages of nanoparticles in drug delivery?

Enhanced bioavailability, targeted delivery, and sustained release.

30. What is entrapment efficiency?

It is the percentage of drug successfully incorporated into the carrier system.

31. How is drug loading different from entrapment efficiency?

Drug loading refers to the amount of drug relative to the total carrier weight.

32. Name a metallic nanoparticle used in medicine.

Silver nanoparticles.

33. What is the use of gold nanoparticles in pharmaceuticals?

They are used for targeted drug delivery and cancer therapy.

34. What are ethosomes?

Soft vesicles enriched with ethanol for enhanced skin penetration.

35. What are transferosomes?

Ultra-deformable vesicles designed for transdermal drug delivery.

36. What is one advantage of ethosomes over liposomes?

Ethosomes penetrate deeper into the skin due to ethanol fluidization.

37. Name one evaluation method for particle size analysis.

Dynamic Light Scattering (DLS).

38. Why is in-vitro release study important?

It predicts how a drug will release over time from its formulation.

39. What type of kinetic models are used in release studies?

Zero-order, first-order, Higuchi, and Korsmeyer-Peppas models.

40. What is a control strategy in QbD formulation development?

A planned set of controls derived from process understanding to ensure consistent quality.

41. What does ICH Q8 emphasize regarding formulation?

Systematic product and process design based on scientific understanding and risk management.

42. Give one example of an FDA-approved nanoformulation.

Doxil® (liposomal doxorubicin).

43. What is the primary goal of computer simulations in drug delivery design?

To predict formulation behavior and optimize parameters before conducting actual experiments.

44. What is GastroPlus™ used for?

For simulating drug absorption, dissolution, and pharmacokinetics.

45. Why are phase diagrams important in formulation?

They help identify stable compositions in multi-component systems.

46. What is meant by the term "design space" in QbD?

It is the multidimensional combination of input variables that assures product quality.

47. Name a real-world application of microemulsions in pharma.

Topical delivery of antifungal drugs like ketoconazole.

48. What is a key challenge in nanoformulation development?

Physical and chemical instability, such as aggregation or degradation.

49. What is the impact of surfactant selection on emulsion properties?

It affects droplet size, stability, drug release, and skin irritation potential.

50. Why is computer-aided formulation development considered essential today?

Because it accelerates innovation, improves success rates, reduces development costs, and ensures regulatory compliance.

MCQS

1. Which technique models drug dissolution and absorption in silico? A. Cryotherapy

   B. GastroPlus™ simulation

   C. Ultracentrifugation

   D. Thermogravimetry

2. Biopharmaceutical characterization mainly helps predict: A. Toxicity

   B. Solubility enhancement

   C. In-vivo performance

   D. Shelf-life

3. The Biopharmaceutics Classification System (BCS) classifies drugs based on: A. Stability and potency

   B. Solubility and permeability

   C. pH and melting point

   D. Half-life and bioavailability

4. A drug with low solubility and high permeability belongs to which BCS class? A. Class I

   B. Class II

   C. Class III

   D. Class IV

5. IVIVC stands for: A. In-Vivo In-Vitro Characterization

   B. In-Vitro In-Vivo Correlation

   C. Intra-Vascular Intra-Venous Comparison

   D. In-Vitro Intra-Cellular Communication

6. What is the main advantage of achieving a Level A IVIVC? A. Early clinical trials elimination

   B. Direct prediction of in-vivo profiles from in-vitro data

   C. Simplified packaging

   D. Reducing excipient usage

7. BCS Class I drugs typically show: A. Low absorption

   B. High solubility and high permeability

   C. Poor oral bioavailability

   D. High hepatic metabolism

8. In computational modeling, permeability prediction often uses: A. Gastrointestinal simulators

   B. Artificial neural networks

   C. MRI scans

    D. Endoscopy

9. Which parameter is critical for oral absorption modeling? A. pKa

    B. Optical rotation

    C. Specific gravity

    D. Surface tension

10. Aqueous solubility of drugs is most affected by: A. Molecular size

    B. pH of the medium

    C. Container material

    D. Stirring speed

11. Permeability studies simulate transport across: A. Bones

    B. Mucosal membranes

    C. Red blood cells

    D. Lymph nodes

12. Which software can simulate drug absorption from different GI segments? A. Photoshop

    B. GastroPlus™

    C. Excel

    D. SketchUp

13. "Sink conditions" in dissolution testing imply: A. Saturation is achieved quickly

    B. Drug does not saturate the medium

    C. Drug evaporates fast

    D. Medium is viscous

14. The "effective permeability coefficient" (Peff) is used in: A. Blood compatibility studies

    B. Intestinal absorption modeling

    C. Eye irritation tests

    D. Lung deposition simulations

15. A Level C IVIVC involves: A. Correlation at multiple time points

    B. Correlation at one parameter

    C. No correlation at all

    D. Only dissolution profile matching

16. PBPK models integrate: A. Organ weights and drug-specific parameters

    B. Only organ sizes

    C. Only molecular weights

    D. Only in-vitro binding data

17. PBPK stands for: A. Physiological Biopharmaceutical Kinetic Modeling

    B. Pharmacological Biopermeability Knowledge

C. Physiology-Based Pharmacokinetic Modeling

D. Pharmacokinetic Binding Knowledge

18. Regulatory agencies encourage IVIVC for: A. Reducing bioequivalence studies

B. Enhancing packaging

C. Accelerating clinical recruitment

D. Skipping Phase III trials

19. Biowaivers can be requested for: A. Class II drugs

B. Class I drugs

C. Class III drugs

D. Both B and C

20. Dissolution media pH commonly used for intestinal simulations is: A. pH 1.2

B. pH 4.5

C. pH 6.8

D. pH 9.0

21. A drug with high solubility but low permeability is classified as: A. BCS Class I

B. BCS Class II

C. BCS Class III

D. BCS Class IV

22. The initial step in IVIVC model development is: A. Statistical validation

B. Formulation optimization

C. Data collection from dissolution and pharmacokinetic studies

D. Packaging study

23. Bioavailability refers to: A. Rate of elimination

B. Extent and rate of drug reaching systemic circulation

C. Metabolic degradation only

D. Drug binding to albumin

24. Gastrointestinal transit time can influence: A. Drug metabolism

B. Drug dissolution and absorption

C. Urinary excretion

D. Plasma protein binding

25. Simulation of gastric emptying is important because it affects: A. Elimination

B. Absorption window

C. Drug stability

D. Renal clearance

26. Which type of model assumes uniform distribution across compartments? A. Non-compartmental model

    B. One-compartment model

    C. Two-compartment model

    D. PBPK model

27. Solubility prediction software is based mainly on: A. Partition coefficient

    B. Molar refractivity

    C. Thermal conductivity

    D. Refractive index

28. The dissolution rate is most dependent on: A. Stirring speed

    B. Drug particle size

    C. Tablet shape

    D. Lid tightness

29. The primary goal of computer-aided biopharmaceutical characterization is to: A. Reduce manufacturing costs

    B. Optimize drug performance predictions

    C. Eliminate toxicology studies

    D. Increase tablet hardness

30. Virtual bioequivalence studies are conducted: A. After regulatory approval

    B. To avoid real human trials where possible

    C. Only in animal studies

    D. Only for generic antibiotics

Answer Key:

1. B
2. C
3. B
4. B
5. B
6. B
7. B
8. B
9. A
10. B
11. B
12. B

13. B
14. B
15. B
16. A
17. C
18. A
19. D
20. C
21. C
22. C
23. B
24. B
25. B
26. B
27. A
28. B
29. B
30. B

CHAPTER SIX

Computer Simulations in Pharmacokinetics and Pharmacodynamics

6.1 Introduction to PK/PD Simulations

6.1.1 Role in Predicting Drug Behavior

Computer-based **pharmacokinetic and pharmacodynamic (PK/PD) simulations** play a critical role in predicting how a drug behaves in the body—both in terms of its movement through the body (pharmacokinetics) and its biological effects (pharmacodynamics). These simulations allow researchers to understand and predict the concentration–time profile of a drug, as well as how that concentration translates into a therapeutic or toxic response. The use of PK/PD models has become an integral part of modern drug development because it offers a science-driven method to support **dose selection, frequency, and treatment duration**, all while minimizing the dependency on expensive and time-consuming clinical trials.

PK simulations describe how a drug is **absorbed, distributed, metabolized, and excreted (ADME)**. These simulations use mathematical models to predict **plasma drug concentration at different time points** after administration. PD simulations, on the other hand, establish a relationship between the drug concentration at the site of action and the observed **pharmacological or toxicological effect**. When combined, PK/PD models provide a comprehensive view of the **exposure–response relationship**, helping researchers make informed decisions regarding **efficacy and safety margins**.

Using computer simulations, researchers can explore "what-if" scenarios without exposing real patients to risk. For instance, they can simulate how a drug behaves in **different populations**, such as pediatric, elderly, renal-impaired, or hepatic-impaired patients. They can also predict how variations in **dose, route of administration, food intake, enzyme activity, or genetic polymorphisms** might affect therapeutic outcomes. These simulations are extremely useful in designing clinical trials, identifying optimal dosing strategies, and reducing the risk of trial failure.

Simulation platforms like **Phoenix WinNonlin, NONMEM, GastroPlus, Simcyp,** and **Berkeley Madonna** are commonly used to build and run PK/PD models. These tools allow incorporation of both **compartmental models** (which assume the body as one or more interconnected compartments) and **physiologically based pharmacokinetic (PBPK) models** (which simulate drug movement through actual organs and tissues). They also help in evaluating **drug-drug interactions, time-dependent effects,** and **nonlinear kinetics,** all of which are essential in both early discovery and late-stage development.

Overall, PK/PD simulations offer a predictive, cost-effective, and ethical approach to drug evaluation, supporting the goals of precision medicine and regulatory science. They allow for better decision-making during drug development and help optimize the benefit–risk balance in clinical practice.

6.1.2 PK/PD Modeling vs. Classical Methods

PK/PD modeling using computer simulations represents a significant advancement over **classical pharmacokinetic and pharmacodynamic methods,** which relied heavily on empirical analysis and limited datasets. Traditional approaches typically involved non-compartmental analysis (NCA), where parameters like **AUC, Cmax, Tmax, clearance, and half-life** were calculated from observed plasma concentration–time data. While this approach provides a good summary of drug exposure, it does not explain the underlying mechanisms or allow for reliable prediction of untested dosing scenarios or patient variability.

In contrast, **computer-based PK/PD modeling** uses mathematical equations to describe the drug's journey through the body and its interaction with biological targets. These models can simulate **dynamic interactions** over time, incorporating real physiological processes such as **enzyme saturation, receptor binding, feedback regulation,** and **tissue distribution.** Classical methods are retrospective, analyzing only what has already happened, whereas modeling and simulation approaches are

prospective—capable of predicting what will happen under different conditions.

For example, a classical method might show that a certain antibiotic achieves a Cmax of 5 µg/mL, which correlates with clinical efficacy. However, a PK/PD model can simulate how **increasing or reducing the dose affects bacterial kill rate**, predict how **missed doses impact therapy**, or show **how drug accumulation might lead to toxicity**. These insights are not possible with classical analysis alone.

Moreover, classical methods often fall short in complex situations involving **nonlinear pharmacokinetics, time-dependent clearance, or indirect response models**, where drug effects occur with a delay or are governed by complex feedback mechanisms. In such cases, mechanistic PK/PD models can integrate these features, offering better predictions of drug behavior and supporting **rational design of dosage regimens**.

Another major difference lies in the ability to **incorporate variability and uncertainty**. While classical methods provide average values, PK/PD modeling can include **population variability**, enabling **population PK/PD modeling** using tools like NONMEM. This is particularly useful in clinical trial simulations, where models are used to **simulate thousands of virtual patients** and assess the probability of achieving desired therapeutic outcomes across different subgroups.

Regulatory agencies are increasingly recognizing the value of PK/PD modeling over classical methods. It is now a part of **model-informed drug development (MIDD)** strategies encouraged by USFDA and EMA, especially in **dose justification, pediatric extrapolation, bridging studies, and bioequivalence**.

6.2 Simulation at Different Biological Levels

6.2.1 Whole Organism Models

6.2.1.1 Physiologically Based Pharmacokinetic (PBPK) Models

Physiologically Based Pharmacokinetic (PBPK) models represent one of the most detailed and mechanistic approaches used in pharmacokinetic simulation. Unlike empirical compartmental models that simplify the human body into abstract compartments, PBPK models aim to replicate the **actual physiological structure and function** of a living organism. These models simulate how a drug is **absorbed, distributed, metabolized, and excreted (ADME)** by incorporating real physiological and anatomical data—such as **organ sizes, blood flow rates, tissue composition, and enzymatic activity**—for each organ or tissue in the body. This makes PBPK modeling particularly powerful for **whole-organism level predictions**.

A typical PBPK model includes compartments for major organs such as the **liver, kidneys, lungs, brain, muscle, fat, gastrointestinal tract, and heart**, each defined by unique parameters like volume, perfusion rate, and specific binding or metabolic capacity. These compartments are connected by systemic circulation, allowing the model to simulate how the drug moves between tissues over time. Organ-specific clearance, active transport, and permeability are also incorporated, enabling detailed predictions of drug concentrations not just in plasma, but in individual tissues and organs.

One of the key advantages of PBPK models is their ability to **integrate drug-specific physicochemical data**—such as **lipophilicity (log P), pKa, solubility, permeability, and molecular weight**—with **individual physiological characteristics** to provide a system-wide simulation. This allows researchers to predict **plasma and tissue concentration–time profiles**, evaluate **dose-exposure relationships**, and assess **variability between individuals** based on factors like **age, gender, disease condition, enzyme expression, or organ impairment**.

PBPK models are especially useful in:

- **First-in-human dose prediction** using preclinical and in vitro data
- **Extrapolation across populations** (e.g., from adults to children or patients with renal impairment)
- **Prediction of drug-drug interactions** by modeling the effect of enzyme inducers or inhibitors

- **Formulation development** by simulating how dosage form and route of administration affect systemic exposure
- **Regulatory decision-making**, including support for biowaivers, clinical trial waivers, and label expansions

Software platforms such as **Simcyp Simulator, GastroPlus, PK-Sim**, and **MATLAB-based PBPK frameworks** are widely used in industry and academia to construct and validate PBPK models. These tools allow for user-defined parameter input, automatic population generation, and integration of enzyme kinetics and transporter mechanisms. Most of them include libraries of predefined physiological values for humans and animals, making model construction efficient and reliable.

Regulatory authorities, including the **USFDA, EMA, and PMDA**, have published guidelines acknowledging the role of PBPK modeling in drug development and encouraging its use in regulatory submissions, especially when clinical studies are not feasible. For example, PBPK simulations have been used successfully to support **dose selection in pediatric studies, predict food effects, model absorption in gastric bypass patients**, and **justify product equivalence in generic applications.**

In summary, PBPK models offer a **mechanistically rich, scientifically rigorous, and physiologically accurate** way to simulate drug behavior at the whole-organism level. They bridge the gap between laboratory data and clinical outcomes, helping pharmaceutical scientists make informed decisions throughout the drug development cycle while reducing dependency on animal and human trials.

6.2.2 Isolated Tissue and Organ Models

6.2.2.1 Liver, Kidney, GI Tract Models

Isolated tissue and organ models represent an intermediate level of pharmacokinetic and pharmacodynamic simulation, where specific organs are modeled independently rather than as part of an integrated whole-body system. These models focus on the **localized handling of drugs within individual tissues,** such as the **liver, kidneys, and gastrointestinal (GI) tract**, to provide deeper insight into **organ-specific processes** like metabolism, secretion, absorption, and transport. This level of simulation is particularly important when a drug's pharmacokinetics is **heavily influenced by a single organ**, or when designing drugs targeted to specific tissues.

The **liver** is the primary site of drug metabolism and is often modeled to evaluate **hepatic clearance, first-pass metabolism**, and **enzyme saturation kinetics**. In isolated liver models, drug input into the liver is typically described by hepatic blood flow, and clearance is calculated using models such as the **well-stirred model, parallel tube model, or dispersion model**. These models incorporate enzyme kinetics, especially **Michaelis–Menten parameters (Km and Vmax)**, to simulate the rate of drug biotransformation. Inputs may include **CYP enzyme levels, liver volume, binding affinity, and transporter activity**, and the output is a prediction of how much drug is metabolized before it reaches systemic circulation. This is crucial in evaluating drugs with high first-pass effect or in predicting the effect of **hepatic enzyme inhibitors or inducers**.

Kidney models simulate renal excretion, including **glomerular filtration, tubular secretion, and reabsorption**. These models help quantify how much of a drug is cleared unchanged via urine and are particularly relevant for hydrophilic drugs with low metabolism. Isolated kidney models may include parameters such as **renal blood flow, glomerular filtration rate (GFR), tubular transporter activity (e.g., OCTs, OATs), and urinary pH**. These models are essential in assessing the impact of **renal impairment** on drug clearance, which directly affects dosing decisions in patients with kidney disease. They also support simulation of **nephrotoxic effects** and drug–drug interactions involving renal transporters.

The **GI tract** is the first site of drug exposure for orally administered drugs and is often modeled to predict **dissolution, degradation, absorption, and interaction with gut enzymes and transporters**. Isolated GI models divide the tract into compartments such as the **stomach, duodenum, jejunum, ileum, and colon**, each with distinct physiological characteristics like **pH, fluid content, bile salt concentration, surface area, and motility**. These models incorporate **permeability coefficients, dissolution kinetics, efflux and uptake transporter activity (like P-gp, PEPT1, OATP), and local metabolism (CYP3A4 in enterocytes)**. Simulating drug behavior within the GI tract allows prediction of **regional absorption, food effects, and formulation performance** under varying conditions.

These isolated models are not used in isolation from clinical reality—they are often validated against **in vitro data from perfused organ systems, tissue slices, or transporter-expressing cell lines**, and integrated into broader models when needed. Tools like **GastroPlus, PK-Sim**, and

Simcyp allow detailed simulations of individual organ behavior and even enable coupling of two or more isolated organ models to simulate **inter-organ interactions**, such as gut-liver first-pass effect.

In summary, isolated tissue and organ models provide a **focused and mechanistic understanding** of how drugs interact with key organs involved in their disposition. They help in **identifying rate-limiting steps, predicting organ-specific toxicity**, and **assessing the influence of diseases or physiological variations**. These models are particularly valuable during early drug development, formulation design, and risk assessment when a detailed evaluation of organ-specific processes is required.

6.2.3 Cellular Level Simulation

6.2.3.1 Receptor Binding and Enzyme Kinetics

Cellular level simulation focuses on the detailed interactions that occur at the site of drug action, particularly involving drug binding to cellular receptors and enzymes. These simulations help explain how molecular-level interactions result in pharmacological effects or biochemical changes. By modeling receptor binding and enzyme kinetics mathematically, researchers can predict the onset, intensity, and duration of a drug's action under various physiological and pathological conditions.

Receptor binding is a critical step in pharmacodynamics. It involves the interaction of a drug molecule with a specific receptor on the surface or inside a cell. This interaction is usually reversible and follows the principles of chemical equilibrium. The simplest model is the law of mass action, where the drug binds to the receptor in a concentration-dependent manner to form a drug-receptor complex. The strength of this interaction is described by the equilibrium dissociation constant, known as the KD value. A lower KD indicates higher affinity between the drug and its receptor. Using simulation tools, this binding process can be modeled over time, allowing prediction of how long the drug remains bound and active.

In more complex models, receptor binding includes additional features such as receptor internalization, desensitization, and up- or downregulation, which occur with prolonged drug exposure. These aspects are important for chronic therapies, especially in conditions like hypertension or psychiatric disorders, where receptor behavior changes over time and affects drug efficacy.

Enzyme kinetics is another important area of cellular-level modeling. Many drugs act by inhibiting or activating enzymes, and their effect can be described using the Michaelis-Menten equation. This equation relates the rate of reaction to the concentration of the drug (acting as a substrate or inhibitor), the maximum rate of reaction (Vmax), and the Michaelis constant (Km), which reflects the drug's affinity for the enzyme. Competitive, non-competitive, and uncompetitive inhibition mechanisms can be simulated to predict how drugs influence metabolic or synthetic pathways in cells.

These models are particularly useful when studying enzyme-mediated drug metabolism or drug interactions. For instance, a drug that inhibits a major liver enzyme like CYP3A4 can slow the metabolism of another co-administered drug, potentially leading to toxicity. Cellular simulations can predict these effects before clinical testing.

Software platforms like MATLAB, COPASI, and PK-Sim can simulate receptor and enzyme interactions at the cellular level. These tools use differential equations to describe the dynamic behavior of these systems and help visualize how changes in concentration, binding affinity, or enzyme levels affect the overall pharmacological response.

In therapeutic areas like oncology, endocrinology, and infectious diseases, cellular level simulations support drug discovery and development by helping researchers understand drug mechanisms, optimize dose-response relationships, and predict the likelihood of resistance or tolerance. These simulations add precision and depth to pharmacodynamic evaluations, linking molecular actions directly to clinical outcomes.:

6.2.4 Protein and Gene-Level Simulation

6.2.4.1 Signal Transduction Pathways

Protein and gene-level simulations represent the most detailed layer of pharmacodynamic modeling. At this level, the focus shifts to understanding how drugs influence complex intracellular networks that regulate gene expression, protein synthesis, and cell signaling. One of the most critical components of this level of simulation is the modeling of signal transduction pathways, which are sequences of molecular events triggered by the activation of cell surface or intracellular receptors. These pathways control a wide range of cellular responses such as proliferation, apoptosis, inflammation, and differentiation.

Signal transduction begins when a drug or endogenous ligand binds to a receptor, usually located on the cell membrane. This interaction leads to a cascade of intracellular events involving secondary messengers, kinases, phosphatases, and adaptor proteins. Each step in this cascade can amplify the signal and produce a rapid and targeted cellular response. Well-known examples include the MAPK/ERK pathway, PI3K/AKT pathway, and JAK-STAT pathway. These pathways are tightly regulated and interconnected, making their simulation highly complex but also highly informative.

In pharmacology, signal transduction pathways are particularly important when studying drugs that target receptors such as G-protein coupled receptors (GPCRs), tyrosine kinase receptors, and nuclear hormone receptors. These drugs may influence not just immediate cellular effects but also long-term changes in gene expression. Simulation of these pathways involves mathematical modeling of the binding interactions, phosphorylation steps, feedback loops, and gene regulatory mechanisms. Ordinary differential equations are typically used to represent the time-dependent concentration changes of each component in the signaling network.

For example, in cancer research, simulations of the EGFR signaling pathway help predict how different inhibitors affect downstream signaling molecules like RAS, RAF, MEK, and ERK. These simulations can identify points of resistance, such as mutations that prevent effective inhibition, and suggest combination therapies that target multiple steps in the pathway. In immunology, modeling cytokine-induced JAK-STAT signaling can explain how immune-modulating drugs alter inflammatory responses at the gene level.

Tools like MATLAB SimBiology, CellDesigner, and COPASI are commonly used to build and simulate these pathway models. These platforms allow users to define each molecular species, reaction rate, and regulatory interaction, and then simulate how the system behaves over time under different drug concentrations or genetic conditions.

Gene-level outputs, such as transcription factor activation or mRNA expression levels, can also be incorporated into the models to connect upstream signaling events with downstream cellular outcomes. These models support systems pharmacology approaches, where the goal is to understand not just the direct effect of a drug but its impact on the entire biological system.

In conclusion, protein and gene-level simulations of signal transduction pathways provide a powerful framework to predict and interpret the molecular basis of drug action. These simulations help bridge the gap between molecular pharmacology and therapeutic outcomes, making them highly valuable in drug discovery, target validation, and precision medicine.

6.2.4.2 Pharmacogenomics and Gene Expression Prediction

Pharmacogenomics and gene expression prediction form a critical part of protein and gene-level simulations, focusing on how individual genetic differences influence drug response, metabolism, and toxicity. These simulations integrate molecular biology with computational modeling to predict how variations in DNA sequences affect the expression and function of proteins involved in drug absorption, distribution, metabolism, excretion, and pharmacological action. By simulating gene expression profiles and genetic variability, researchers can develop models that support personalized medicine and improve drug safety and efficacy across diverse patient populations.

Pharmacogenomics deals primarily with the simulation of genetic polymorphisms in drug-metabolizing enzymes, transporters, and drug targets. For example, cytochrome P450 enzymes such as CYP2D6, CYP2C9, and CYP3A4 exhibit significant genetic variability between individuals and populations. These polymorphisms result in phenotypes like poor, intermediate, extensive, or ultra-rapid metabolizers. Simulation platforms use genetic data to predict how these variations impact systemic drug exposure, clearance, and therapeutic outcomes. For instance, a patient with a poor metabolizer genotype for CYP2D6 may exhibit increased plasma concentrations of certain antidepressants or beta-blockers, leading to higher risk of adverse effects. Simulating these scenarios helps guide dose adjustments based on genotype.

Gene expression prediction focuses on modeling how drug exposure influences the transcription and translation of specific genes. These models often simulate the activation of nuclear receptors such as PXR, CAR, or AhR, which regulate the expression of metabolic enzymes and transport proteins. For example, some antiepileptic drugs induce the expression of CYP3A4 through PXR activation, which in turn increases the metabolism of co-administered drugs. Simulation of such drug-induced gene expression changes allows researchers to anticipate drug-drug interactions, enzyme induction effects, and the potential for loss of efficacy over time.

These simulations involve the integration of multiple data sources including gene sequences, promoter activity, transcription factor binding affinities, and mRNA stability. They use mathematical frameworks such as Boolean logic models, ordinary differential equations, and machine learning algorithms to predict how gene networks respond to internal and external stimuli. Systems biology tools like MATLAB SimBiology, GenePattern, and BioUML are often used to develop these models. Some platforms also incorporate publicly available databases like PharmGKB, dbSNP, and ENCODE to strengthen the predictive capacity.

Simulation of pharmacogenomic effects is especially valuable in oncology, cardiology, psychiatry, and infectious diseases, where inter-individual variability can significantly affect treatment outcomes. For example, predicting the effect of UGT1A1 polymorphisms on irinotecan metabolism helps avoid severe toxicity in patients undergoing chemotherapy. In infectious disease treatment, genetic simulation can predict the risk of hypersensitivity reactions to drugs like abacavir in patients carrying HLA-B*57:01 allele.

In clinical development, these simulations support biomarker identification, patient stratification, and individualized dose selection. Regulators are increasingly open to submissions that include pharmacogenomic simulations, especially when they are used to justify genotype-guided dosing or label warnings.

In conclusion, pharmacogenomics and gene expression prediction simulations add a molecular-level understanding of variability in drug response. They enable a shift from population-based treatment strategies to personalized approaches, improving therapeutic outcomes and minimizing adverse effects. As data quality and computational power continue to improve, these simulations are expected to become a standard component of precision pharmacotherapy.

6.3 Modeling Techniques in PK/PD

6.3.1 One-Compartment and Two-Compartment Models

One-compartment and two-compartment models are fundamental mathematical tools used in pharmacokinetics to describe how a drug distributes and is eliminated in the body over time. These models form the backbone of classical pharmacokinetic analysis and are still widely used in clinical and research settings due to their simplicity, interpretability, and ease of application. They help predict plasma drug concentration at different time points after administration, supporting decisions on dose, frequency, and route of administration.

In the one-compartment model, the body is assumed to act as a single, homogeneous unit where the drug instantly distributes throughout upon entering the systemic circulation. This model assumes that the drug concentration in the blood is representative of the entire body. Once administered, the drug is absorbed (if not given intravenously), distributed uniformly, and eliminated according to first-order kinetics, meaning that the rate of elimination is proportional to the drug concentration. This model works well for drugs that distribute quickly and extensively, such as paracetamol or theophylline, and provides estimates of key pharmacokinetic parameters like volume of distribution, clearance, half-life, and area under the curve (AUC).

The two-compartment model introduces greater physiological realism by dividing the body into two interconnected compartments: the central compartment and the peripheral compartment. The central compartment typically includes the blood and highly perfused organs like the liver and kidneys, while the peripheral compartment represents tissues such as muscle or fat where the drug distributes more slowly. After administration, the drug first enters the central compartment and then redistributes into the peripheral compartment. Elimination usually occurs from the central compartment. The concentration–time profile in a two-compartment model typically shows two phases: an initial distribution phase where drug levels drop rapidly due to distribution into peripheral tissues, followed by a slower elimination phase once equilibrium is reached.

Two-compartment models are more suitable for drugs with complex distribution kinetics, such as digoxin or vancomycin, which distribute slowly into certain tissues. These models help in understanding drug accumulation, delayed tissue distribution, and biphasic elimination profiles. They are particularly useful in drugs with narrow therapeutic windows, where accurate dosing is essential to avoid toxicity or subtherapeutic exposure.

Mathematically, both models are described using differential equations that simulate drug concentration over time. One-compartment models use a single exponential decay equation, whereas two-compartment models involve a sum of two exponentials representing distribution and elimination phases. Software like WinNonlin, NONMEM, and MATLAB is often used to estimate parameters and simulate concentration–time curves based on these models.

While more advanced models like physiologically based pharmacokinetic (PBPK) models and nonlinear mixed-effects models offer deeper insights, one- and two-compartment models remain valuable, especially in early-stage development, clinical pharmacology, and therapeutic drug monitoring. They provide a foundation for more complex simulations and remain essential tools in the pharmacokinetic modeling toolbox.:

6.3.2 Non-Linear Mixed Effects (NONMEM) Modeling

Non-linear mixed effects modeling, commonly referred to as **NONMEM modeling**, is a powerful and flexible approach used to describe the variability in pharmacokinetics and pharmacodynamics across a population. This technique goes beyond simple compartmental models by allowing simultaneous analysis of data from multiple individuals, while accounting for both the fixed effects that apply to the entire population and the random effects that represent variability between individuals. NONMEM is not just a software platform—it is a statistical modeling framework that has become the gold standard for population pharmacokinetic and pharmacodynamic modeling.

In NONMEM, the total variability in drug response is separated into two components: **inter-individual variability** and **residual unexplained variability**. Inter-individual variability refers to differences in pharmacokinetic parameters like clearance or volume of distribution between subjects, which may arise due to age, weight, genetics, disease state, or co-medications. Residual variability accounts for random errors in measurement, data collection, or model misspecification. NONMEM allows these sources of variability to be explicitly modeled, providing a more accurate and realistic description of drug behavior in real-world populations.

The modeling process begins by defining a structural model, which may be a one-compartment, two-compartment, or more complex system, depending on the drug's kinetics. The next step involves specifying a statistical model that incorporates random effects to account for variability in parameters across individuals. Covariates such as body weight, creatinine clearance, liver function tests, or genotype can then be included in the model to explain some of this variability, leading to a better understanding of which patient characteristics influence drug exposure or response.

For example, in a population study of an antibiotic, NONMEM modeling might reveal that renal function significantly influences drug clearance, allowing for dose adjustment recommendations in patients with impaired kidney function. Similarly, the model may predict that children metabolize the drug faster than adults, supporting age-specific dosing. The ability to identify such covariate relationships is one of the major strengths of NONMEM.

NONMEM models are constructed and analyzed using the NONMEM software developed by ICON plc, often in combination with tools like PsN (Perl-Speaks-NONMEM), Xpose, and R for diagnostics and visualization. These tools help perform model building, validation, simulation, and visual predictive checks. The results are typically presented as goodness-of-fit plots, residual plots, and predictive performance assessments, which help in evaluating the reliability and accuracy of the model.

NONMEM modeling is widely used in clinical pharmacology, particularly in phase I and phase II trials, to support dose selection, trial design, and evaluation of special populations. It is also used post-marketing to support labeling updates, therapeutic drug monitoring, and regulatory submissions. Regulatory agencies such as the USFDA and EMA encourage the use of NONMEM for model-informed drug development, especially when variability in response is a concern.

In summary, NONMEM modeling provides a comprehensive and quantitative framework to understand variability in drug response across a population. By integrating clinical, demographic, and biological data into a unified model, it enables more precise and individualized drug therapy, improves clinical trial efficiency, and supports data-driven regulatory decisions.

6.3.3 Time-Concentration and Effect Relationship Models

Time-concentration and effect relationship models are essential tools in pharmacokinetics and pharmacodynamics, as they describe how the concentration of a drug in the body over time translates into a therapeutic or toxic effect. These models help bridge the gap between drug exposure and drug response, enabling researchers to predict not just how long a drug stays in the system, but also how long and to what extent it produces a desired pharmacological effect. This relationship is particularly important for dose optimization, determining dosing intervals, and designing controlled-release formulations.

The most basic approach assumes a direct relationship between drug concentration and effect, often represented by the Emax model. In this model, the effect increases with concentration up to a maximum value (Emax), beyond which additional drug does not produce further benefit. The shape of this curve depends on the EC50 value, which is the concentration that produces half of the maximum effect. This model is widely used for drugs where the effect is immediate and directly related to plasma concentration, such as inotropic agents or antihypertensives.

However, many drugs do not produce immediate effects that correspond directly to plasma concentrations. In such cases, more advanced models are needed. One common approach is the use of effect compartment models, which introduce a hypothetical biophase compartment that accounts for the time delay between plasma concentration and effect. This delay may be due to distribution to the site of action, slow receptor binding, or intracellular signaling cascades. The concentration in the effect compartment, not the central compartment, is then linked to the observed pharmacodynamic response.

Another widely used method is the indirect response model, which assumes that the drug does not directly produce the observed effect, but rather modifies the rate of synthesis or elimination of an endogenous substance. For example, corticosteroids suppress inflammatory markers not by acting directly, but by altering the transcription of related proteins. Indirect response models include equations to describe the stimulation or inhibition of production or removal processes, and are suitable for drugs with delayed onset or offset of action.

Sigmoid Emax models, which include a Hill coefficient, are also used to describe cases where the relationship between concentration and effect is steeper or more gradual than a simple Emax curve. These models help in fine-tuning the predicted therapeutic window and in evaluating how steep dose-response curves may impact the safety margin.

These models are implemented in simulation platforms such as NONMEM, Phoenix WinNonlin, and MATLAB, and are validated by comparing predicted effects with observed clinical or experimental data. Model outputs are typically used to predict the magnitude and duration of effect for different dosing regimens, helping to identify optimal dose ranges and anticipate potential adverse effects.

In clinical development, time-concentration and effect relationship models support decisions on starting doses, dose titration schemes, and dosing frequency. They are also critical in understanding tolerance development, drug accumulation, and the impact of missed doses. For chronic therapies, such as antihypertensives or antidiabetics, these models help ensure consistent therapeutic effect while minimizing risk.

In conclusion, modeling the time course of both drug concentrations and drug effects is fundamental to understanding and predicting therapeutic outcomes. These models provide a quantitative framework for translating pharmacokinetic data into meaningful pharmacodynamic predictions, forming the basis for rational and personalized pharmacotherapy.

6.4 Software Used in PK/PD Simulation

6.4.1 WinNonlin, NONMEM, Phoenix

Several specialized software platforms are used in pharmacokinetic and pharmacodynamic (PK/PD) modeling and simulation to evaluate drug behavior and predict therapeutic outcomes. Among the most widely adopted tools in the pharmaceutical industry and academia are **WinNonlin**, **NONMEM**, and **Phoenix**. Each of these tools plays a unique role in supporting model-based drug development by allowing detailed analysis of drug concentration–time data, modeling population variability, and simulating different dosing scenarios.

WinNonlin is one of the most commonly used tools for non-compartmental analysis (NCA) and basic compartmental PK modeling. It provides a user-friendly interface that enables pharmacologists to quickly estimate key parameters such as area under the curve (AUC), peak concentration (Cmax), half-life, clearance, and volume of distribution. It supports standard one- and two-compartment models and is often used in the early phases of drug development and for routine bioequivalence studies. It is especially useful when dealing with small datasets or when a rapid, reliable PK analysis is needed.

NONMEM (Nonlinear Mixed Effects Modeling), developed by ICON plc, is considered the gold standard for population PK/PD modeling. It allows researchers to analyze data from multiple individuals simultaneously, accounting for both fixed effects (parameters common to the population) and random effects (variability between individuals). NONMEM is especially valuable in late-stage clinical development, where it supports dose optimization, trial simulations, covariate analysis, and variability assessment. NONMEM is also widely used in regulatory submissions, particularly when model-informed decisions are made for special populations like pediatrics or patients with renal impairment.

While NONMEM itself uses a command-line interface and requires scripting knowledge, it is often used in conjunction with companion tools such as PsN (Perl-Speaks-NONMEM) for model automation, and Xpose or R for data visualization and diagnostics. These tools help manage large datasets and evaluate model performance through goodness-of-fit plots, residuals, and prediction-corrected visual predictive checks.

Phoenix is a complete suite that includes WinNonlin as one of its core modules, offering additional capabilities for PK/PD modeling, IVIVC (in vitro–in vivo correlation), and data visualization. It is designed to provide both the simplicity of a graphical user interface and the flexibility of advanced modeling techniques. Phoenix allows for both individual and population PK/PD modeling and integrates tools for handling complex models such as indirect response models, effect compartment models, and covariate relationships.

One of the major advantages of Phoenix is its accessibility for users without programming backgrounds. It provides workflows and templates that streamline analysis while still offering robust mathematical modeling options. It is commonly used in industry settings for report generation, regulatory documentation, and method validation.

Together, WinNonlin, NONMEM, and Phoenix form a powerful toolkit for PK/PD modeling. These tools are supported by regulatory agencies and are integral to model-informed drug development. They help researchers analyze clinical and preclinical data, predict outcomes in untested scenarios, optimize dosing strategies, and ensure safe and effective use of new medicines across diverse populations. Their continued development reflects the growing importance of simulation and modeling in modern pharmaceutical science.

6.4.2 GastroPlus, SimBiology, MATLAB

In addition to classical PK/PD tools like WinNonlin and NONMEM, more advanced and mechanistic modeling platforms such as **GastroPlus**, **SimBiology**, and **MATLAB** have become increasingly important in modern pharmacokinetic and pharmacodynamic simulations. These tools enable the development of detailed models that simulate drug absorption, distribution, metabolism, excretion, and effect at various biological levels. They also allow the integration of physiological, biochemical, and molecular data to support decision-making in formulation design, virtual trials, and regulatory submissions.

GastroPlus, developed by Simulations Plus, is a widely used platform for physiologically based pharmacokinetic (PBPK) modeling and biopharmaceutics simulations. It specializes in predicting oral absorption based on the drug's physicochemical properties and gastrointestinal physiology. One of its key features is the Advanced Compartmental Absorption and Transit (ACAT) model, which divides the gastrointestinal tract into multiple compartments, each representing a segment like the stomach, duodenum, jejunum, and colon. The software simulates dissolution, precipitation, permeability, metabolism, and transporter effects within each segment, providing a highly detailed picture of how a drug behaves during its journey through the body.

GastroPlus is also used for virtual bioequivalence studies, food-effect simulations, in vitro–in vivo correlation (IVIVC), and biowaiver justifications. It supports different populations, including pediatrics, geriatrics, and disease-specific cohorts. Because of its comprehensive built-in physiological databases, it allows formulation scientists and clinical pharmacologists to test a wide range of scenarios with minimal in vivo data.

SimBiology, a toolbox in MATLAB developed by MathWorks, is designed for modeling, simulating, and analyzing systems biology and PK/PD models. It uses a graphical block diagram approach, allowing users to construct models by connecting components such as compartments, reactions, and species. SimBiology is especially valuable for modeling at cellular and molecular levels, such as enzyme kinetics, receptor binding, gene regulation, and signal transduction pathways. However, it also supports classical pharmacokinetic models like one- and two-compartment systems and advanced approaches like target-mediated drug disposition and indirect response models.

SimBiology allows the implementation of ordinary differential equations, parameter estimation, and sensitivity analysis. It is particularly helpful for exploratory research and early-stage modeling when the user wants to visualize biological interactions in a customizable environment. Its integration with MATLAB provides powerful computation and visualization options, making it suitable for both academic research and industrial development.

MATLAB itself is a general-purpose scientific computing environment that can be customized for PK/PD modeling through custom scripts or with the help of toolboxes like SimBiology. Experienced users can build tailored models, solve complex sets of differential equations, and perform Monte Carlo simulations, global sensitivity analyses, and parameter optimization. Its flexibility and scalability make it ideal for creating large-scale simulations or modeling non-standard pharmacokinetic behavior.

Together, GastroPlus, SimBiology, and MATLAB offer powerful capabilities beyond standard compartmental or population modeling. They support systems pharmacology, mechanistic modeling, and hypothesis testing across different biological scales. These platforms are increasingly adopted in industry and regulatory science to inform early decision-making, reduce clinical trial burden, and support model-informed precision dosing. As pharmaceutical research becomes more complex and individualized, such advanced tools are essential for capturing the depth and variability of biological systems.

Review questions

1. What is pharmacokinetics (PK)?
Pharmacokinetics studies how the body absorbs, distributes, metabolizes, and excretes a drug over time.

2. What is pharmacodynamics (PD)?
Pharmacodynamics examines how the drug affects the body, including the mechanism of action and drug-receptor interactions.

3. What is the role of computer simulations in PK/PD studies?
They predict drug concentration-time profiles and drug effects, helping in dose optimization without extensive experimental studies.

4. Name two major software platforms used in PK/PD modeling.
NONMEM and Phoenix WinNonlin.

5. Define compartmental modeling.
It simplifies the body into compartments where drug movement and elimination are mathematically modeled.

6. What is a one-compartment model?
A model where the body is considered a single, homogenous compartment for drug distribution.

7. What is a two-compartment model?
A model with a central and a peripheral compartment, representing rapid and slow distribution phases.

8. What is meant by first-order elimination?
A constant fraction of the drug is eliminated per unit time.

9. What is zero-order elimination?
A constant amount of drug is eliminated per unit time, independent of concentration.

10. What is clearance (CL) in pharmacokinetics?
It represents the volume of plasma from which the drug is completely removed per unit time.

11. Define half-life ($t\frac{1}{2}$) of a drug.
It is the time required for the plasma concentration of a drug to reduce by

half.

12. What is volume of distribution (Vd)?

It indicates how extensively a drug distributes into body tissues compared to plasma.

13. Why are computer models used before clinical trials?

They help predict dosing regimens, identify risks, and reduce the need for early human testing.

14. What is non-compartmental analysis (NCA)?

An analysis based on minimal assumptions about drug distribution, relying on statistical moment theory.

15. What is bioavailability (F)?

It is the proportion of an administered drug that reaches systemic circulation unchanged.

16. Define Cmax in a PK profile.

Cmax is the maximum plasma concentration achieved by the drug after administration.

17. Define Tmax in a PK study.

Tmax is the time required to reach the maximum plasma concentration after dosing.

18. What is AUC (Area Under the Curve)?

It measures the total drug exposure over time after administration.

19. What is physiologically based pharmacokinetic (PBPK) modeling?

A detailed modeling approach that integrates drug properties with human physiology to predict ADME behavior.

20. Give one application of PBPK models.

Predicting drug-drug interactions and special population pharmacokinetics (e.g., pediatrics, elderly).

21. What does Emax represent in pharmacodynamics?

The maximum effect a drug can produce regardless of dose.

22. What is EC50?

It is the concentration of a drug that produces 50% of its maximum effect.

23. Define the term "dose-response relationship."

It describes how drug effect changes with varying doses.

24. What is a sigmoid Emax model?

A pharmacodynamic model describing a sigmoidal (S-shaped) dose-response curve.

25. Why is modeling drug absorption important?

It helps in predicting how different formulations and routes affect drug bioavailability.

26. What is lag time (Tlag) in PK studies?

It is the delay between drug administration and the start of its absorption.

27. How does renal impairment affect pharmacokinetics?

It reduces clearance and prolongs half-life, necessitating dose adjustment.

28. What is the role of sensitivity analysis in PK/PD modeling?

It identifies which parameters most influence the simulation results.

29. What is population pharmacokinetics (PopPK)?

It studies drug behavior variability across a patient population rather than in a single individual.

30. Name one software commonly used for population PK modeling.

NONMEM (Nonlinear Mixed-Effect Modeling).

31. What is the main advantage of PBPK over simple compartmental models?

PBPK models allow prediction across different populations and dosing scenarios based on biological principles.

32. What is Monte Carlo simulation in PK/PD?

It uses repeated random sampling to predict variability and uncertainty in pharmacokinetic and pharmacodynamic models.

33. What is model validation in PK/PD modeling?

It confirms that the model reliably predicts drug behavior in different datasets.

34. What does the term "model fitting" mean?

Adjusting model parameters so that the model's output best matches observed experimental data.

35. What is a residual error in model fitting?

The difference between observed and model-predicted values.

36. What is the significance of goodness-of-fit plots?

They assess whether the model adequately describes the observed data.

37. Name a key regulatory agency encouraging PBPK submissions.

The U.S. Food and Drug Administration (FDA).

38. What is exposure-response modeling?

It relates drug exposure levels (AUC, Cmax) to therapeutic or toxic effects.

39. What is a target-mediated drug disposition (TMDD) model?

A model used when drug pharmacokinetics are significantly influenced by binding to its biological target.

40. What is a virtual bioequivalence trial?

A simulation study comparing two formulations to predict bioequivalence outcomes without conducting physical trials.

41. How does machine learning assist in PK/PD modeling today?
It can uncover complex relationships between patient characteristics and drug responses.

42. What is cross-validation in model development?
It splits the data into parts to train and test the model for assessing predictive accuracy.

43. Why are covariates important in PopPK models?
They explain sources of variability in drug behavior, such as age, weight, or genetics.

44. What are prediction-corrected visual predictive checks (pcVPC)?
They are graphical tools used to assess the predictive performance of a pharmacometric model.

45. What is the therapeutic index and its relevance to PK/PD?
The ratio between toxic and therapeutic doses; PK/PD modeling helps maintain drug levels within the therapeutic window.

46. What is an example of a biologic drug requiring complex PK/PD modeling?
Monoclonal antibodies like trastuzumab.

47. What are software examples for PBPK modeling?
Simcyp Simulator and GastroPlus™.

48. Why is time-to-peak effect sometimes different from Tmax?
Because drug action often depends on more than just plasma concentration, involving receptor kinetics or distribution delays.

49. Define steady-state concentration.
It is the condition where the drug intake equals drug elimination, leading to a constant plasma concentration over time.

50. What is NONMEM primarily used for?
Population pharmacokinetics and nonlinear mixed-effects modeling in clinical research.

MCQS

1. What does PK modeling primarily describe?
   A. Drug absorption rates
   B. Drug distribution patterns
   C. Drug movement in the body over time

    D. Drug metabolism only

2. Pharmacodynamics (PD) modeling relates drug concentration to:
   A. Metabolism
   B. Elimination
   C. Biological effect
   D. Absorption

3. Which of the following is a compartmental model assumption?
   A. Drug distributes uniformly within compartments
   B. Drug enters and leaves organs randomly
   C. No metabolism occurs
   D. Elimination occurs only after distribution

4. In PK modeling, clearance refers to:
   A. Volume of drug distribution
   B. Rate of absorption
   C. Volume of plasma cleared per unit time
   D. Half-life of the drug

5. A two-compartment model describes:
   A. Only blood circulation
   B. Only tissue accumulation
   C. Central and peripheral compartments
   D. Only kidney filtration

6. The time taken for plasma concentration to reduce by half is called:
   A. Tmax
   B. Bioavailability
   C. Half-life
   D. Clearance

7. What is the main goal of PK/PD simulations?
   A. Reduce sample size
   B. Predict clinical outcomes
   C. Increase manufacturing speed
   D. Lower trial costs

8. NONMEM software is widely used for:
   A. Manufacturing
   B. Toxicology reports
   C. Population pharmacokinetic modeling
   D. Inventory management

9. Volume of distribution relates the drug dose to:
   A. Rate of metabolism

B. Plasma drug concentration

C. Excretion

D. Clearance

10. The initial spike in drug concentration after dosing is known as:

    A. Steady-state

    B. Peak plasma concentration

    C. Distribution phase

    D. Elimination phase

11. Which parameter indicates the extent of drug exposure over time?

    A. Tmax

    B. AUC (Area Under Curve)

    C. Clearance

    D. Half-life

12. In pharmacodynamics, EC50 refers to:

    A. Maximum response

    B. Dose needed to kill 50% of cells

    C. Concentration producing 50% of maximum effect

    D. Half-life of the effect

13. In a one-compartment model, the body is treated as:

    A. Multiple separate organs

    B. Uniform compartment

    C. Central nervous system only

    D. Metabolic compartment

14. PBPK modeling stands for:

    A. Plasma Bioavailability and Pharmacokinetics

    B. Physiology-Based Pharmacokinetic Modeling

    C. Protein Binding Pharmacokinetics

    D. Pharmacokinetics Based on Population

15. Which software helps simulate oral absorption profiles?

    A. Simcyp®

    B. MS Word®

    C. Excel®

    D. ChemDraw®

16. Bioavailability is measured as:

    A. Volume of distribution

    B. Fraction of administered drug reaching systemic circulation

    C. Time to maximum concentration

    D. Peak drug concentration

17. PD models often use which kind of relationship?
    A. Exponential growth
    B. Linear decrease
    C. Concentration–effect relationship
    D. Volume–mass relationship
18. Steady-state concentration occurs when:
    A. Drug input equals drug elimination
    B. Drug metabolism stops
    C. Only drug absorption is occurring
    D. Only excretion is occurring
19. Flip-flop kinetics occurs when:
    A. Absorption is slower than elimination
    B. Elimination is slower than absorption
    C. Distribution is instant
    D. Excretion is zero
20. Saturable metabolism often follows:
    A. Linear kinetics
    B. Michaelis-Menten kinetics
    C. First-order kinetics
    D. Second-order kinetics
21. Which term refers to how a drug binds to its target?
    A. Pharmacokinetics
    B. Pharmacodynamics
    C. Binding affinity
    D. Distribution
22. AUC is primarily influenced by:
    A. Clearance
    B. Volume of distribution
    C. Protein binding
    D. Half-life
23. Physiological variables considered in PBPK models include:
    A. Tablet size
    B. Blood flow rates
    C. Shelf life
    D. Capsule weight
24. An increase in clearance leads to:
    A. Longer half-life
    B. Higher plasma concentration

    C. Lower drug exposure

    D. Increased volume of distribution

25. What does Tmax indicate?

    A. Time to reach peak plasma concentration

    B. Total drug exposure

    C. Maximum elimination rate

    D. Absorption rate constant

26. What characterizes zero-order kinetics?

    A. Constant fraction eliminated per time

    B. Constant amount eliminated per time

    C. Exponential decline

    D. Linear increase

27. Which is an example of a PD parameter?

    A. Volume of distribution

    B. Clearance

    C. Emax (maximum effect)

    D. Half-life

28. Simulation of drug dosing helps predict:

    A. Manufacturing requirements

    B. Best packaging methods

    C. Optimal therapeutic regimens

    D. Shortest expiry dates

29. A sigmoidal Emax model describes:

    A. Simple elimination

    B. Exponential distribution

    C. Drug concentration-effect curve

    D. First-pass metabolism

30. Which of the following helps link PK and PD?

    A. Metabolic clearance

    B. Pharmacometric modeling

    C. Bioequivalence study

    D. Stability testing

Answer Key:

1. C

2. C

3. A

4. C
5. C
6. C
7. B
8. C
9. B
10. B
11. B
12. C
13. B
14. B
15. A
16. B
17. C
18. A
19. A
20. B
21. C
22. A
23. B
24. C
25. A
26. B
27. C
28. C
29. C
30. B

CHAPTER SEVEN

Computers in Clinical Development

7.1 Computer-Aided Clinical Trial Design

7.1.1 Role in Protocol Development

Computer-aided tools play a foundational role in the development of clinical trial protocols by enabling the efficient design, simulation, and validation of study parameters before actual patient enrollment begins. The protocol is the most critical document in a clinical trial as it defines the study objectives, methodology, inclusion and exclusion criteria, dosing strategy, assessment schedules, and statistical plans. Traditionally, protocol development was a manual and time-consuming process, prone to inconsistencies and human errors. Today, computer-assisted systems offer structured frameworks and decision-support tools that help streamline this process, reduce ambiguity, and ensure regulatory compliance.

One of the primary uses of computer-based systems in protocol development is the incorporation of clinical trial simulation tools. These tools allow researchers to test various design scenarios, such as different dosing schedules, inclusion criteria, or patient stratification strategies, and evaluate their impact on trial outcomes such as power, effect size, and patient recruitment timelines. By simulating the expected pharmacokinetics, pharmacodynamics, and clinical endpoints in virtual populations, these systems help identify the most efficient and scientifically sound trial design before any patient is exposed.

In addition, electronic protocol templates embedded in clinical trial management systems (CTMS) and electronic data capture (EDC) platforms ensure that essential elements required by regulatory bodies like the

USFDA, EMA, and CDSCO are included. These systems automatically flag missing sections, prompt for consistency between trial objectives and assessments, and link protocol components to operational procedures such as visit schedules and data collection forms.

Advanced software also supports integration of historical data, literature-based evidence, and real-world data into protocol planning. This allows developers to build protocols that are not only scientifically justified but also practical and reflective of real clinical settings. For instance, leveraging prior trial outcomes or observational studies can guide inclusion criteria or help forecast dropout rates, which significantly affects trial timelines and cost.

Furthermore, protocol authoring tools now include version control, audit trails, and collaborative access, allowing multidisciplinary teams—such as clinical pharmacologists, statisticians, medical writers, and regulatory experts—to work together in real time. This collaborative environment reduces miscommunication, shortens review cycles, and enhances the overall quality of the protocol.

Computers also aid in standardizing protocol language using CDISC standards such as Protocol Representation Model (PRM), which improves interoperability across systems, facilitates data sharing, and accelerates regulatory review. Ultimately, by enhancing precision, reducing redundancy, and enabling data-driven decisions, computer-aided protocol development leads to more efficient clinical trials and faster drug development timelines.

7.1.2 Adaptive Trial Design Using Simulations

Adaptive trial design is a modern and flexible approach to clinical research that allows for planned modifications to a study based on accumulating data without undermining the validity and integrity of the trial. The increasing complexity of therapeutic interventions and the need for faster, more efficient development processes have made adaptive designs highly attractive. These designs are now strongly supported by computer simulations, which allow researchers to predefine possible adjustments and evaluate their statistical and clinical implications before the trial begins.

Computer simulations play a central role in the planning and implementation of adaptive designs. Using statistical software and modeling platforms, researchers can simulate thousands of virtual clinical trials under various assumptions, such as different patient response rates, dropout patterns, or effect sizes. These simulations help in identifying the best possible design features, such as sample size reassessment points, stopping boundaries for futility or efficacy, dose adjustments, or even changes in randomization ratios.

One of the most common types of adaptive designs is sample size re-estimation. Here, simulations help determine the likelihood of achieving statistical power if recruitment is extended or if variability in responses is higher than expected. Similarly, in seamless phase II/III trials, simulations enable the merging of two phases into one continuous study, which helps eliminate delays between trial phases and reduces costs.

Another key application is in dose-finding studies, where adaptive designs allow for real-time adjustment of doses based on tolerability or efficacy signals. Model-based adaptive designs such as the continual reassessment method (CRM) use simulations to update dose-escalation decisions dynamically during the trial, which improves patient safety and trial efficiency.

Bayesian adaptive designs are also supported by simulation tools, where prior knowledge is mathematically combined with observed data to update probabilities of success. These models are especially useful in rare diseases or oncology, where patient populations are small, and traditional fixed designs are not practical.

Software platforms like EAST, FACTS, ADDPLAN, and R packages such as 'gsDesign' and 'bayesCT' are commonly used to design and simulate adaptive trials. These tools allow trial designers to assess the operating characteristics of the study under different scenarios, including type I error control, power, and bias. They also provide visualizations like decision boundaries, sample size curves, and predictive probabilities to support transparent planning.

Regulatory agencies now recognize the value of adaptive designs when they are planned properly and supported by robust simulations. The USFDA and EMA have published guidance documents that outline the statistical considerations and documentation required for such trials. When used appropriately, adaptive designs increase the chance of trial success, reduce unnecessary exposure to ineffective treatments, and accelerate the path from research to approval.

In conclusion, computer simulations are indispensable in adaptive trial design, enabling scientifically rigorous and operationally flexible studies. By anticipating a range of real-world possibilities through simulations, developers can design trials that are more ethical, efficient, and responsive to emerging data.

7.2 Clinical Data Collection Systems

7.2.1 Electronic Data Capture (EDC) Systems

Electronic Data Capture (EDC) systems have transformed the way clinical trial data is collected, managed, and monitored. These computer-based platforms are designed to replace traditional paper-based data collection methods with secure, structured, and real-time electronic data entry systems. EDC systems are now a standard in clinical research because they improve data accuracy, streamline trial operations, reduce errors, and facilitate faster decision-making during studies.

In a typical clinical trial, data is collected from multiple sites, often across countries. With paper-based systems, this process is time-consuming and error-prone, involving manual data entry, transcription errors, delayed data availability, and difficulties in monitoring. EDC systems solve these issues by allowing investigators to enter data directly into electronic case report forms (eCRFs) using an internet-based interface. This enables real-time access to trial data for sponsors, contract research organizations (CROs), and monitors, regardless of geographic location.

Modern EDC systems are built with built-in validation checks that prevent incorrect, incomplete, or inconsistent data entries. These checks ensure that the data complies with protocol-specific logic, which significantly reduces the need for repeated data cleaning or queries. For example, if a lab value entered is outside the permissible range, the system can immediately flag the entry and prompt the user for verification or correction.

One of the major advantages of EDC systems is their support for centralized monitoring. Regulatory bodies and sponsors can view updated trial data instantly, enabling proactive tracking of recruitment, protocol deviations, adverse events, and overall data quality. This helps in identifying problems early and reduces the time and cost associated with on-site monitoring visits.

Most EDC systems are compliant with global regulatory standards, such as 21 CFR Part 11 (from USFDA) and Good Clinical Practice (GCP) guidelines. This means they offer secure user access, audit trails, electronic signatures, and data integrity features that meet stringent regulatory requirements. These features also facilitate easier data retrieval during inspections or audits.

Popular commercial EDC systems include Medidata Rave, Oracle Clinical, Veeva Vault EDC, REDCap, and OpenClinica. Each of these platforms provides varying levels of customization, scalability, and integration with other systems such as randomization tools, laboratory data systems, and pharmacovigilance databases.

EDC systems also support faster trial closeout by enabling immediate database locking once data verification is complete. This has a direct impact on reducing the overall trial timeline and cost, making them an essential component of modern clinical development programs.

In summary, Electronic Data Capture systems provide a secure, efficient, and accurate platform for managing clinical trial data. By eliminating the inefficiencies of manual data collection, they help ensure high data quality, improve compliance, and accelerate drug development timelines.

7.2.2 Remote Data Entry and Patient-Reported Outcomes (PROs)

Remote data entry and patient-reported outcomes (PROs) have become integral components of modern clinical trials, enabled largely by advancements in digital health technologies and electronic data capture systems. These tools allow for direct data input from patients and investigators outside traditional clinical settings, supporting decentralized trials, real-time monitoring, and improved participant engagement. Their growing adoption is driven by the need for more flexible, patient-centric, and cost-effective approaches to data collection, especially in multi-site and global trials.

Remote data entry refers to the ability of clinical trial sites or healthcare professionals to enter data directly into a centralized database using secure, web-based platforms from any geographic location. This eliminates the delays and errors associated with paper-based collection and manual transcription. Investigators can enter laboratory values, clinical observations, adverse events, and concomitant medications from remote or satellite locations, making trial operations more scalable and efficient. Built-in validation rules, drop-down menus, and time stamps ensure that the data captured is accurate, complete, and audit-ready.

Parallel to remote data entry is the increasing use of electronic systems to collect patient-reported outcomes. PROs are data provided directly by the patient about their health condition, symptoms, or treatment experience, without interpretation by clinicians or others. These include metrics such as pain intensity, fatigue, quality of life, functional status, and treatment satisfaction. Electronic PRO systems (ePROs) allow patients to report this information using web portals, smartphone apps, tablets, or interactive voice response systems from their home or any convenient location.

The use of ePROs offers several advantages over traditional paper diaries. First, it improves data accuracy by reducing recall bias and transcription errors. Second, it supports real-time monitoring, allowing investigators to identify symptom changes or adverse events more quickly. Third, the time-stamped entries improve compliance and ensure that data is collected according to protocol-defined schedules. Additionally, alerts and reminders can be integrated into the system to prompt patients when they forget to make entries.

ePROs are particularly useful in therapeutic areas such as oncology, psychiatry, dermatology, and chronic pain, where subjective patient experiences are central to evaluating treatment benefits. Regulatory agencies like the USFDA and EMA increasingly recognize the value of well-designed PRO measures in assessing drug efficacy and tolerability, and they encourage their inclusion in clinical trials when appropriate.

Both remote data entry and PRO collection platforms must adhere to data privacy and security regulations such as GDPR and 21 CFR Part 11. Encryption, secure login protocols, and role-based access are essential to ensure the confidentiality and integrity of clinical data. Many systems are also integrated with EDC platforms, allowing for seamless data consolidation, query management, and statistical analysis.

In conclusion, remote data entry and patient-reported outcome systems represent a major step toward decentralized and patient-focused clinical research. By allowing real-time, accurate, and flexible data collection, they not only improve trial efficiency and participant experience but also enhance the quality and relevance of the clinical evidence generated.

7.3 Clinical Data Management

7.3.1 Data Cleaning and Discrepancy Management

Data cleaning and discrepancy management are core processes in clinical data management, aimed at ensuring the accuracy, consistency, and completeness of data collected during a clinical trial. The quality of clinical trial outcomes, including the reliability of safety and efficacy assessments, heavily depends on the integrity of the data. Therefore, cleaning the data and resolving discrepancies in a systematic, traceable, and timely manner is essential for regulatory compliance and scientific credibility.

Data cleaning begins as soon as data is entered into the Electronic Data Capture (EDC) system. Pre-programmed validation rules within the system check for common errors such as missing fields, out-of-range values, inconsistent dates, or illogical entries. For example, if a patient's age is recorded as 150 years or the date of death precedes the date of birth, the system flags the entry. These automated checks allow for real-time identification of errors and reduce the need for extensive manual review later.

Once errors are identified, they are categorized as discrepancies. Discrepancy management involves reviewing these flagged data points and initiating queries to the site for clarification or correction. Clinical data managers use query management modules within the EDC platform to track, communicate, and resolve these issues. The resolution process must be documented in detail, including who made the changes, when they were made, and the rationale behind each correction. This traceability is critical for audit readiness and regulatory acceptance.

In addition to automated validations, data managers conduct manual reviews, often referred to as data listings review or manual edit checks. These reviews help capture complex inconsistencies that are beyond the scope of automated logic, such as unusual dosing patterns, contradictions in medical history, or inconsistencies between lab values and adverse event reports.

The entire process of data cleaning and discrepancy management is iterative and continues throughout the trial until the database is locked. A clean database reflects a high level of data quality and readiness for final statistical analysis and regulatory submission.

7.3.2 Audit Trails and Version Control

Audit trails and version control are essential components of secure and compliant clinical data management systems. They ensure that every change made to the data or study documentation is recorded, tracked, and recoverable, thereby maintaining the transparency and reliability of the data handling process.

An audit trail is a system-generated, chronological record that captures all user interactions with the clinical data. This includes every instance of data entry, modification, deletion, and query resolution. For each change, the system logs key details such as the user's identity, timestamp, the original value, the updated value, and the reason for the change (if applicable). These audit trails are not only critical for maintaining data integrity but are also required under regulations like 21 CFR Part 11 and ICH-GCP, which mandate that electronic records must be trustworthy and trackable.

Audit trails play a major role during regulatory inspections, where authorities may request detailed histories of how and when specific data were altered. The ability to present a complete, unaltered audit trail is often a key determinant of a sponsor's credibility and compliance status. Furthermore, audit logs help sponsors detect patterns of error, identify training needs at sites, and prevent potential data manipulation.

Version control, on the other hand, applies to clinical trial documents and database structures. Protocols, case report forms (CRFs), data dictionaries, and standard operating procedures (SOPs) often undergo multiple revisions during the life of a clinical study. Version control ensures that each iteration of these documents is properly numbered, time-stamped, and archived. It allows all stakeholders to refer to the correct version of a document and prevents the accidental use of outdated or incorrect forms.

In EDC systems, version control is also applied to CRFs. If a CRF design is updated mid-trial—for example, to capture a new safety parameter—the system must log which version of the form was used for each subject and site. This is essential for consistent data interpretation during statistical analysis.

7.4 Regulatory Guidelines for Computer Systems

7.4.1 21 CFR Part 11 Compliance

21 CFR Part 11 is a key regulation issued by the United States Food and Drug Administration (FDA) that governs the use of electronic records and electronic signatures in clinical trials and other regulated pharmaceutical activities. It applies to any system used in the creation, modification, maintenance, archiving, retrieval, or transmission of electronic records that are required by FDA regulations. Compliance with Part 11 ensures that electronic data are trustworthy, reliable, and equivalent to paper records.

One of the main requirements of 21 CFR Part 11 is **system validation**. All computerized systems used in the capture or management of regulatory data must be validated to demonstrate that they operate as intended. This includes testing for functionality, data integrity, access control, and audit trail capabilities. Validation must be documented thoroughly and updated whenever the system is modified.

Another major component is **secure access and user authentication**. Systems must limit access to authorized users and require unique user credentials. Two-factor authentication and strong password policies are typically implemented to prevent unauthorized access. Every user action, including data entry and modifications, must be linked to a specific individual to ensure accountability.

Electronic records must be **protected against accidental or intentional loss or corruption**. This is achieved through controlled access rights, automatic backups, secure storage, and disaster recovery protocols. Systems must also maintain **audit trails**, which log all data-related actions with details such as the user's name, timestamp, and changes made. These logs should be tamper-proof and must not be editable by users.

The regulation also includes provisions for **electronic signatures**, which must be unique to an individual and verifiable. Electronic signatures must include the signer's name, date and time of signing, and the purpose of the signature (such as approval, review, or verification). Organizations must establish policies to ensure that electronic signatures cannot be misused or replicated.

In addition, systems must maintain **data integrity and version control** throughout the record's life cycle. Every data point should be traceable to its origin, and systems must prevent the deletion or overwriting of original data without traceability. The ability to produce accurate and complete copies of records in both human-readable and electronic formats is also a requirement under 21 CFR Part 11.

Overall, compliance with 21 CFR Part 11 ensures that electronic systems used in clinical development and pharmaceutical operations meet the same standard of quality, security, and reliability as traditional paper-based processes. This regulation is enforced during FDA inspections, and non-compliance can result in warning letters, trial delays, or product rejections.

7.4.2 ALCOA+ Principles

ALCOA+ is a set of principles that describe the core attributes of data integrity in regulated environments such as clinical trials, drug development, and manufacturing. Originally derived from Good Documentation Practices (GDP), ALCOA stands for **Attributable, Legible, Contemporaneous, Original, and Accurate**. The "+" extension includes additional expectations such as **Complete, Consistent, Enduring, and Available**. These principles are recognized by regulatory bodies including the USFDA, EMA, MHRA, and WHO.

Attributable means that every data entry must be linked to a specific individual who generated or modified it. This ensures accountability and supports traceability in case of audits or investigations.

Legible refers to the requirement that all data must be readable and understandable throughout its lifecycle. In electronic systems, this includes ensuring that information can be displayed clearly and that metadata, like time stamps or system logs, are easily interpretable.

Contemporaneous data are recorded at the time the activity is performed, not afterward. Electronic systems help enforce this principle by using automatic time stamps and real-time data capture, reducing the risk of backdating or delayed entries.

Original indicates that the data should be the first capture of information or a verified copy of the original. In electronic systems, the source data must be preserved in its original form, including audit trails and metadata.

Accurate data must be error-free and faithfully represent what actually occurred. Systems should include built-in validation rules to check for logical errors, out-of-range values, or inconsistencies.

The "+" elements extend the integrity framework:

Complete means that all data—including repeated measurements, corrections, and deleted entries—must be preserved and available for review.

Consistent refers to data being collected and recorded in a uniform manner, according to protocol, standard operating procedures, or regulatory guidance.

Enduring means that records must be retained for the required period of time in a durable format. Electronic data must not be stored in temporary systems or volatile media that cannot ensure long-term accessibility.

Available ensures that data are readily accessible for review, audits, and inspections. This includes having appropriate retrieval systems in place and ensuring that authorized users can access records when needed.

In practice, ALCOA+ principles are embedded into the design and operation of electronic data capture systems, clinical trial management systems, and quality management systems. Compliance with ALCOA+ is crucial for maintaining data integrity, passing regulatory inspections, and ensuring that clinical and manufacturing decisions are based on reliable data.

Together, 21 CFR Part 11 and ALCOA+ principles form the backbone of computerized system compliance in pharmaceutical and clinical research environments. They guide system design, data handling practices, and quality assurance strategies, helping ensure that electronic records are complete, trustworthy, and legally defensible.

7.4.3 GAMP 5 and CSV (Computer System Validation)

GAMP 5 (Good Automated Manufacturing Practice) and Computer System Validation (CSV) are essential frameworks used to ensure that computer systems used in pharmaceutical and clinical environments are reliable, accurate, and compliant with global regulatory standards. These systems may include software platforms for clinical trials, laboratory instruments, manufacturing systems, or any digital application used to support regulated processes. Together, GAMP 5 and CSV ensure that electronic systems perform consistently, protect patient safety, and support data integrity.

GAMP 5, developed by the International Society for Pharmaceutical Engineering (ISPE), is the most widely recognized guidance for validating computerized systems in life sciences. The latest version of this framework, titled *GAMP 5: A Risk-Based Approach to Compliant GxP Computerized Systems*, focuses on aligning validation activities with the **risk posed to product quality and patient safety**. Rather than applying the same level of testing to all systems, GAMP 5 recommends a **risk-based approach**.

Systems that have a direct impact on product quality or regulatory data require more extensive validation than those used for non-critical functions.

GAMP 5 classifies software into categories, ranging from simple configuration (Category 3) to custom-developed applications (Category 5). For example, a commercially available EDC system with no modifications would be lower risk compared to a custom-built clinical data management system that controls patient data flow. Based on this categorization, developers define a validation strategy that includes testing activities like Installation Qualification (IQ), Operational Qualification (OQ), and Performance Qualification (PQ).

In parallel, **Computer System Validation (CSV)** refers to the **structured process of testing and documenting** that a computer system meets its intended use and regulatory requirements. CSV ensures that the system performs consistently, maintains data integrity, and includes safeguards such as user access controls, audit trails, and secure data storage. The CSV process typically follows a life cycle that includes the following phases:

1. **User Requirements Specification (URS):** A document that defines what the system is expected to do.
2. **Functional Specification (FS):** Describes how the system will meet user requirements.
3. **Design Specification (DS):** Provides technical details about how the system is constructed or configured.
4. **Risk Assessment:** Identifies which parts of the system have a direct impact on GxP compliance and data integrity.
5. **Validation Plan:** Outlines the approach, scope, responsibilities, and testing to be performed.
6. **Testing Phases:**

   - **Installation Qualification (IQ):** Verifies that the system is installed correctly.
   - **Operational Qualification (OQ):** Confirms that the system operates according to specifications under normal conditions.
   - **Performance Qualification (PQ):** Demonstrates that the system performs as intended in the user's environment.

Each validation activity is supported by documentation that includes test scripts, acceptance criteria, deviation logs, and summary reports. These records serve as proof during audits or inspections and must be retained throughout the system's life cycle.

Validation doesn't end after deployment. GAMP 5 and CSV emphasize **change control, periodic reviews, and re-validation** when systems are updated or their environment changes. This ensures continued compliance throughout the system's operational life.

GAMP 5 also introduces the concept of **supplier involvement and leveraging vendor documentation**, especially for pre-validated or off-the-shelf systems. When properly evaluated, this can reduce the validation burden for end-users while still ensuring system compliance.

In clinical development, CSV is particularly important for systems like **Electronic Data Capture (EDC), Clinical Trial Management Systems (CTMS), Pharmacovigilance tools, Laboratory Information Management Systems (LIMS), and Document Management Systems (DMS)**. Any system that handles regulatory data or impacts patient safety must be validated according to GAMP and CSV guidelines.

7.5 Case Studies of Digital Clinical Trials

7.5.1 Examples of AI-Enabled Trials

Artificial Intelligence (AI) is reshaping the landscape of clinical research by enabling smarter, faster, and more adaptive trial designs. Case studies of AI-enabled clinical trials highlight how machine learning, natural language processing, and predictive analytics are being used to optimize everything from patient recruitment to real-time monitoring and outcome prediction. These technologies are not only making trials more efficient but also improving data quality, reducing trial costs, and accelerating decision-making processes.

One notable example is the use of AI in **patient recruitment and matching**, where machine learning algorithms analyze electronic health records (EHRs), social media activity, and genomic data to identify suitable participants. In a large oncology trial conducted by Tempus and several U.S. cancer centers, AI algorithms were used to screen patient EHRs across multiple hospitals to match individuals with rare tumor markers to targeted therapy studies. This approach significantly reduced recruitment time and improved enrollment rates for trials that traditionally faced challenges due to narrow inclusion criteria.

Another significant case is from the **Pfizer-BioNTech COVID-19 vaccine trials**, where AI tools were used to process incoming clinical data in near real-time to monitor patient safety, adverse events, and protocol deviations. By using AI-driven dashboards, trial monitors were able to detect anomalies quickly and address them without delays. This real-time data review supported rapid regulatory submissions and played a part in the accelerated approval timelines for the vaccine.

In **neurological and psychiatric research**, companies like Verge Genomics and IBM Watson Health have applied AI to identify new biomarkers and predict disease progression. In one Alzheimer's disease trial, AI tools analyzed imaging data and cognitive performance scores to predict which patients were most likely to show progression within a 12-month window. This enabled trial enrichment by selecting participants with higher probability of clinical deterioration, increasing the study's statistical power and reducing sample size.

Another groundbreaking example comes from the use of **digital twins**—a virtual simulation of a patient created using AI to model how they would respond to a specific drug or treatment. In trials conducted by Novartis and MIT, digital twin simulations were used alongside traditional trial arms to predict long-term outcomes and side effects, allowing early go/no-go decisions for compounds in development.

AI has also been applied in **remote patient monitoring** using wearable devices and smart sensors. For instance, in cardiovascular studies, AI algorithms interpret data from wearable ECG monitors, step counters, and sleep trackers to detect subtle signs of deterioration or treatment response. In a heart failure trial conducted by Stanford Medicine, AI processed millions of data points from home-monitoring devices and predicted hospitalization risk days in advance, enabling early intervention and reduced emergency visits.

These case studies demonstrate that AI-enabled trials are not limited to data analysis—they support the entire trial life cycle. They enable **adaptive trial designs**, where interim analyses are driven by AI predictions, and **automated data cleaning**, where inconsistencies are flagged instantly based on learned data patterns. AI also enhances **regulatory compliance** by maintaining traceability, validating protocols against real-world data, and supporting standardized data formatting.

In conclusion, AI-enabled clinical trials represent a shift toward more intelligent, data-driven research methodologies. As case studies show, the integration of AI leads to faster recruitment, smarter monitoring, more personalized treatment strategies, and ultimately, more efficient and successful clinical outcomes. These examples underline the transformative potential of AI in bringing the next generation of clinical research into practice.

7.5.2 Use of Wearables and IoT

The integration of **wearable devices** and the **Internet of Things (IoT)** into clinical trials has opened new possibilities for continuous, real-time, and patient-centric data collection. These technologies allow the remote monitoring of physiological parameters, activity levels, and even environmental conditions, transforming how clinical data is gathered, analyzed, and used in decision-making. The use of wearables and IoT supports decentralized trial designs, improves patient compliance, and reduces the need for frequent site visits, all while maintaining high-quality, real-world data.

One of the most common applications of wearables in clinical trials is in **cardiovascular research**, where smartwatches and chest-worn monitors continuously record heart rate, rhythm, and variability. For example, in atrial fibrillation trials, wearable ECG patches such as the Zio Patch or Apple Watch ECG feature have been used to detect arrhythmias over extended periods. These devices capture data passively and transmit it securely to cloud platforms, where it is analyzed to identify abnormal patterns that might otherwise go undetected in intermittent clinic-based assessments.

Another important use is in **neurological and movement disorder studies**, where wristbands, accelerometers, and motion sensors measure gait, tremors, and sleep patterns. In Parkinson's disease trials, companies like Verily Life Sciences have developed multi-sensor wearables to capture fine motor movements and medication response. These data help assess disease progression more objectively than traditional clinical scoring systems and allow for more precise evaluation of treatment effects.

In **diabetes research**, continuous glucose monitors (CGMs) such as the Dexcom G6 and FreeStyle Libre have been used to collect real-time blood glucose data without finger pricks. This allows for a more comprehensive view of glycemic control over days or weeks. When combined with insulin pump data or dietary input through mobile apps, these systems provide a complete picture of patient management and outcomes, enabling individualized treatment adjustment and improved endpoint monitoring.

IoT platforms extend the functionality of wearables by connecting devices like **digital pillboxes, smart inhalers, connected blood pressure monitors, and even home spirometers.** These devices transmit usage data directly to trial databases, ensuring that adherence and real-time health status are accurately recorded. For example, in asthma trials, smart inhalers equipped with sensors track when and how patients use their medication. This data has been used to correlate adherence with treatment response and to send real-time reminders, improving compliance and clinical outcomes.

The use of wearables and IoT also supports **early detection of adverse events.** In oncology trials, wearable temperature sensors and activity trackers have helped predict neutropenic fever or fatigue, prompting timely intervention. Similarly, in sleep and mental health studies, wearable devices track rest patterns, physical activity, and heart rate variability, providing insight into anxiety, depression, and other behavioral symptoms.

To ensure data integrity, wearable and IoT data are collected in **Good Clinical Practice (GCP)-compliant** systems, with encryption, secure data transmission, and audit trails. Integration with electronic data capture systems and centralized monitoring platforms allows investigators to visualize trends, set thresholds for alerts, and generate reports in real-time.

Despite these benefits, challenges remain, including **data standardization, battery life limitations, device calibration, and user adherence.** However, many of these issues are being addressed through validated algorithms, machine learning-driven data correction, and patient education programs.

In conclusion, the use of wearables and IoT in clinical trials has revolutionized data collection, enabling a more patient-centric and continuous approach to monitoring health outcomes. By capturing high-frequency, real-world data in natural environments, these technologies improve trial efficiency, enrich data quality, and contribute to more responsive and adaptive clinical research designs.

Review questions

1. What is clinical development in pharmaceuticals?
Clinical development refers to the process of testing new drugs in humans to ensure safety, efficacy, and quality before regulatory approval.
2. What is the role of computers in clinical development?
Computers assist in planning, managing, monitoring, and analyzing clinical

trial data efficiently and securely.

3. What is an Electronic Data Capture (EDC) system?

An EDC system is a computerized system used to collect clinical trial data electronically instead of using paper case report forms.

4. Name one popular EDC software.

Medidata Rave is a widely used EDC platform.

5. What is a Clinical Trial Management System (CTMS)?

CTMS helps manage clinical trial operations, including site management, subject tracking, budgeting, and reporting.

6. Name a common CTMS tool.

Oracle Siebel CTMS.

7. What is a Case Report Form (CRF)?

A CRF is a tool used to collect data from each participating patient in a clinical trial.

8. How have computers improved CRF handling?

Electronic CRFs (eCRFs) enable faster data entry, validation, and real-time access across sites.

9. What is a Trial Master File (TMF)?

The TMF contains essential documents demonstrating compliance with regulatory requirements during a clinical trial.

10. What is eTMF?

eTMF is an electronic version of the Trial Master File for secure, organized document management.

11. What is Interactive Web Response System (IWRS)?

IWRS systems manage randomization, drug assignment, and inventory tracking online during clinical trials.

12. How do computers help with patient recruitment?

They use algorithms to match eligible patients to specific trials based on inclusion and exclusion criteria.

13. What is Risk-Based Monitoring (RBM)?

RBM uses data analytics to prioritize monitoring resources toward higher-risk sites or patients.

14. How do computers facilitate RBM?

By analyzing site performance metrics and flagging deviations automatically.

15. What is source data verification (SDV)?

SDV ensures that data recorded in CRFs matches source documents like medical records.

16. How does electronic SDV (eSDV) work?

eSDV allows remote verification of scanned source documents, reducing site visits.

17. What is a Data Management Plan (DMP)?

It is a document detailing how clinical trial data will be collected, processed, and validated.

18. What is a Data Clarification Form (DCF)?

DCF is used to query and correct discrepancies or missing information in clinical data.

19. What is clinical data cleaning?

The process of reviewing, querying, and correcting clinical data to ensure accuracy before analysis.

20. How do statistical software tools assist clinical trials?

They perform data analysis, interim analyses, and final statistical evaluations of study results.

21. Name two statistical software commonly used in clinical trials.

SAS and R.

22. What is the importance of audit trails in EDC systems?

They maintain records of all data changes for regulatory compliance and traceability.

23. What is Good Clinical Practice (GCP)?

GCP is an international ethical and scientific quality standard for designing, conducting, and reporting clinical trials.

24. How do computers ensure GCP compliance?

By maintaining secure, time-stamped audit trails and controlled user access in clinical systems.

25. What is adverse event reporting?

It refers to the documentation and reporting of any undesirable experience during a clinical trial.

26. How is adverse event data managed electronically?

Through electronic safety databases like Argus Safety or ARISg.

27. What is pharmacovigilance?

It is the science of monitoring, detecting, and preventing adverse effects or any drug-related problems after approval.

28. What is electronic patient-reported outcomes (ePRO)?

ePRO systems allow patients to report symptoms and outcomes directly through digital devices.

29. How do ePRO systems benefit clinical trials?

They reduce data entry errors and enable real-time symptom tracking.

30. What are electronic informed consent (eConsent) systems?

Digital platforms that help patients review, understand, and electronically sign consent documents.

31. What is metadata in clinical trials?

Metadata refers to information about collected data, like collection time, method, and device used.

32. How do computers help in interim analysis?

They allow rapid real-time analysis to decide on trial continuation, modification, or termination.

33. What is the importance of data security in clinical systems?

To protect patient confidentiality and comply with regulatory requirements such as HIPAA and GDPR.

34. What is a Clinical Data Repository (CDR)?

A centralized database where clinical trial data from multiple studies are stored for analysis and retrieval.

35. What is data integration in clinical development?

It combines data from different systems like EDC, CTMS, and lab systems for holistic analysis.

36. What is the purpose of Clinical Study Reports (CSR)?

CSRs summarize clinical trial results and are submitted to regulatory agencies for drug approval.

37. What is the role of computers in CSR preparation?

They streamline data extraction, statistical analysis, and automated document formatting.

38. What is regulatory submission of clinical data?

Submitting complete clinical data electronically to regulatory bodies like the FDA or EMA.

39. Name a platform used for electronic regulatory submissions.

eCTD (electronic Common Technical Document) submission systems.

40. What is an Investigator's Brochure (IB)?

A compilation of clinical and non-clinical data about the investigational product for investigators.

41. How do Clinical Data Management Systems (CDMS) help?

They ensure efficient capture, validation, and storage of clinical data throughout the study lifecycle.

42. Name one commonly used CDMS.

Medidata Rave CDMS.

43. What are protocol deviations?

Instances where trial procedures differ from the approved protocol.

44. How are protocol deviations tracked electronically?

Through CTMS and EDC systems with automated deviation recording modules.

45. What is Centralized Monitoring?

The remote, real-time monitoring of trial sites using clinical and operational data analytics.

46. What is real-world data (RWD)?

Data collected outside controlled clinical trials, such as from electronic health records or insurance databases.

47. How is RWD used in clinical development?

For designing pragmatic trials, understanding drug performance, and supplementing regulatory submissions.

48. What is the role of artificial intelligence in clinical development?

AI predicts patient recruitment rates, identifies adverse event patterns, and enhances protocol optimization.

49. What are common data formats in clinical trials?

CDISC standards like SDTM (Study Data Tabulation Model) and ADaM (Analysis Data Model).

MCQS

1. What is the full form of EDC in clinical research?

- a) Electronic Data Capture
- b) Electronic Drug Control
- c) Evaluation Data Center
- d) Entry Drug Certificate

1. Which system is used for managing clinical trial operations?

- a) ERP
- b) CTMS
- c) LIMS
- d) DMS

3. Electronic Case Report Forms (eCRFs) primarily help in:

- a) Recording financial transactions
- b) Tracking laboratory supplies
- c) Collecting patient clinical data
- d) Manufacturing batch records

4. Clinical trial randomization is managed through:

- a) LIMS
- b) IWRS
- c) EDC
- d) ERP

5. What is the main purpose of an eTMF?

- a) Manage manufacturing data
- b) Maintain trial master files

- c) Monitor patient adherence
- d) Track adverse events

6. Which software supports statistical analysis of clinical trial data?

- a) AutoDock
- b) SAS
- c) ChemDraw
- d) Fluent

7. Which regulatory guideline defines good clinical practice?

- a) ICH E6
- b) ICH Q8
- c) ICH Q9
- d) ICH M7

8. What does CDMS stand for?

- a) Clinical Data Management System
- b) Computerized Drug Management Structure
- c) Clinical Decision Making Software
- d) Clinical Documentation Management Setup

9. Validation of computer systems in clinical trials is essential for:

- a) Aesthetic design
- b) Regulatory compliance
- c) Marketing approval
- d) Financial reporting

10. Real-time monitoring of patient enrollment is enabled through:

- a) IWRS
- b) ERP
- c) CAD
- d) CRM

11. What is a major advantage of EDC systems over paper-based methods?

- a) Increases time of data entry
- b) Decreases accuracy of data
- c) Enhances data quality and speed
- d) Prevents drug discovery

12. CTMS software helps primarily in:

- a) Designing lab tests
- b) Tracking clinical trial activities
- c) Filing patents
- d) Submitting market reports

13. Electronic signatures in clinical data are regulated by:

- a) 21 CFR Part 11
- b) 21 CFR Part 210
- c) ISO 9001
- d) GAMP 5

14. Adverse event data in clinical trials is managed using:

- a) LIMS
- b) Safety databases
- c) CAD software
- d) Labeling systems

15. Which database stores information on investigational products?

- a) ERP
- b) IWRS
- c) CTMS
- d) LIMS

16. Data integrity issues in clinical development can lead to:

- a) Faster approvals

- b) Trial failures
- c) Higher drug potency
- d) Extended patent protection

17. Risk-based monitoring (RBM) in clinical trials uses:

- a) CAD software
- b) Predictive analytics
- c) Wet lab experiments
- d) Non-digital filing

18. A digital audit trail ensures:

- a) Drug dissolution improvement
- b) Secure and traceable data changes
- c) Faster drug degradation
- d) Poor data verification

19. Clinical trial supply management is handled through:

- a) LIMS
- b) IWRS
- c) HPLC
- d) CAD

20. What is the main goal of clinical data validation?

- a) Maximize enrollment speed
- b) Ensure data accuracy and consistency
- c) Predict future trials
- d) Increase protocol deviations

21. What supports secure remote access to clinical trial data?

- a) VPNs
- b) Printed reports
- c) Courier services
- d) Fax systems

22. What system is used for storing laboratory results in clinical trials?

- a) CTMS
- b) EDC
- c) ERP
- d) SCM

23. What process checks for missing or inconsistent trial data?

- a) Data cleaning
- b) Patient randomization
- c) Informed consent
- d) Drug labeling

24. Which tool helps in sample size calculation during trial design?

- a) LIMS
- b) JMP
- c) CTMS
- d) SAP

25. Which technology has improved trial participant recruitment through online platforms?

- a) CAD
- b) E-Recruitment
- c) LIMS
- d) E-Labelling

26. Site monitoring reports in trials are stored in:

- a) TMF
- b) LIMS
- c) SAP
- d) LIMS

27. Secure storage and sharing of informed consent forms is ensured through:

- a) EDC
- b) E-Consent platforms
- c) HPLC
- d) Minitab

28. Which platform supports medical coding in clinical research?

- a) MedDRA
- b) AutoCAD
- c) ChemDraw
- d) Fluent

29. Clinical trial progress dashboards are part of:

- a) EDC
- b) CTMS
- c) ERP
- d) RIMS

30. In clinical development, electronic diaries (eDiaries) help capture:

- a) Investigator notes
- b) Patient-reported outcomes
- c) Staff attendance
- d) Protocol amendment

Answer Key

1. a) Electronic Data Capture
2. b) CTMS
3. c) Collecting patient clinical data
4. b) IWRS
5. b) Maintain trial master files
6. b) SAS
7. a) ICH E6
8. a) Clinical Data Management System
9. b) Regulatory compliance
10. a) IWRS

11. c) Enhances data quality and speed
12. b) Tracking clinical trial activities
13. a) 21 CFR Part 11
14. b) Safety databases
15. b) IWRS
16. b) Trial failures
17. b) Predictive analytics
18. b) Secure and traceable data changes
19. b) IWRS
20. b) Ensure data accuracy and consistency
21. a) VPNs
22. b) EDC
23. a) Data cleaning
24. b) JMP
25. b) E-Recruitment
26. a) TMF
27. b) E-Consent platforms
28. a) MedDRA
29. b) CTMS
30. b) Patient-reported outcomes

CHAPTER EIGHT

Artificial Intelligence, Robotics and Computational Fluid Dynamics (CFD)

8.1 Overview of Artificial Intelligence in Pharma

8.1.1 Machine Learning, Deep Learning, Natural Language Processing (NLP)

Artificial Intelligence (AI) has emerged as a transformative force in the pharmaceutical industry, offering intelligent systems that mimic human cognition and learn from complex datasets to make decisions or predictions. Among the most impactful AI techniques in pharmaceutical applications are **machine learning**, **deep learning**, and **natural language processing (NLP)**. These methods are widely used in drug discovery, formulation development, clinical trials, pharmacovigilance, and regulatory affairs, enabling the pharmaceutical sector to work faster, more efficiently, and with greater precision.

Machine learning is a branch of AI that enables computers to learn patterns from data and make predictions or decisions without being explicitly programmed for every scenario. In pharma, machine learning algorithms are used to analyze high-dimensional datasets such as chemical libraries, gene expression profiles, and clinical trial records. Supervised learning models can predict drug activity, toxicity, or formulation stability, while unsupervised methods like clustering can identify patient subgroups, compound classes, or biological pathways.

One common application is in virtual screening, where machine learning models trained on historical structure-activity relationship (SAR) data are used to predict which chemical compounds are most likely to bind to a specific biological target. This significantly reduces the number of compounds that need to be tested experimentally, saving time and cost. These models are also applied to optimize synthetic routes in process chemistry by predicting reaction outcomes and yields.

Deep learning is a subset of machine learning that uses artificial neural networks with multiple layers to analyze complex and unstructured data. Deep learning is particularly powerful in image and signal analysis. In pharmaceutical research, it is used in high-content screening, histopathological image interpretation, and radiological analysis for clinical trials. For example, deep convolutional neural networks (CNNs) can analyze tissue biopsy slides to detect cancer subtypes, predict prognosis, or assess drug response. In drug formulation, deep learning models can analyze particle morphology or distribution from microscopy images to predict dissolution behavior or stability.

Deep learning also supports generative models such as variational autoencoders (VAEs) and generative adversarial networks (GANs), which can create novel molecular structures with desired pharmacological properties. These algorithms are increasingly used in de novo drug design to suggest candidate compounds that fit a specified binding site or exhibit predefined ADMET (Absorption, Distribution, Metabolism, Excretion, and Toxicity) profiles.

Natural Language Processing (NLP) enables computers to read, interpret, and generate human language. It is extremely useful in the pharmaceutical domain, where large volumes of unstructured text data—such as scientific publications, clinical trial protocols, patient records, regulatory documents, and social media posts—need to be analyzed for decision-making. NLP algorithms are used to extract adverse event signals from pharmacovigilance databases, identify relevant studies for meta-analyses, or summarize research findings from literature.

One real-world application is in automatic protocol review, where NLP tools analyze clinical trial protocols to identify inconsistencies, missing sections, or regulatory non-compliance. Another example is drug repurposing, where NLP mines biomedical literature to find associations between existing drugs and new therapeutic targets based on co-occurrence, semantic similarity, or causal statements.

These AI techniques are implemented through platforms like TensorFlow, PyTorch, SciKit-learn, and commercial tools developed specifically for the pharmaceutical industry. Data security, model interpretability, and regulatory acceptability are key challenges in deploying these AI systems, but advancements in explainable AI (XAI) and validation frameworks are making them more trustworthy and compliant.

In conclusion, machine learning, deep learning, and NLP have become essential tools in the modern pharmaceutical landscape. They enable data-driven decision-making, accelerate drug development, and improve patient outcomes by transforming how data is analyzed and used across the entire pharmaceutical value chain.

8.1.2 AI Tools in Drug Discovery (e.g., DeepChem, AlphaFold)

The application of Artificial Intelligence (AI) in drug discovery has evolved from a theoretical possibility to a practical necessity, particularly due to the increasing complexity of biological targets, rising development costs, and the need for faster innovation. Several AI-based tools and platforms have been developed to support drug discovery by predicting molecular properties, modeling protein structures, identifying lead compounds, and optimizing drug-target interactions. Among these, **DeepChem** and **AlphaFold** are two prominent tools that represent distinct but complementary applications of AI in the early stages of drug development.

DeepChem is an open-source machine learning library specifically designed for the life sciences and drug discovery. Built in Python, DeepChem provides a framework for applying deep learning algorithms to chemical, biological, and structural data. The library supports tasks such as molecular property prediction, bioactivity classification, quantitative structure–activity relationship (QSAR) modeling, and toxicity forecasting. Researchers can input molecular data in the form of SMILES strings or molecular graphs and train neural networks to predict properties like solubility, binding affinity, or permeability.

One of the key strengths of DeepChem is its ability to handle **graph-based molecular representations**, where atoms are nodes and bonds are edges. This structure is highly suitable for convolutional neural networks that operate on non-Euclidean data, making DeepChem ideal for building graph neural network (GNN) models in cheminformatics. The platform includes pre-built datasets like Tox21, MoleculeNet, and DrugBank, enabling rapid experimentation and benchmarking. It is widely used in academia and industry for high-throughput virtual screening and early-stage compound evaluation.

AlphaFold, developed by DeepMind, is another groundbreaking AI system that has revolutionized **protein structure prediction**. Understanding the three-dimensional structure of a protein is essential for rational drug design, as it reveals the shape and properties of binding sites where drugs can interact. Traditionally, solving a protein's structure through X-ray crystallography or cryo-electron microscopy is time-consuming, expensive, and not always feasible.

AlphaFold uses a deep learning approach trained on known protein structures from the Protein Data Bank (PDB) to accurately predict the 3D conformation of a protein based solely on its amino acid sequence. Its second version, AlphaFold2, demonstrated performance comparable to experimental methods, solving many previously unsolved protein structures with high accuracy. This advancement allows drug developers to model novel or mutated targets quickly and design molecules that can interact with them effectively.

The availability of AlphaFold's predictions has greatly enhanced target identification and validation in diseases like cancer, infectious diseases, and genetic disorders. Structural data generated from AlphaFold can be used in docking simulations, molecular dynamics, and pharmacophore modeling to accelerate hit-to-lead processes.

In addition to DeepChem and AlphaFold, other AI tools are being integrated into drug discovery workflows. For instance:

- **AtomNet** uses deep convolutional networks to predict bioactivity directly from protein-ligand structures.
- **Insilico Medicine's PandaOmics** applies AI to target discovery using omics data and literature mining.
- **IBM RXN** applies NLP-based AI models to automate chemical synthesis planning.

All of these tools share the ability to learn from massive biological and chemical datasets and make predictive decisions that guide experimental work. By reducing the need for trial-and-error in the lab, AI tools improve the success rate and cost-efficiency of drug discovery pipelines.

In summary, tools like DeepChem and AlphaFold represent a new era in drug discovery, where AI systems complement human expertise by generating accurate, scalable, and actionable insights. Their integration into discovery workflows is shortening the timeline from molecule to medicine and opening the door to innovations that were previously limited by experimental constraints.

8.2 Robotics in Pharmaceutical Research

8.2.1 Laboratory Automation and High-Throughput Screening (HTS)

Robotics has become an essential component of modern pharmaceutical research, particularly in the domains of laboratory automation and high-throughput screening (HTS). These technologies enhance the speed, accuracy, and reproducibility of experimental workflows, allowing researchers to process large volumes of samples and generate reliable data with minimal manual intervention. In drug discovery, robotics-driven automation is central to the efficient identification of active compounds, optimization of formulations, and quality control processes.

High-throughput screening refers to the rapid testing of thousands to millions of chemical compounds against a biological target to identify potential hits—compounds that show the desired activity such as enzyme inhibition, receptor binding, or antimicrobial action. Traditional methods of compound screening were limited by manual handling, pipetting, and plate reading, which were time-consuming and error-prone. With robotic systems, these steps are now fully automated, making it possible to conduct large-scale screening campaigns in a fraction of the time.

Automated HTS platforms typically include robotic arms, liquid handling systems, automated incubators, plate stackers, barcode scanners, and multi-well plate readers. The process begins with automated dispensing of compounds and reagents into microplates—commonly 96, 384, or 1536 wells—followed by incubation, reaction monitoring, and signal detection using fluorescence, luminescence, or absorbance technologies. Robotic arms transfer plates between stations without human contact, ensuring uniform processing conditions and eliminating operator variability.

One of the key advantages of robotics in HTS is consistency. Robotic systems deliver precise volumes and maintain strict timing across all wells and assays, which is crucial when screening thousands of compounds in parallel. The systems are programmed using standardized protocols and can operate continuously for long durations, including overnight or over weekends, increasing laboratory productivity without increasing staffing needs.

In pharmaceutical discovery labs, robotic HTS systems are integrated with software that manages experimental scheduling, data acquisition, and analysis. These systems generate vast datasets that are often fed into machine learning algorithms to identify promising leads, structure-activity relationships, or unexpected off-target effects. Robotic systems are also used in follow-up assays such as dose-response studies, secondary screenings, and cytotoxicity profiling.

Beyond HTS, laboratory automation also supports:

- **Automated synthesis and purification** of compounds in medicinal chemistry labs
- **Robotic sample preparation** for LC-MS or HPLC analysis
- **Automated cell culture** systems for biological assays
- **Liquid handling in ELISA and PCR workflows**

In recent years, advancements in miniaturization, microfluidics, and robotic software have further enhanced HTS capabilities, allowing for ultra-high-throughput screening (uHTS) with even smaller reagent volumes and higher data density. These developments have made it feasible to screen entire chemical libraries or natural product extracts for rare or novel biological activities.

In conclusion, robotics has revolutionized laboratory workflows in pharmaceutical research by enabling high-throughput, high-precision, and high-efficiency operations. In HTS, robotics supports the rapid and reproducible screening of massive compound libraries, playing a critical role in the identification of lead compounds and accelerating the early phases of drug discovery.

8.2.2 Robotic Arms in Synthesis and Sample Preparation

Robotic arms are a cornerstone of laboratory automation in pharmaceutical research, particularly in chemical synthesis and sample preparation tasks. These programmable, multi-jointed mechanical systems replicate the motion of a human arm with far greater precision, speed, and consistency. In research and development settings, robotic arms are employed to carry out repetitive and technically demanding procedures such as weighing reagents, transferring liquids, capping and uncapping vials, mixing solvents, filtering solutions, and loading samples into analytical instruments. By automating these labor-intensive steps, robotic arms reduce manual errors, minimize cross-contamination, and increase throughput significantly.

In medicinal chemistry laboratories, robotic arms are often integrated with automated synthesis workstations. These systems perform parallel or sequential reactions, measure reaction conditions like temperature or pH, and can be coupled with real-time analytics such as in-line spectroscopy or chromatography. For example, a robotic system may prepare reaction mixtures in a multi-well format, heat them to specific temperatures, then transfer reaction products to purification columns, all without human involvement. This approach accelerates lead optimization studies by generating hundreds of analogues in a fraction of the time required by manual methods.

In sample preparation for bioanalysis or quality control, robotic arms are used to carry out routine tasks such as pipetting plasma or serum samples into vials, adding extraction solvents, mixing, centrifuging, and reformatting plates. These automated workflows are particularly valuable in large clinical trials or stability testing, where hundreds of samples must be processed daily with minimal variability. Robotic systems ensure that each step is performed exactly the same way, preserving sample integrity and improving data consistency.

Robotic arms are also essential in high-risk environments, such as handling highly potent active pharmaceutical ingredients (APIs), infectious agents, or radiolabeled compounds. In these cases, automation not only improves efficiency but also protects laboratory personnel from exposure. Enclosed robotic systems with HEPA filtration and glove-free interfaces allow sterile or contained operations to be conducted safely and reproducibly.

8.2.3 AI-Guided Robotic Systems

AI-guided robotic systems represent the next evolution in laboratory automation by combining the mechanical precision of robotics with the intelligent decision-making capabilities of artificial intelligence. These systems are not just following pre-programmed instructions—they actively learn, adapt, and optimize experimental workflows based on real-time data analysis and feedback loops.

In pharmaceutical research, AI-guided robotic platforms are being developed to autonomously plan and execute experiments, analyze outcomes, and refine their strategies in an iterative manner. For instance, in automated drug synthesis, an AI algorithm may evaluate the yield and purity of a set of reactions and use this data to modify reaction conditions in the next round, such as changing the temperature, catalyst, or solvent. This form of closed-loop experimentation enables continuous learning and process improvement without human intervention.

One widely known example is the self-driving lab concept, where robotic systems are trained to explore chemical space using machine learning models that predict reaction success, solubility, or biological activity. In a study conducted by the University of Liverpool, an AI-driven robot autonomously ran thousands of experiments to discover new photocatalysts, optimizing conditions and learning from failures in real-time.

AI-guided robotics also play a role in formulation development, where models predict the most promising excipient combinations, mixing speeds, or process parameters. The robotic platform then prepares multiple formulations, measures key properties such as particle size or dissolution rate, and feeds the results back into the AI model for the next iteration. This approach significantly accelerates development timelines and reduces resource consumption.

In biologics research, AI-robotics integration enables automated cell culture, colony picking, and protein expression screening, where the robot decides which cell lines or expression conditions to continue based on output data. The same principle is applied in automated screening of vaccine candidates or antibody optimization.

These AI-guided robotic systems are further enhanced by integration with laboratory information management systems (LIMS) and cloud-based data analytics platforms. This connectivity allows seamless communication between devices, centralized data storage, and automated interpretation of results across multiple instruments and experiments. The AI component continuously analyzes patterns in data, detects anomalies, and suggests experimental pathways with higher success probability, significantly reducing the need for manual trial-and-error.

A practical example is the use of AI-driven robotics in **structure–activity relationship (SAR) studies**, where hundreds of analogues of a lead molecule are synthesized and tested for biological activity. The AI algorithm analyzes the results, learns which molecular modifications enhance activity or reduce toxicity, and directs the robotic system to synthesize the next batch of optimized compounds. This dynamic feedback loop can lead to quicker identification of potent leads with favorable pharmacological profiles.

In **high-throughput formulation screening**, AI systems use prior data on viscosity, stability, or bioavailability to predict promising excipient combinations. The robotic arms then assemble formulations using precise micro-dosing of components, conduct characterization tests like particle sizing or dissolution, and automatically refine the inputs for the next round. This intelligent screening can identify optimized formulations in days instead of weeks or months.

Another emerging application is in **automated analytical method development**, where AI models guide robotic systems to adjust parameters such as solvent composition, pH, or gradient slope in liquid chromatography or electrophoresis. By learning from retention times, resolution, and peak shapes, the AI helps fine-tune methods much faster than manual optimization.

Despite these advantages, implementing AI-guided robotic systems requires careful system integration, validated algorithms, and regulatory alignment. Validation of such systems must demonstrate that AI-based decisions lead to reproducible and scientifically sound outcomes. Compliance with GAMP 5, 21 CFR Part 11, and data integrity guidelines such as ALCOA+ remains essential to ensure that automated operations meet the rigorous standards of pharmaceutical R&D.

8.3.3 Robotic Filling, Packaging, and Sterile Processing

Robotic systems have significantly transformed pharmaceutical manufacturing, particularly in the critical stages of **filling, packaging, and sterile processing**. These processes demand high precision, reproducibility, and compliance with strict regulatory standards to ensure product safety and integrity. Robotics provides a level of consistency and contamination control that manual operations cannot achieve, especially in sterile environments.

In **filling operations**, robotic arms and automated dispensing systems are used to fill vials, syringes, cartridges, and ampoules with exact volumes of liquid or powdered drug formulations. These systems are equipped with sensors and vision technologies that verify fill volume, detect misalignment, and reject defective containers. Robotics ensures precise filling even with highly viscous or sensitive biologics, minimizing product loss and exposure to environmental variables.

Packaging involves automated labeling, sealing, inspection, and assembly into secondary containers such as cartons or blister packs. Robotic arms handle each unit delicately and efficiently, reducing the risk of damage or mislabeling. Vision systems scan barcodes, QR codes, and imprints to ensure compliance with serialization requirements under global track-and-trace regulations. These systems are scalable, allowing quick changeovers for different product lines and packaging formats.

In **sterile processing**, robotics offers a contamination-free solution for handling aseptic operations. In cleanrooms and isolators, robots perform activities such as transferring sterile containers, capping, stoppering, and terminal sterilization without direct human contact. Advanced robotic cells can maintain Grade A environments and are integrated with environmental monitoring systems. These setups are essential for parenterals, vaccines, and monoclonal antibody formulations where sterility is critical.

Automation in sterile processing also reduces the risk of occupational exposure to cytotoxic or high-potency compounds, ensuring operator safety. These systems are validated under GMP guidelines and must demonstrate consistent performance during media fill trials and simulation runs.

In summary, robotic filling, packaging, and sterile processing systems enhance product quality, operational efficiency, and regulatory compliance in pharmaceutical manufacturing. They are essential for modern, high-throughput, and contamination-sensitive production environments.

8.4 Computational Fluid Dynamics (CFD)

8.4.1 Introduction to CFD Principles

Computational Fluid Dynamics (CFD) is a simulation-based technique used to analyze and predict fluid flow, heat transfer, and mass transport within a defined system using numerical methods and algorithms. In pharmaceutical applications, CFD provides detailed insights into the behavior of air, liquid, or gas within equipment, rooms, or product environments without the need for costly physical experiments. It plays a vital role in optimizing manufacturing processes such as tablet coating, mixing, drying, and HVAC design.

CFD divides the physical space into small discrete elements and solves the governing equations of fluid motion for each element over time. This allows researchers and engineers to visualize and evaluate complex flow patterns, velocity fields, pressure distribution, and turbulence that are otherwise difficult to observe directly.

8.4.2 Governing Equations: Navier-Stokes

At the core of CFD lies the **Navier-Stokes equations**, which describe the motion of viscous fluids. These equations are derived from Newton's second law and account for the conservation of mass, momentum, and energy within a fluid. The fundamental equations include:

- **Continuity equation**: Ensures mass conservation.
- **Momentum equations**: Represent the forces acting on the fluid, including pressure, viscous, and external forces.
- **Energy equation**: Describes heat transfer and thermal effects.

These partial differential equations are solved numerically using methods such as finite volume, finite element, or finite difference methods. Because of the complexity and non-linearity of these equations, especially in turbulent or multiphase flows, powerful computational resources and robust solvers are required.

8.4.3 Meshing, Boundary Conditions, and Simulation Setup

To perform a CFD simulation, the first step is to create a **geometric model** of the system and divide it into small elements or **mesh cells**. The **meshing process** significantly affects the accuracy and computational load of the simulation. Finer meshes are used in regions with high gradients or detailed geometry, such as impellers, baffles, or coating nozzles.

Boundary conditions define how the fluid behaves at the edges of the simulation domain. These may include inlet velocities, outlet pressures, wall temperatures, no-slip conditions, or moving boundaries. Defining realistic and application-specific boundary conditions is critical to obtaining valid results.

The **simulation setup** also includes selecting physical models such as laminar or turbulent flow, heat transfer, species transport, and multiphase interactions. After solving, the data is post-processed to visualize flow vectors, temperature gradients, or mixing patterns using color maps, streamlines, or 3D animations.

8.4.4 CFD Applications in Pharma

8.4.4.1 Tablet Coating Uniformity

In tablet coating processes, uniform distribution of coating material over tablet surfaces is critical for functionality, taste masking, and controlled release. CFD simulations are used to model the airflow, spray patterns, and particle motion inside coating pans. By simulating droplet trajectories and temperature distribution, CFD helps optimize nozzle placement, pan rotation speed, and drying air parameters to ensure even coating without defects such as over-coating or chipping.

CFD also assists in predicting the effect of scale-up from lab-scale coaters to commercial-scale systems, ensuring that performance remains consistent across production batches.

8.4.4.2 Mixing and Stirring Optimization

Efficient mixing of powders, liquids, or suspensions is essential for content uniformity in pharmaceutical formulations. CFD allows detailed visualization of how fluids move within reactors, blenders, or tanks. By simulating parameters such as vortex formation, shear rate, and impeller speed, engineers can identify dead zones, optimize baffle placement, and improve agitator designs.

CFD is also valuable in blending operations involving non-Newtonian fluids or shear-sensitive compounds where excessive agitation may degrade product quality. Simulations reduce the need for trial-and-error experiments and shorten development timelines.

8.4.4.3 HVAC and Clean Room Simulations

In pharmaceutical manufacturing, maintaining controlled environmental conditions is critical to product safety and compliance with Good Manufacturing Practices (GMP). HVAC systems regulate air quality, pressure differentials, humidity, and temperature within cleanrooms. CFD simulations are extensively used to model airflow distribution, identify contamination risks, and validate cleanroom designs.

CFD simulations in **HVAC and cleanroom design** help visualize how air flows through vents, filters, and exhausts within controlled environments. These simulations are critical in ensuring **laminar flow**, preventing **turbulence near critical zones**, and confirming that airborne contaminants are effectively removed from areas where sterile or sensitive operations take place. By modeling airflow at different pressure settings, CFD helps confirm that **pressure cascades** are properly maintained between rooms of different cleanliness classifications (e.g., from Grade B to Grade A areas in aseptic processing facilities).

One of the key benefits of CFD in this context is the ability to test **what-if scenarios** without physically altering the facility. For example, CFD can predict how introducing a new machine, changing HEPA filter location, or altering personnel movement will impact air quality and particulate flow. This predictive capability supports **risk assessments** and helps ensure **regulatory compliance** with standards such as ISO 14644, EU GMP Annex 1, and USFDA aseptic processing guidelines.

Moreover, CFD allows engineers to assess **clean-up time** after particle-generating events, like door openings or equipment cleaning, and optimize **air change rates (ACR)** to balance cleanliness and energy efficiency. By simulating **thermal loads** and **humidity gradients**, CFD also ensures comfort and compliance with **temperature and RH requirements** for specific pharmaceutical operations.

CFD in cleanroom validation supports continuous improvement by identifying airflow short-circuits, stagnation points, and backflow risks, allowing proactive design modifications. It is also used during facility retrofitting or expansions to maintain air cleanliness without compromising ongoing manufacturing.

In conclusion, **Computational Fluid Dynamics** has become a powerful digital engineering tool in the pharmaceutical industry. Whether optimizing tablet coating, improving mixing efficiency, or ensuring air quality in cleanrooms, CFD offers detailed, physics-based insights that are difficult to obtain through traditional methods. As pharmaceutical systems grow more complex, CFD provides a **cost-effective, non-invasive, and scalable** solution to designing and validating processes that are both compliant and efficient.

8.5 Advantages and Disadvantages of Automation and AI

8.5.1 Benefits in Speed, Accuracy, and Compliance

The integration of automation and artificial intelligence (AI) in pharmaceutical research and manufacturing brings significant benefits across all phases of drug development. One of the most prominent advantages is **speed**. Automated systems perform repetitive tasks such as sample preparation, formulation screening, data entry, and report generation much faster than human operators. AI further accelerates this process by identifying patterns, generating predictions, and making data-driven decisions in seconds, reducing the time from discovery to delivery.

In terms of **accuracy**, automation eliminates variability introduced by human errors. Robots consistently dispense reagents, operate instruments, and perform quality checks with extreme precision. AI algorithms improve the accuracy of data analysis, reducing false positives or negatives in high-throughput screening, image analysis, and signal interpretation. This leads to more reliable results and improved decision-making.

Compliance is another major area where automation and AI offer value. Automated systems are designed with built-in audit trails, user authentication, and error logging, ensuring **21 CFR Part 11**, **GAMP 5**, and **ALCOA+** compliance. AI-powered tools can automatically flag protocol deviations, validate entries, and support documentation processes for regulatory submissions. These technologies streamline adherence to Good Clinical Practice (GCP) and Good Manufacturing Practice (GMP) requirements, minimizing the risk of non-compliance during audits.

8.5.2 Limitations: Cost, Validation, and Ethical Concerns

Despite their advantages, automation and AI come with limitations that must be considered. The **cost** of implementing robotic systems, AI infrastructure, and high-performance computing platforms can be significant. Small to mid-sized pharmaceutical companies may find it difficult to invest in advanced automation without compromising other operations. Initial investments also include software licenses, staff training, maintenance, and infrastructure upgrades.

Validation is another major challenge. Automated and AI-driven systems must be rigorously validated to ensure they function consistently, maintain data integrity, and comply with regulatory standards. For AI systems, validation is more complex due to the adaptive and opaque nature of machine learning models. Black-box algorithms, which make decisions without clear traceability, are difficult to justify in regulatory submissions. This creates a need for explainable AI and standardized validation protocols.

There are also **ethical concerns**, especially in clinical applications. The use of AI in patient selection, trial monitoring, and predictive diagnostics must be handled carefully to avoid bias, discrimination, or data misuse. Additionally, increased reliance on automation can lead to job displacement in areas such as laboratory operations, data entry, and manual QC, raising concerns over workforce changes and reskilling.

8.6 Current Challenges and Future Directions

8.6.1 Regulatory Hurdles in AI Adoption

One of the biggest barriers to widespread AI adoption in the pharmaceutical industry is the **regulatory uncertainty**. While agencies like the USFDA and EMA acknowledge the value of AI, there are limited standardized frameworks for its validation and approval. AI algorithms used in regulated environments must demonstrate transparency, reproducibility, and traceability—criteria that many current AI systems struggle to meet due to their complexity.

For example, adaptive learning systems that evolve over time raise questions about version control and change management. Regulatory authorities require locked algorithms or clear documentation of changes. Until clear and harmonized guidelines are established, the approval of AI-integrated systems will remain cautious and slow.

8.6.2 Data Integration, Interoperability, and Standardization

Pharmaceutical research generates vast amounts of data from various platforms—clinical trials, omics studies, laboratory systems, manufacturing equipment, and patient health records. A major challenge is **integrating** this data in a consistent and meaningful way. Different systems often use incompatible formats, data dictionaries, and standards, leading to silos and inefficiencies.

Interoperability between laboratory information management systems (LIMS), electronic data capture (EDC), hospital information systems (HIS), and AI platforms is crucial for maximizing the value of automation. Achieving this requires standardized data models, application programming interfaces (APIs), and global data governance policies. Regulatory guidance like CDISC standards and HL7 FHIR for clinical data are steps in this direction, but widespread adoption remains uneven.

8.6.3 Future Outlook: Digital Twins, Real-Time Monitoring

The future of pharmaceutical automation is moving towards **digital twins, real-time monitoring**, and **fully autonomous systems**. A digital twin is a virtual replica of a physical process, product, or system that mirrors real-world behavior using live data and simulation models. In pharma, digital twins can simulate drug manufacturing lines, bioreactor performance, or patient response to therapy, enabling proactive decision-making and optimization.

Real-time monitoring through sensors, IoT, and cloud-connected platforms will support continuous manufacturing, adaptive clinical trials, and predictive maintenance. Combined with AI, these technologies allow for self-correcting systems that ensure quality, compliance, and efficiency.

In the long term, the integration of quantum computing, advanced neural networks, and global health data may unlock even more sophisticated models for disease prediction, molecule design, and personalized medicine. However, realizing this vision will require collaborative efforts across industry, academia, regulators, and technology developers to build robust, secure, and ethical frameworks for digital transformation in pharmaceuticals.

Review questions

1. What is Artificial Intelligence (AI)?
AI refers to the simulation of human intelligence processes by machines, especially computer systems.

2. Name two subfields of AI commonly used in pharmaceuticals.
Machine Learning (ML) and Natural Language Processing (NLP).

3. What is the role of AI in drug discovery?
AI accelerates target identification, molecule screening, and lead optimization.

4. Give an example of AI software used in drug discovery.
DeepMind's AlphaFold for protein structure prediction.

5. What is Machine Learning?
Machine Learning is a subset of AI where algorithms learn from data to make predictions or decisions.

6. How does AI assist in toxicity prediction?
AI models analyze chemical structure and biological data to predict potential toxicity before animal studies.

7. What is the role of robotics in pharmaceutical research?
Robots automate repetitive tasks such as high-throughput screening and sample handling.

8. What is high-throughput screening (HTS)?
HTS is a method that uses automation to quickly test thousands of compounds for biological activity.

9. Name one robotic system used in pharmaceutical labs.
Hamilton Microlab STAR for liquid handling.

10. How does AI help in clinical trial design?
AI predicts patient enrollment rates and identifies suitable study sites.

11. What is a digital twin in clinical development?
It is a virtual model of a patient or system used to simulate and predict real-world behavior.

12. How does NLP benefit pharmaceutical research?
NLP extracts useful information from scientific literature, patents, and clinical notes.

13. What is computational drug repurposing?
Using AI to find new therapeutic uses for existing drugs.

14. Define Robotics Process Automation (RPA) in pharma.

RPA automates administrative tasks like data entry, reporting, and regulatory submissions.

15. What is an example of AI in vaccine development?

AI models were used to speed up COVID-19 vaccine development by predicting immune responses.

16. What are collaborative robots (cobots)?

Cobots work alongside human workers to perform delicate tasks in pharma manufacturing.

17. What is predictive modeling in AI?

It forecasts outcomes (e.g., patient response) based on historical and real-time data.

18. Mention one advantage of using robots in drug manufacturing.

They improve consistency, reduce contamination, and increase throughput.

19. What is the role of AI in personalized medicine?

AI analyzes genetic, lifestyle, and clinical data to tailor treatments to individuals.

20. How does AI assist in pharmacovigilance?

By detecting adverse event patterns from large healthcare databases and social media.

21. What does Computational Fluid Dynamics (CFD) study?

CFD studies the flow of fluids (liquids and gases) using computer simulations.

22. Why is CFD important in pharmaceutical development?

CFD helps optimize processes like mixing, granulation, coating, and drying.

23. Name a popular CFD software used in pharma.

ANSYS Fluent.

24. How does CFD aid in tablet coating?

It simulates airflow and droplet deposition patterns in coating pans to improve uniformity.

25. What is mesh generation in CFD?

It is the process of dividing a computational domain into smaller elements for numerical analysis.

26. How does CFD help in optimizing mixing processes?

It predicts fluid behavior inside reactors or tanks, improving homogeneity.

27. What parameters does CFD typically measure?

Velocity, pressure, temperature, turbulence, and concentration fields.

28. How is CFD useful in inhalation product development?

It models airflow and drug particle deposition in human airways.

29. What is boundary condition in CFD?

It defines how fluids interact with surfaces at the edges of the simulation domain.

30. What is the significance of turbulence modeling in CFD?

It helps simulate realistic fluid behavior in complex systems like granulators and mixers.

31. What is the advantage of combining AI and CFD?

AI can optimize CFD simulations by predicting the best process parameters faster.

32. How is AI used in pharmaceutical quality control?

AI identifies manufacturing defects through automated vision systems.

33. What is process analytical technology (PAT)?

PAT uses real-time measurements and models to control pharmaceutical processes, often integrating AI and CFD.

34. How does robotics improve laboratory safety?

By handling hazardous substances and repetitive tasks, reducing human exposure.

35. Give an example of AI in regulatory submissions.

AI algorithms assist in writing and checking electronic Common Technical Document (eCTD) files.

36. How does AI help reduce time-to-market for new drugs?

By predicting molecular properties, optimizing trials, and automating documentation.

37. How are robotic arms used in pharmaceutical packaging?

They automate blister packing, vial filling, and labeling with high precision.

38. What are CFD simulations used for in biopharmaceutical manufacturing?

Modeling bioreactor mixing, oxygen transfer, and cell culture environments.

39. What is the Navier-Stokes equation?

It is the fundamental mathematical model that describes fluid motion in CFD.

40. What is validation in CFD modeling?

Comparing CFD simulation results to experimental or real-world data to ensure accuracy.

41. What challenges exist in applying AI to pharma R&D?

Data quality issues, regulatory acceptance, and model interpretability challenges.

42. Name a robotic process used in cell culture automation.

Automated pipetting and media exchange systems.

43. What is generative design in AI?

An AI-based method that creates multiple optimal design solutions for given constraints.

44. How does AI assist in dose prediction?

By analyzing pharmacokinetic and pharmacodynamic data for individualized dosing.

45. How is AI applied in clinical site selection?

AI evaluates site performance history, patient demographics, and operational capabilities.

46. What are smart factories in pharma?

Digitally connected manufacturing facilities using AI, robotics, and real-time monitoring.

47. How is AI used in stability studies?

Predictive models forecast product degradation under various storage conditions.

48. What is computational granulation modeling?

Using CFD and discrete element modeling (DEM) to simulate granule formation processes.

49. How does AI impact pharma supply chains?

It predicts demand, optimizes inventory, and enhances logistic planning.

50. What future trends are expected for AI, robotics, and CFD in pharma?

Fully automated labs, AI-driven personalized drug development, and virtual clinical trials.

MCQS

1. Which field uses machines to mimic human intelligence? a) Artificial Intelligence

   b) Robotics

   c) CFD

   d) Simulation

2. In pharmaceutical R&D, AI is commonly used for: a) Predicting drug toxicity

   b) Tablet compression

   c) Capsule filling

   d) Coating thickness

3. Machine Learning is a subset of: a) Robotics

   b) Artificial Intelligence

   c) CFD

   d) Mechanistic modeling

4. Which of the following focuses on autonomous mechanical systems? a) CFD

   b) AI

   c) Robotics

   d) Clinical trial management

5. Deep learning models are particularly useful for: a) Analyzing blood pressure manually

   b) Image-based drug screening

   c) Conducting interviews

   d) Manual record keeping

6. In pharmacy, robotic arms are commonly used for: a) Literature review

   b) Automated liquid handling

   c) Protocol writing

   d) Drug coding

7. Computational Fluid Dynamics primarily simulates: a) Drug-receptor interaction

   b) Blood flow and air dynamics

   c) Enzyme kinetics

   d) Gene editing

8. Which software is widely used for CFD simulations? a) AutoDock

   b) ANSYS Fluent

   c) SPSS

   d) Phoenix WinNonlin

9. What is a "digital twin" in pharmaceutical research? a) Twin brother of a scientist

   b) Virtual model of a process or organ

   c) Duplicate data entry

   d) Cloning a robot

10. Natural Language Processing (NLP) is important for: a) Liquid chromatography

    b) Analyzing scientific literature

    c) Emulsion formulation

    d) Tablet hardness

11. A chatbot used to answer drug information queries uses: a) Manual input

    b) Robotics

    c) NLP

    d) Spectrophotometry

12. Which robotic platform is famous for automated drug discovery? a) Roomba

    b) Labcyte Echo

    c) WinNonlin

    d) JMP

13. Reinforcement learning teaches a machine: a) By example only

    b) By reward and penalty

    c) Through manual coding

    d) Through fixed instructions

14. One major challenge in AI-based drug discovery is: a) Lack of robots

    b) Data bias and quality issues

    c) Power shortage

    d) Lack of laboratories

15. AI in clinical trials helps in: a) Manual data entry

    b) Patient recruitment prediction

    c) Capsule filling

    d) Coating pan cleaning

16. CFD can simulate: a) Heat transfer during drying

    b) DNA sequencing

    c) Plasma protein binding

d) Chromatographic peaks

17. Robotics improves which aspect in pharmaceutical production? a) Batch size reduction

    b) Human error minimization

    c) Document writing

    d) Taste masking

18. AI models like CNN are particularly effective for: a) Statistical regression

    b) Image pattern recognition

    c) Manual dissolution studies

    d) Mass spectrometry

19. In CFD, the study of mixing patterns during granulation is called: a) Pharmacokinetics

    b) Flow dynamics analysis

    c) Ligand docking

    d) Drug recall management

20. In drug delivery, CFD is used for: a) Modeling nanoparticle distribution

    b) Predicting genetic disorders

    c) Managing databases

    d) Approving regulatory forms

21. Robotics is useful for high-throughput: a) Documentation

    b) Sample screening

    c) Label printing

    d) Financial auditing

22. One limitation of robotics in pharma is: a) Lack of power supply

    b) High initial setup cost

    c) Slow processing speed

    d) Low accuracy

23. AI is applied in pharmacovigilance to: a) Store hard copies

    b) Detect adverse drug events

    c) Perform HPLC

    d) Capsule polishing

24. The AI subfield focusing on decision trees is: a) Deep learning

    b) Supervised learning

    c) Robotics

    d) Fluid dynamics

25. CFD models use which type of mathematical equations? a) Linear algebra only

    b) Partial differential equations

    c) Arithmetic sequences

    d) Matrix inversion

26. AI helps in reducing: a) Lab floor area

    b) Time for hypothesis testing

    c) Room temperature

    d) Water usage

27. Robotics can replace humans in: a) Subjective decision-making

    b) Manual pipetting tasks

    c) Policy formulation

    d) Scientific interpretation

28. CFD can simulate tablet coating uniformity by studying: a) Surface tension

    b) Fluid flow over tablet surfaces

    c) Genetic mutations

    d) Dissolution curves

29. AI-based modeling often requires: a) High-quality datasets

    b) Manual quality control sheets

    c) Hard copy storage

    d) Random manual trials

30. The future role of AI and robotics in pharma includes: a) Eliminating regulatory processes

    b) Personalized drug manufacturing

    c) Manual labeling improvement

    d) Fossil fuel usage

Answer Key

1. a) Artificial Intelligence
2. a) Predicting drug toxicity
3. b) Artificial Intelligence
4. c) Robotics
5. b) Image-based drug screening
6. b) Automated liquid handling
7. b) Blood flow and air dynamics
8. b) ANSYS Fluent
9. b) Virtual model of a process or organ

10. b) Analyzing scientific literature
11. c) NLP
12. b) Labcyte Echo
13. b) By reward and penalty
14. b) Data bias and quality issues
15. b) Patient recruitment prediction
16. a) Heat transfer during drying
17. b) Human error minimization
18. b) Image pattern recognition
19. b) Flow dynamics analysis
20. a) Modeling nanoparticle distribution
21. b) Sample screening
22. b) High initial setup cost
23. b) Detect adverse drug events
24. b) Supervised learning
25. b) Partial differential equations
26. b) Time for hypothesis testing
27. b) Manual pipetting tasks
28. b) Fluid flow over tablet surfaces
29. a) High-quality datasets
30. b) Personalized drug manufacturing

About Authors

Ms. M.Durga Bhavani

Ms. M.Durga Bhavani is working as Asst.Professor, Department of Pharmaceutical Chemistry, Narasaraopeta Institute of Pharmaceutical Sciences (Autonomous), Narasaraopet.

She has completed her M.Pharm, Pharmaceutical Chemistry from Krishna University, Machilipatnam. And having 10 years of teaching experience. The author has to her credit many scientific publications in National and International journals.

Dr. Saritha Karnati

Dr. Saritha Karnati Professor, Department of Pharmaceutical Chemistry, K.V. Subba Reddy Institute of Pharmacy (Autonomous), Kurnool.

Dr.Saritha holds a Bachelor's from Bapatla college of Pharmacy, Bapatla , Master's degree in Pharmaceutical Chemistry from G. Pulla Reddy College of Pharmacy, Hyderabad and Ph.D from Sri Padmavati Mahila Visvavidyalayam(University for Women) Tirupati. She has over Eighteen years of experience in Drug design and specializing in computer aided drug designing and synthetic chemistry. **Dr. Saritha** has published more than 15 articles in reputed journals, 4 patents and one book chapter and has been actively involved in the scientific community presenting at various conferences and serving on editorial boards. She guided more than sixteen project works for UGs. Her area of interest *Insilico* studies by using different softwares. She maintains active involvement in the pharmacy community as a registered pharmacist and member of several professional bodies

Dr K. Ravi Shankar

Dr K. Ravi Shankar completed B. Pharm from KVSR Siddhartha College of Pharmaceutical Sciences, Vijayawada, M. Pharmacy from AU College of Pharmaceutical Sciences, Andhra University, Visakhapatnam and Ph. D from JNTU, Hyderabad. He is having a total of 14 years' experience in Teaching and Research. He Qualified in Gate 2008 with AIR 447. He published 75 research articles in national and international journals of repute. At present he is working as Associate Professor at KVSR Siddhartha College of Pharmaceutical Sciences, Vijayawada.

He has been actively involved in the scientific community presenting at various conferences and serving on editorial boards. He guided more than 24 PG projects and 20 UG project works. His area of interest is NDDS, Solubility Enhancement, and Controlled Drug Delivery. He maintains active involvement in the pharmacy community as a registered pharmacist and member of several professional bodies.

Dr. Raghavendra Kumar Gunda

Dr. Raghavendra Kumar Gunda Associate Professor, Faculty-In-Charge, Department of Pharmaceutics, Narasaraopeta Institute of Pharmaceutical Sciences (Autonomous), Narasaraopet.

Dr. Raghavendra holds a Bachelor's and Master's degree in Pharmaceutics from Acharya Nagarjuna University, Guntur, and a Ph.D. from the School of Pharmaceutical Sciences, Vels Institute of Science, Technology and Advanced Studies, Pallavaram, Chennai. He has over Thirteen years of experience in Pharmaceutical Product Development, specializing in novel drug delivery systems. **Dr. Raghavendra** has published more than 100 research and review papers, 2 Books, 6 Book Chapters and has been actively involved in the scientific community, presenting at various conferences and serving on editorial boards. His contributions have earned him numerous accolades, including the Bharath Shiksha Gaurav Puraskar from KTK Outstanding Achievers & Education Foundation; Global Ambassador of Education Excellencefrom International Institute of Education & Management and Best Researcher Award from the Association of Pharmacy Professionals. He maintains active involvement in the pharmacy community as a registered pharmacist and member of several professional bodies (IPA, APTI, IPGA, APP, AAPNA).